"A perceptive and thought-provoking invitation to reconsider typical approaches to both youth ministry and public worship in congregations, parachurch organizations, Christian schools, and campus ministries. Mathis writes with deep awareness of the pastoral riches of historic patterns of Christian worship and with deep gratitude for the gifts, insights, and capacities that God lavishes on teenagers. This book challenges simplistic limits that we too often impose on intergenerational communities and particular generational cohorts and invites us to a richer and deeper way of worshiping together. This is also an ideal book for parents, guardians, and grandparents to read to glimpse new possibilities for providing spiritual encouragement to their teenagers—and for learning from them and with them."

—**John D. Witvliet**, Calvin Institute of Christian Worship, Calvin University, and Calvin Theological Seminary

"While there are plentiful resources for youth ministry, worship scholar Mathis perceptively observes that there is a serious lack of scholarship on adolescent spiritual formation. Having read *Worship with Teenagers*, I am impressed by the careful investigative work supporting Mathis's bold claim that 'when congregations choose to engage teenagers in the worship life of the church, all ages in the church are enriched, connected, encouraged, and strengthened for the ministry of the gospel of Jesus Christ.' Indeed, Mathis's book is essential reading for church leaders wanting to revitalize their congregation."

—**Lim Swee Hong** (林瑞峰), Emmanuel College, Victoria University, University of Toronto

WORSHIP WITH TEENAGERS

Adolescent Spirituality and Congregational Practice

ERIC L. MATHIS

Foreword by **Kenda Creasy Dean**

Baker Academic

a division of Baker Publishing Group
Grand Rapids, Michigan

Published by Baker Academic
a division of Baker Publishing Group
PO Box 6287, Grand Rapids, MI 49516-6287
www.bakeracademic.com

Printed in the United States of America

Library of Congress Cataloging-in-Publication Data
Names: Mathis, Eric L., author.
Title: Worship with teenagers : adolescent spirituality and congregational practice / Eric L. Mathis ; foreword by Kenda Creasy Dean.
Description: Grand Rapids, Michigan : Baker Academic, a division of Baker Publishing Group, [2022] | Includes index.
Identifiers: LCCN 2020049526 | ISBN 9781540960603 (paperback) | ISBN 9781540964441 (casebound)
Subjects: LCSH: Christian teenagers—Religious life. | Spiritual formation. | Public worship. | Church work with teenagers.
Classification: LCC BV4531.3 .M365 2022 | DDC 264.00835—dc23
LC record available at https://lccn.loc.gov/2020049526

Baker Publishing Group publications use paper produced from sustainable forestry practices and post-consumer waste whenever possible.

22   23   24   25   26   27   28   7   6   5   4   3   2   1

✦ For my grandmother, who loved to worship God ✦
and inspired me to do the same

Contents

Foreword

Kenda Creasy Dean

I spent the summer of my sixteenth year trying to make my church's worship look more like camp. The reason was screamingly obvious (to me): worship in my congregation felt like a flat Sprite, while worship at camp felt fizzy and alive, which made Jesus feel alive as well. Obviously (I surmised), my church was doing it wrong. Clearly, they needed my help.

Trying to discern just what made worship "alive"—what makes you sure God is in the house—turned out to be trickier. Was it the singing? (Strong chance, but soaring songs from camp sounded cheesy in the sanctuary.) Was it the peer-led service or the youth-friendly sermon? (Possibly, but back home Youth Sunday came up only once a year.) Was it the Communion liturgy, when teary young people streamed forward to receive the elements from peers and counselors who meted out love and affirmation along with bread and cup? (Likely; sacraments seemed holy in both contexts, but our congregation only celebrated sacraments a few times a year.) At camp, the unapologetic emotion, the palpable sense of divine connection, the peer leadership, the embodied physicality, the participative spirit—all were at play. I left camp worship believing God was afoot. I left church worship convinced that God was at camp.

I was lucky to attend a small, struggling congregation, one of those churches where you need everyone with a pulse to pitch in or the whole thing falls apart. So youth participation in worship was not revolutionary; teens sang, read Scripture, prayed, played instruments, served as greeters, lit the candles (I didn't know what an acolyte was until seminary), and occasionally shared relevant announcements or experiences. The congregation received our offerings with unabashed "joy-joy-joy-joy down in their hearts." Most people in the pews were retired (whatever that means if you're a farmer), but they knew us by name, asked about our school activities when the service ended, and let us call them *Ed* and *Marcia*. Bob Whiteside doled out Tootsie Rolls after every service as a reward for getting through it.

Nothing much came of my "worship reform" summer save for some bad guitar playing on my part. I still wanted to put a fork in my eye on most Sunday mornings. I counted ceiling tiles, stared at the stained glass, and practiced crossing my eyes slightly to take in the altar candles (the blurry flames seemed more magical). I became ridiculously well acquainted with the hymnal since it was the only reading material in the pew other than a Bible. Sermons evaporated from memory before the benediction landed. Baptism and Communion Sundays were the exceptions; these mysteries needed no commentary. As babies wailed, resisting the water, grace sank into them (and me) unbidden. As the Communion elements entered my digestive tract, bread and juice, body and blood, girl and God all became one mysterious entanglement.

Something took.

This book is not about doing worship wrong—or right. It is about the multiplicity of ways we invite young people into worship (I had never counted how many different ways we do this until now) and what is at stake in each of them. Eric Mathis has written a book unlike any I have read in youth ministry. He explores, with impressive depth and scope, the various ways young people worship and how these experiences both reflect and shape their faith and lives. He shows how sticky wickets (like emotions) can also be holy portals, and he never once blames youth for "shallow" worship. In fact, he avoids judgment altogether; after all, today's youth weren't even born during the "worship wars" of the 1990s. He does all this with disarming honesty and joy—hallmarks of his character as well as his writing.

For as long as people have cared that young people have faith, youth have worshiped. Somehow Mathis manages to view everything we have learned to call youth ministry—from revivals to YMCAs to parachurch ministries to staid youth groups in church basements—through the aperture of worship, which, after all, is the point. Worship, as he points out, is many things, not least of which is a way of life. Both because of us and in spite of us, worship is where many, many young people—in many, many ways—have encountered God's encounter of them.

Patricia Snell's research on youth groups found that youth who attend religious youth groups (and 51 percent of US teens do)[1] experience more adult

1. Jeff Diamant and Elizabeth Podrebarac Sciupac, "10 Key Findings about the Religious Lives of U.S. Teens and Their Parents," Pew Research Center, September 10, 2020, https://www

support, are more comfortable around adults, are more likely to attend church (and less likely to think it's boring), and receive better reinforcement of moral codes than their peers. Interestingly, teenagers who attend worship but who do *not* attend youth group experience the same benefits.[2] Meanwhile, one national study found that "the most consistent predictor of youths' religiosity was their experience leading worship" through music, serving as an acolyte or altar boy/girl, teaching a lesson or giving a sermon or testimony, serving as an usher or greeter, or collecting offerings. Youth who did several of these activities attended church more often, engaged in more personal prayer and Scripture reading, volunteered more, and found religion helpful for making "big decisions." Compared to their peers, these youth had a stronger commitment to their faith tradition and a greater desire for others to know about their commitment.[3]

In these youth, something—apparently—took.

The metric that matters seems to be *participation*, not style of worship; young people who lead worship don't leave worship, at least not until the faith community has formed them (and vice versa) in significant ways. The truth is that feeling "alive" is a terrible measure of divine presence; God is alive in *all* worship. The issue is whether we have the wherewithal to notice. Worship, in its myriad forms and endless contexts, reliably acts as a burning bush that helps young people behold God. It's an occasion when they turn aside and take note: something has happened. God is afoot. Something took. *Sit laus deo.*

.pewresearch.org/fact-tank/2020/09/10/10-key-findings-about-the-religious-lives-of-u-s-teens-and-their-parents/.

2. Strengthening faith does not appear to be a strong benefit of religious youth group participation. See Patricia Snell, "What Difference Does Youth Group Make? A Longitudinal Analysis of Religious Youth Group Participation Outcomes," *Journal for the Scientific Study of Religion* (September 1, 2009), https://doi.org/10.1111/j.1468-5906.2009.01466.x.

3. Marjorie Lindner Gunnoe and Claudia DeVries Beversluis, "Youth, Worship, and Faith Formation," *Reformed Worship* 91 (March 2009), https://www.reformedworship.org/article/march-2009/youth-worship-and-faith-formation.

Acknowledgments

In "A Variation on Deuteronomy 6:11," the late Reverend Peter Raible wrote,

> We build on foundations we did not lay.
> We warm ourselves by fires we did not light.

Raible's words are true for this book, for the work reflected here has been shaped and formed by many people. That forming began with foundations laid by ministers who engaged me in life-changing experiences when I was a teenager who thrived in worship leadership. Later, mentors and teachers at Wheaton College, Baylor University, and Fuller Theological Seminary stoked my passions for worship ministry and youth ministry and encouraged me to pursue them.

The administration, faculty, and staff at Samford University provided me with a full-time teaching position and their trust to birth and lead the Center for Worship and the Arts, where my colleagues—Tracy, Kara, Stacy, Wen, Meagan—invested abundantly in work with teenagers, whether they wanted to or not. A host of university students rotated in and out of our work each semester and engaged it with curiosity and passion. I am particularly indebted to Christian, Matthew, and Nathan, undergraduate and graduate residents at the center, who helped me survey research, create bibliographies, and develop outlines, while making many trips across the quad to the library on my behalf. My faculty colleagues Paul, Emily, Joe, and especially Chuck believed in my scholarship, teaching, and research in this area; contributed to it; and made it better. Colleagues across the country provided invaluable advice, mentoring, and guidance for my teaching and scholarship: David Bailey, Randall Bradley, Kenda Creasy Dean, Mark DeVries, Brad Griffin, Mary Hopper,

Sarah Kathleen Johnson, Todd Johnson, Tony Payne, Abigail Visco Rusert, Paul Ryan, Sandra Maria Van Opstal, Ed Willmington, and John Witvliet. Their generosity and open-handed approach to advice and time is unparalleled in my experience.

The work of the center would not have happened without numerous private donors, including the C.I.O.S. Foundation and the Lilly Endowment. The endowment has established and sustained centers and institutes for youth ministry across the United States for decades, and my work at Samford built on the rich legacy of the experiences, research, and resources of those institutes. The efforts of this book represent only a small fraction of the rich network into which the endowment's staff enculturated me.

Many scholars, ministers, and individuals I did not know influenced this work, especially the large team at Baker Academic, which was immensely patient with me—a first-time author—throughout the publication process. Individuals I have known well—especially faith communities, teenagers, ministers, and family members—also have their fingerprints on this text.

I am grateful to those communities of faith where I have served as a minister: First Baptist Church of Wheaton, Illinois; First Baptist Church of Valley Mills, Texas; Calvary Baptist Church of Waco, Texas; Glenkirk Presbyterian Church of Glendora, California; and Dawson Memorial Baptist in Birmingham, Alabama. These congregations adopted and supported me, and many times their leadership allowed me to minister alongside them as an equal. I learned the most about worship with teenagers serving alongside John Woods, the music and worship pastor at Dawson Memorial Baptist, who weekly inspires teenagers to worship God with honesty, serve the church with humility, and follow Christ into the world with conviction.

In each of these communities, a number of teenagers let me into their sphere of work, worship, and play as a participant observer. Most recently this was a small group of eleventh-grade guys—Carson, Cole, Grant, and Josh—who regularly shared openly about their lives, asked how my writing was going, and genuinely cared about my response. Like all teenagers, their energy was contagious, their trust humbling, and their faith honest.

My parents, Greg and Lisa, have supported me at every turn in my journey, even though many of the paths I have chosen have been unfamiliar to them. My grandmother June Coffey instilled in me a love for church music and worship leadership at a very young age and ensured I received musical and theological training that would prepare me to serve God in full-time ministry. Brittany, my partner in life for more than eight years, shared the lived experience of this book with me. That included unwavering support and companionship while birthing a program at Samford, enduring long days of Animate, traveling as a sponsor on youth trips, hosting teenagers in our home, and losing sleep over this manuscript. She consistently offered rigorous honesty and unwavering loyalty, and I will always regret I did not offer the same to her.

Shortly after submitting this manuscript, I resigned from my academic and church positions to seek help for personal issues. In that process, the individuals acknowledged above did not abandon me; they extended grace, care, and compassion in ways I did not expect or deserve. Moreover, they gave me the confidence I needed to believe that in the midst of my brokenness, the work reflected in this book can still be used for the good of the church and for the glory of God. This is as it should be.

Introduction

In 2003 I stumbled my way into working with teenagers. I had just graduated from college and moved to Waco, Texas, to begin seminary at Baylor University. I took a part-time job as a minister of music at a two-hundred-member congregation in a rural Texas community. The congregation had a remarkable music ministry for a church of its size, and its adult choir, children's choirs, and other programs attracted a number of individuals from the community who enjoyed making music but had no other outlet for artistic expression. But the music ministry had one problem, made clear to me by a longtime church member in my second week on the job. The problem was that though teenagers had always been engaged in the music ministry of the church, they were not engaged at the present—and they needed to be. I could solve this problem, she said, by starting a choir to "get teenagers off the streets and into the church."

While I don't remember the exact impetus—my own desire to please this devoted church member or to create a comprehensive music ministry, or my genuine interest in teenagers—I took her words to heart and started a youth choir the following spring. Thirty-four teenagers from grades seven through twelve showed up to the first rehearsal, probably because I offered food and promised a trip in early summer. Of the thirty-four, only one could read music, none of them had experience singing in a choir, and they sounded terrible when we tried to sing a familiar worship song. "What on earth have I done?" I wondered. Left with no other option, I continued meeting those teenagers every Sunday night that semester and for the next two years that I served the congregation. That student choir became a nucleus for youth ministry in the little congregation. The teenagers who participated in it became participants in and students of worship. They sat in front each Sunday morning eager to participate in worship, they led worship as individuals and as a group, they traveled and served together, they read Scripture and prayed with one another, they sang for graduation ceremonies, and they offered their voices at the funeral of a beloved friend. This work continued well beyond my tenure in that beloved congregation.

Twenty years later, I reflect on that season of my life. I now know that while my job title was Minister of Music, I was actually serving as Minister of Youth under the auspices of public worship. This experience, and others like it, prompted questions in my own soul about the spiritual formation of teenagers in the context of worship.

In 2013 I became founding director of the Center for Worship and the Arts at Samford University in Birmingham, Alabama. My work focused on teaching teenage worshipers, training teenage worship leaders, and equipping the adults in the congregations, schools, and faith communities in which they reside. Through grant-based initiatives, we engaged in the qualitative and quantitative study of teenage worship practices. Part of this research included a weeklong intensive summer program, Animate, for seventh- through twelfth-grade students on Samford's campus. While running Animate, I worked with faculty in sociology and undergraduate and graduate students to collect data on teenage worship practices through surveys, focus groups, and site visits of more than five hundred teenagers and twenty-five congregations across the United States. A number of summer programs like ours have recently developed at universities across the country thanks to generous funding from Lilly Endowment. These programs have enhanced the conversation and awareness of teenage worship practices and have increased dialogue opportunities with program leaders and the individuals, congregations, and schools associated with them. They have provided me with excellent opportunities to see, ponder, critique, and ask questions about the broader teenage worship landscape in the United States.

The central question of this book might be articulated in this way: What happens when teenagers are intentionally engaged in the worship life of a congregation? The short answer is that when congregations choose to engage teenagers in the worship life of the church, all ages in the church are enriched, connected, encouraged, and strengthened for the ministry of the gospel of Jesus Christ. While much of my work focusing on the relationship between teenagers and worship has been positive, it has also brought up a number of challenges and questions that have necessitated further study of teenage worship practices. In some instances I have found answers; in other instances I have ended up with more questions than when I began.

The aim of this book is to present my observations to you, the reader. Does my work reflect your experience, leadership, reading, and research? At times I will suggest answers—or at least the starting point for answers—for some questions in which the relationship between faith, teenagers, formation, and worship is cloudy. At other times, I will not be able to provide clear-cut answers because I am still searching myself. In these instances, I will hope for opportunities to continue the dialogue with you in person, online, or through additional publications.

Observations, Questions, and Opportunities

Before we get started, it is worth naming a few key observations about the landscape of teenage worship practices. These key observations and their accompanying pastoral questions set the backdrop for most, if not all, of the chapters in this book.

First, there is no shortage of communal worship opportunities for teenagers engaged in the Christian church in the United States. Teenagers typically participate in weekly worship gatherings with all ages in the church, in services otherwise known as all-church worship. They also participate in worship gatherings beyond these intergenerational worship experiences throughout the week, such as when their youth group worships together on Sunday or Wednesday evenings. Some of them worship in one or multiple chapel services at Christian high schools, others in Bible studies and small groups before and after school, and on and on the list goes. I've met teenagers who say they participate in a worship gathering three or four times a week. This weekly list omits other opportunities for communal worship, such as seasonal and annual youth ministry events. Indeed, teenagers participate in multiple youth camps, retreats, mission trips, denominational youth gatherings, and other conferences where worship services might take place three, four, five, or more times in a period of twenty-four or forty-eight hours. These observations lead me to a series of questions: What is the relationship between worship and the spiritual formation of teenagers participating in these worship practices? How do we teach teenagers about the multifaceted activity of worship? How are we forming teenagers in the Christian faith as they engage communal worship?

Second, teenagers on the whole are a discrete minority in most congregations, and the worship gatherings that teenagers participate in are nearly always the product of adult planning and leadership. Even where teenagers lead the music or speak or play another leadership role in adult or youth worship, teenagers remain influenced by the adults who mentor them and who bear responsibility for their actions. In intergenerational worship, teenagers are often lumped together with children or with college students and emerging adults. On the one hand, it is logical that adults would preside over and lead worship since most teenagers are not able to assume the pastoral role that worship planning and leadership requires in some traditions. On the other hand, teenagers may experience a gap between the worship practices of a primarily adult community and the more juvenile ways adults teach children to worship. The end product is a cumulative disparity among the worship experiences of teenagers in the church. Some teenagers leave for college understanding worship as an event that caters to their specific wants and needs, while other teenagers leave for college understanding worship as a rhythm of spiritual formation disconnected from personal preference. This reveals a failure of initial primary enculturation into a faith community. Of course, "The mistaken hope is that this alternative enculturation would in any way lead people to return to the primary enculturating community and its practices, but that's just hardly ever how it works."[1] How do we best equip those responsible for planning and leading the worship gatherings in which teenagers participate?

Third, despite the many opportunities teenagers have to participate in communal worship gatherings, they are attuned to experiences of God in individual or private worship experiences. These experiences are as important—if not more important—than the communal worship of the church, and teenagers often describe these experiences as more significant, meaningful, or impactful than experiences of corporate worship. At Samford we have spent the last five years documenting teenagers' responses to questions such as "Where do you worship?" and "Where do you find God?" The answers are, "When I'm outside," "When I'm singing 'that song' in my school choir," "When I'm driving with my windows down on a sunny day," "When I'm curled up reading a book that wasn't assigned," "When I'm running cross-country," or "When I attended that concert with my friends." These are the times teenagers feel closest to God. Teenagers need these experiences of God beyond the walls of the church, to be sure. But this raises important questions about the role of Christian community in a teenager's life and important questions about the connection between worship on the Lord's Day and worship in all of life: How does the church encourage teenagers to engage worship as full, conscious, active participants? How does our communal worship on Sunday inform our individual worship throughout the week? Are worship experiences limited to only those times when teenagers feel God?

---

1. Taylor Burton-Edwards, email to the author, September 29, 2015.

Fourth, a significant number of teenagers are currently serving as worship leaders in their communities, schools, and congregations. Communities of faith have seen and observed particular skills in teenagers. They have encouraged teenagers to use these skills, and teenagers have found themselves in worship leadership. This leadership is often connected to a specific adult's recognition of a gift and encouragement to use that gift. I have regularly asked teenage worship leaders how they started leading worship at their churches/schools. They often respond, "Well, I played [insert instrument], and [insert name/role of adult] asked me to help out." While their leadership often happens in an area of the arts such as music, worship leadership is not limited to the arts. Teenagers lead worship by making music, speaking, running audio and video, creating prayer spaces, making graphics, and welcoming friends, among other things. Burnout is a common challenge among these teenage worship leaders. This observation leads to another series of questions: How do we balance worship leadership roles for teenage worship leaders with their own need for mentoring and formation through worship? How do we teach and train teenage worship leaders? How do we prevent leadership burnout among these teenage worship leaders?

Fifth, in the web of teenage worship practices, a number of individuals, most of whom are adults, bear responsibility for planning and leading these all-church and youth-only worship gatherings. These people include youth ministers, chaplains, music teachers, worship ministers, pastors, and thoughtful laypersons, as well as teenagers themselves. When I ask adult mentors of these teenagers how they started working with teenage worship leaders, they often say things like, "I'm a youth minister, and our youth group worships on Wednesday nights. I never took a class on worship in seminary, but I spend a lot of time planning worship times for our youth group." Or, "I'm a science teacher at a Christian high school and sing on the praise team at my church. We needed someone to help with the music in chapel services, and I agreed to do it." In the best instances, adults who mentor these young people are able to devote time to work with and train worship leaders. In other instances, adults are overwhelmed or don't know how to coach young worship leaders, and as a result, some teenagers have no one to invest in them as a worship leader. One challenge for all these faithful adults is that very few of them have had extensive training in worship ministry. Few seminaries require students to take courses in worship, and many congregations and schools do not require worship leaders to have formal education in worship leadership or from a seminary. Those in higher education circles have often debated what theological and musical requirements we should place on those who lead faith communities in worship (no matter their age). We should ask,

How do we balance (what some articulate as) a lack of formal education with the meaningful experience of a number of young worship leaders who were taught through apprenticeship and mentoring models?

Finally, there seems to be a gap in resources and literature about and for teenage worshipers, teenage worship leaders, and their adult mentors. Despite the large number of worship services that teenagers participate in, the large number of teenage worship leaders, and the many church leaders responsible for overseeing their work, few resources address these topics. There are few books and articles about what happens when teenagers worship, and there are even fewer books, articles, and resources for teenagers about how to lead worship for peers or a congregation of adults. How do we best equip the church for the task of forming faithful teenagers who are disciples through the process of worshiping, worship planning, and worship leading?

Youth Ministry and Worship Ministry

Examining a Relationship

Taken as a whole, the above observations, questions, and opportunities point to a very specific question: What is the relationship between youth ministry and worship ministry? Academic research in the twenty-first century has focused on the developmental trajectories of teenagers and the need for the church to provide deep spiritual formation to support and encourage lifelong faith. Despite the numerous research projects, books, articles, and resources that have been published about teenagers in recent years, the role of public Christian worship in adolescent spiritual formation has been only peripherally addressed. In ecclesial practice, teenagers often function as marginalized worshipers. Congregations tend to group teenagers with older children or young adults where worship principles and practices are concerned. Yet the process of spiritual formation in worship is unique for teenagers. These critiques are not intended to be indictments, but they do demonstrate that a gap exists in both the scholarship and the practice of youth ministry and worship ministry.

It seems there are misperceptions about worship from teenagers as well as adults. In some instances, teenagers perceive worship as irrelevant, a show, a ritual, or something to be done in private outside the worshiping community, while adults tend to overcompensate for such misperceptions by turning worship into a spectacle or game. Adults come to critique worship practices they participate in through the lens of sentimentality, the way they remember feeling when they worshiped as teenagers.

Engaging the gap between scholarship and practice, between youth ministry and worship ministry, has the potential to help the church reach a healthier place in worship practice, and I believe the cumulative effect will be a significant reframing of conversations surrounding both youth ministry and worship ministry for the twenty-first-century church. To that end, the purpose of this book is to build a bridge between these two disciplines by identifying the gap between adolescent spirituality and liturgical studies in academic and pastoral literature, illustrating the importance of the reciprocal relationship between youth ministry and worship ministry, and initiating conversations in academic and ecclesial circles about teenagers and worship. Aside from my personal experiences, questions, hopes, and challenges, this book is an invitation to consider how to engage the worship life of the faith community and cultivate a generative faith among teenagers—a faith rooted in the story of the Triune God, nurtured by the Christian community, and important enough to extend beyond adolescence.

A Word of Caution

As we examine worship ministry and youth ministry, we will find much to celebrate as well as much to lament. We will learn about the successes and failures of those who have gone before us, and we will identify repetitive cycles that cater to or ignore teenagers altogether. We might also realize we have much to learn. Both the generalities and the particularities of our learning can provide a way to frame ministry in the present as well as in the future.

Worship ministry influences youth ministry, and youth ministry influences worship ministry. This has been the pattern throughout history, at times for the better and at other times for the worse. As we examine the histories of worship ministry and youth ministry and attend to their narratives side by side, we will uncover a story we must hold carefully—namely, that the two ministries have not been the best ministry partners. Too often youth ministry has become the scapegoat for worship ministry, and church leaders blame youth programs for not having enough young people in worship. At the same time, worship ministry can become the scapegoat for youth ministry, and congregations change worship styles without critical reflection to "attract the young people."

Perhaps the most infamous chasm between worship ministry and youth ministry occurred throughout the latter half of the twentieth century. While life in the sanctuary progressed "as usual" with choirs and organs, youth ministry discovered the guitar and created a shift in worship ministry.[2] This

2. Randall Bradley uses a helpful metaphor here, describing how worship moved "up the stairs" from the youth room in the basement to the sanctuary throughout the 1960s and 1970s.

period became defined as the "worship wars," and though this type of "war" occurred most recently in the late twentieth century, the concept is not new.[3] This chapter will allude to the story of the worship wars, but it will also tell the story of how worship in the youth room can move teenagers toward full, active, and conscious participation in the worship life of the church. Indeed, God is present in the sanctuary, but God is also present in the youth room. When God finds teenagers and teenagers find God in either place, adolescents can expand the worship and mission of the church.

However, we must hold that possibility in tension with the vast amounts of literature that describe America's teenagers as "inarticulate" about matters of faith, especially the overarching narrative of the gospel and its relevance for life today. It is difficult to place the blame for this in a single place because the problem is so complex. But the heartbeat of this book is a belief that the most public pronouncement of the Christian story happens in Christian worship. If teenagers are participating in communal worship week in and week out yet still cannot articulate the God story and their place in it, then our approach to worship must change.

This change will need to come from all sides: evangelicals, Catholics, and mainline Protestants. It will need to come from youth ministry and worship ministry. It will need to come from every ministry area of the church. Ultimately, this is a Christian problem that impacts every age group and ministry in the church in the past, present, and future. Making this change will require collaboration among all ministries in the church, and this change will not be a change in the style of worship; it will be a change in the content of worship. Before we approach how to make this shift, we must first define worship in more specific terms, which we will do below.

What is largely missing from the historical narratives of youth ministry and worship ministry is a reciprocal relationship and dialogue between both ministries. If the ministries cannot work together, the church loses its capacity to celebrate, appreciate, and uphold the gifts of the Christian tradition. It also loses its ability to imagine, inspire, and adapt ministry practices for faithful transmission in the current culture. Upholding the story and tradition

---

See C. Randall Bradley, *From Memory to Imagination: Reforming the Church's Music*, Calvin Institute of Christian Worship Liturgical Studies (Grand Rapids: Eerdmans, 2012), 16–18.

3. These battles are internal (within the church) as well as external (from church to culture). As an example of worship against the prevailing societal culture, see the example from Scripture in Walter Brueggemann, *Israel's Praise: Doxology against Idolatry and Ideology* (Philadelphia: Fortress, 1988). As an example of worship among Protestant congregations and denominations, see Terry W. York, *America's Worship Wars* (Peabody, MA: Hendrickson, 2003). For illustrations from the Roman Catholic Church, see James Empereur, "Worship Wars in the Roman Catholic Church," *Liturgy* 19, no. 4 (2004): 15–24.

of the church is the gift and calling of worship ministry. Adapting ministry practices to the current culture is the gift and calling of youth ministry. The twenty-first century needs the collective gifts, which combine the best of faithful improvisation and careful discernment, from these two ministries in the church.

Disclaimers

A few disclaimers and definitions are in order. Whenever I speak to an individual or a group, three questions are nearly always asked. The first question sounds something like this: "When you say the word *teenagers*, what ages are you talking about?" I define a teenager as any young person between thirteen and eighteen years old. This distinguishes them from *older children*, who are typically eight to twelve years of age, and *emerging and young adults*, who are nineteen to twenty-nine years of age.[4] While some of the things I say about the thirteen- to eighteen-year-old population may apply to older children or emerging adults, this text intentionally focuses on the thirteen- to eighteen-year-old age group. From time to time, I will interchange the word *teenagers* with *youth* or *students* to keep it interesting for the reader.

The second question sounds something like this: "When you talk about the value of teenagers worshiping with their peers, are you saying intergenerational worship is not important?" Here, it is worth noting that I value intergenerational worship, I believe intergenerational worship practices are biblically grounded, and I believe they are the best model of worship the church can foster. At times, I will use the words *intergenerational worship* and *all-church worship* interchangeably.

The third question I receive is the inverse of the second: "When you say intergenerational worship is important, are you saying that the youth group is an outdated model of ministry?" My response is that to do intergenerational worship well, we must know and understand each generational segment in the population. While I advocate for intergenerational worship and activities, I am not denying that age-specific ministries are vital, necessary, and can contribute to the spiritual well-being of all ages, particularly teenagers.

We know from James Fowler's *Stages of Faith* that each of us moves through a progression of spiritual development in the same way we move

4. See Jeffrey Jensen Arnett, *Adolescence and Emerging Adulthood: A Cultural Approach*, 5th ed. (Upper Saddle River, NJ: Pearson Education, 2012).

through progressions in physical and emotional development.[5] Teenagers are in a different place from children, college-age students, middle-aged adults, and senior adults. Most of them are in what Fowler labels as stage 3 of faith development, "Synthetic-Conventional faith." This stage is characterized by questions of belonging (Who am I? Do I matter? Do I belong?) and is a season during which teenagers make their faith their own, as opposed to the faith of their parents. Like all of us, teenagers benefit from ministries that acknowledge this specific place on the faith development journey.

Defining Worship

Every fall semester, I start my Introduction to Worship Leadership class with a clip from the movie *Mean Girls*. In a famous scene from this movie, Cady, the new girl at North Shore High School, is introduced to the school lunchroom. Her friends Janis and Damian tell her, "Where you sit in the cafeteria is crucial." Then they carefully map out the cafeteria using stereotypical labels: freshmen, ROTC guys, jocks, nerds, hotties, wannabes, burnouts, band geeks, plastics, and so on. Their labels for each subset of students at each table in the cafeteria represent accurate stereotypes of high school students.

Sadly, their approach to talking about the lunchroom is similar to our approach to talking about worship. *Worship* is a problematic term. In fact, we have given it so many meanings that it has lost its meaning. The terms we use for worship presuppose particular values, often relating to style, quality, and quantity. Regarding style, we use terms like *contemporary* or *traditional*. Regarding quality, we use terms like *good* or *bad*. And when we speak of quantity, we refer to the size of the gathered congregation. When we talk about worship with these labels, we imply one alternative is good and one is bad, just like Janis and Damian did.

Really, these labels indicate our preferences, and rarely are we able to prevent ourselves from neutrality. There are multiple ways to worship God, and we live in an era of liturgical pluralism. Yet while our worship practices may look different, our conversations about worship should not polarize or claim superiority. We should have common values that guide our different worship practices, and we should be willing to enter conversations about those values.

5. James W. Fowler, *Stages of Faith: The Psychology of Human Development and the Quest for Meaning* (San Francisco: Harper & Row, 1981).

In an article addressing the challenges of talking about worship, John Witvliet says that the word *worship* has at least three meanings and probably more.[6] He suggests we conceive of these three meanings as forming concentric circles: worship in life, worship in the church, and small acts of worship.

Figure I.1
Three Meanings of Worship

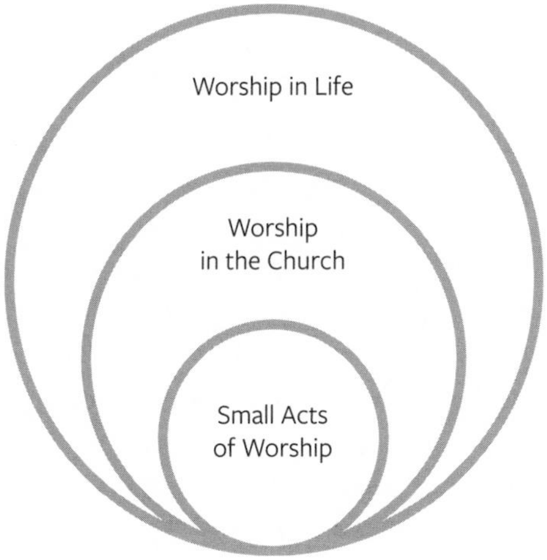

Worship in Life

Worship
in the Church

Small Acts
of Worship

Worship in Life

First, worship is the way in which we live all of life. We offer our work, leisure, family, and every other aspect of life to the Lord. In that sense, our entire life is a sacrifice of praise to God. This aligns with Romans 12:1, where Paul admonishes believers "to present your bodies as a living sacrifice, holy and acceptable to God, which is your spiritual worship." No matter how we define worship, we can never diminish the importance of worship in the way we live life and the way those around us live their lives. Mark Labberton says it this way: "Worship names what matters most: the way human beings are created to reflect God's glory by embodying God's character in lives that seek righteousness and do justice. Such comprehensive worship redefines all

6. These three meanings are borrowed from John Witvliet, "On Three Meanings of the Term Worship," *Reformed Worship* 56 (June 2000), https://www.reformedworship.org/article/june-2000/three-meaning-term-worship. I have added to and developed his meanings with additional materials.

we call ordinary. Worship turns out to be the dangerous act of waking up to God and to the purposes of God in the world, and then living lives that actually show it."[7]

Worship in the Church

The second definition of worship is an event, ritual practice, or liturgy that we often call a worship service. Congregations around the world gather on the Lord's Day for public worship. Worship is the sum of what happens when people show up on Sunday mornings, and this is synonymous with the meaning of the Greek word that we translate as *liturgy*, which means work performed for the benefit of another. This term was brought into the church from society to describe the goods (often food) that people brought to the Lord's Table as offerings: grapes, olives, cheese, bread, and wine. This food was given to clergy to eat, and the remains were given to the poor. The meaning of *liturgy* is corporate by nature, and every congregation, whether high church or low church, has a liturgy that is written or extemporaneous in worship. Worship is more than a printed bulletin; it is what occurs when people embody the text on the page. We see a biblical example of this meaning in John 4:21, where Jesus explains, "The hour is coming when you will worship the Father neither on this mountain nor in Jerusalem." Christopher Ellis emphasizes this definition of Christian worship, which he defines as "a gathering of the church, in the name of Jesus Christ and in the power of the Holy Spirit, in order to meet God through Scripture, prayer, proclamation and sacraments, and to seek God's Kingdom."[8]

Worship Is a Specific Act

A third and equally common understanding of worship suggests that worship is a specific act, such as adoration or praise. We ascribe worth to God in public worship and in our own lives. We might sing a song of praise to God, or we might see a new baby and give thanks to God. Psalm 95:6 uses the word in this sense, "Come, let us bow down in worship, let us kneel before the LORD, our maker" (NIV). This is the narrowest sense of the word *worship*. It closely matches the Old English word *weorthship*, which means "to give the worth due a person." Evelyn Underhill, a twentieth-century

---

7. Mark Labberton, *The Dangerous Act of Worship: Living God's Call to Justice* (Downers Grove, IL: IVP, 2007), 13.

8. Christopher J. Ellis, *Gathering: A Theology and Spirituality of Worship in Free Church Tradition* (London: SCM, 2004), 20–21.

lay theologian, claims that orientation is the key to worship. She identifies worship as a specific act that directs our attention to God and prompts us to say, "God is God and I am not."[9] Therefore, "worship will include all those dispositions and deeds which adoration wakes up in us, all the responses of the soul to the Uncreated, all the Godward activities of [humans]."[10] The true test of worship is whether we have reoriented ourselves, or allowed others to reorient themselves, in light of encountering God.

We often confuse various meanings of worship, emphasize one over the other, and even forget some of these components. But when we talk about public Christian worship, we shouldn't ignore any of these definitions. Rather, we should seek to understand how they might work together. But before we can comprehend them, we need to examine the object of our worship by asking, Who is worship for?

Who Is Worship for?

Worship is a multifaceted event that involves many people, places, things, and beliefs. It engages at least three major entities: God, the church, and the world. In worship, these three entities converse with one another. Worship is a conversation that occurs in the present while engaging the past and anticipating the future. God speaks to us, we speak to God, and we learn God's vision for the world.

Figure I.2
The Focus of Worship

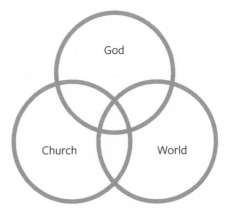

9. Evelyn Underhill, *Worship* (New York: Harper, 1937), 8.
10. Underhill, *Worship*, 8.

Worship Is for God

First, worship cultivates knowledge and imagination about who God is and what God has done. This means worship does not begin with our needs and priorities. Rather, worship begins with acknowledging, recognizing, praising, and honoring God, along with the psalmist who wrote, "One thing I asked of the LORD, that will I seek after: to live in the house of the LORD all the days of my life, to behold the beauty of the Lord, and to inquire in his temple" (Ps. 27:4). Philippians 2:6–11 is an ancient hymn from the church that describes the passion of Christ. The final verses, 9–11, remind us that Christ is the object of our worship: "Therefore, God also highly exalted him and gave him the name that is above every name, so that at the name of Jesus every knee should bend, in heaven and on earth and under the earth, and every tongue should confess that Jesus Christ is Lord, to the glory of God the Father."

Worship Is for the Church

Worship is not only for God; worship is for the church. Through the full, conscious, and active participation of all worshipers as an intergenerational community, worship acknowledges the covenant relationship we have with God and one another. These themes are prominent in the Old Testament, especially where Yahweh articulates the covenant with Israel in Jeremiah 31:33: "I will put my law within them, and I will write it on their hearts; and I will be their God, and they shall be my people."

Nehemiah 8 describes a rich scene of worship where Ezra the scribe brings out the book of the law before all the assembled people—"both men and women and all who could hear with understanding" (v. 2). This community acts when Ezra "blessed the LORD, the great God," and the people respond by raising their hands. Then, they bow their heads and worship God by lying facedown on the ground (v. 6). After instructing them in the Scriptures, Nehemiah says to them, "Go your way, eat the fat and drink sweet wine and send portions of them to those for whom nothing is prepared" (v. 10).

Finally, 1 Peter 2:9–10 identifies the church as the community of God: "But you are a chosen people, a royal priesthood, a holy nation, God's special possession, that you may declare the praises of him who called you out of darkness into his wonderful light" (NIV). As individual members of the church, we have needs when we enter the church. By the grace of God, these needs have the potential to be met in worship. Through communal actions of giving thanks and praise, extending hospitality, and clarifying our commitment to God, we are strengthened and enriched as the body.

Worship Is for the World

Third, worship is for the world. We seek the kingdom of God, and this inevitably involves God's vision for the whole world. Acts 2:42–47 tells of the many wonders and signs done by the apostles. All "would sell their possessions and goods and distribute the proceeds to all, as any had need" (2:45). Finally, passages like Revelation 5:9 remind us of the final consummation, when all tribes, tongues, nations, and languages will worship together singing a new song: "You are worthy to take the scroll and to open its seals, for you were slaughtered and by your blood you ransomed for God saints from every tribe and language and people and nation." Worship reminds us that, indeed, "the God on whom we focus is the One who is passionately concerned about the world, and our worship must reflect that reality. Any worship which avoids the needs of the world for which Christ died is not going to be worship which is true to the gospel."[11]

Worship is difficult to define in a few words. It is the way we live life, it is the worship event, and it is small acts of adoration. It is for God, the gathered community, and the world.

An Overview of the Book

I have presented most, but not all, of the topics in this book at academic conferences or regional or national gatherings of youth ministers, worship ministers, and denominations within the last five years. These discussions have developed through seasons of full- and part-time youth ministry, graduate studies in Christian worship, continued studies in adolescent culture and spirituality, and the administration of two Lilly Endowment grants related to teenage worship leaders and the adults who mentor them.

This book is divided into three parts with three chapters each: "Cultural Perspectives," "Liturgical Perspectives," and "Pastoral Perspectives." The first part, "Cultural Perspectives," provides an analysis of teenagers, youth ministry, and worship ministry from literature in these three fields from the late nineteenth century to the present day. This is a broad segment of history to cover, and my aim is to give an aerial view that will get us to the present-day context. Chapter 1 paints a picture of the American teenager using cultural studies from the first two decades of the twenty-first century with a broad focus on the National Study of Youth and Religion (NSYR). Chapter 2 traces

11. Christopher J. Ellis, *Approaching God: A Guide for Worship Leaders and Worshippers* (London: SCM, 2009), 26.

the history of youth ministry and worship ministry, interpreting those histories for lessons that we can use to think about student worship ministry in the twenty-first-century church. Chapter 3 is the heartbeat of this book. It outlines a telos for teenage worshipers that builds on the work of James K. A. Smith.

The second part, "Liturgical Perspectives," looks at key issues with worship practices of congregations where teenagers are concerned. The chapters are organized around the theology of worship I teach teenagers and articulated earlier in this introduction: that worship is about God, the church, and the world. Chapter 4 demonstrates how God's story and teenagers' stories have become lost in our worship and provides perspectives for uncovering both. Chapter 5 advocates for intergenerational worship as the crucible in which teenagers find acceptance and belonging, even though worshiping with all generational cohorts presents immense complexities as well as deep hope. Chapter 6 looks at the worship experiences teenagers have in the world—namely, those down the street, in soup kitchens, on mission trips, and at summer camps and seasonal retreats.

The third part, "Pastoral Perspectives," holds up a mirror to the first two parts of this book by asking how we should reframe our worship practices with teenagers in the sanctuary and in the youth group. Chapter 7 uses philosophy, psychology, and anthropology to describe the role of emotions in the worship of the American teenager. Chapter 8 is written for worship pastors, and it examines models of worship with teenagers in the present-day context through the lens of worship systems. Chapter 9 is written for youth pastors and provides a framework for youth ministers to think about worship in the context of the youth group. Two appendixes at the end expound on practical elements of student worship ministry: mentoring teenage worship leaders and planning worship with teenagers.

A Final Word

I am an inherent optimist, and I hope to approach conversations about worship like Witvliet, who always argues that the study and practice of worship must be undertaken with wisdom, discernment, gratitude, and a "hermeneutic of charity":

> Every act of Christian ministry . . . reflects a certain undertone, often an undertone of fear, guilt, pride, or gratitude. It is terribly tempting to teach worship with an undertone of guilt ("if you don't do it this way, be shamed"), fear ("worship practices out there are pretty bad, and getting worse"), or pride ("how

fine indeed it is that we don't pray like those [fill in the blank] publicans"). But a gospel undertone for both worship and discussion about worship—even in the bleakest days—is most fittingly that of gratitude. Ultimately, gratitude itself is a gift we receive. We can't engineer it. But we can hope for it, pray for it, and celebrate it when it arrives, even in the middle of a college or seminary class. Two moves—from legalism to wisdom, from didacticism to doxology—set the tone for a more fruitful kind of learning environment, better attuned to the topic of worship.[12]

Some of my dearest friends and family members are pessimists, and they lose sleep at night worrying that because of the shape of today's young people, Christianity as a whole is on a downward spiral into a pit from which it will never recover. Similarly, many books about ministry begin by stating a problem and explaining how readers can fix that problem by mobilizing the forces or changing that one thing or overhauling an entire system. So a book about teenagers or a book about worship that starts by articulating a problem is not surprising. Writers have sold many books about youth ministry and worship ministry by articulating a gospel of fear: Christianity is languishing, and we should do something about it, like better mobilize our young people or change our worship style. This has been the practice of the church throughout much of the twentieth century, it seems, and more often than not, this practice has gotten us nowhere. It has hurt congregations and ministries of all shapes and sizes.

While I am aware of the challenges of the twenty-first-century church in the United States, I do not share their sentiments. I am optimistic when it comes to the faith of our teenagers, and I believe others should be as well. For instance, research shows us that rather than a 40 to 50 percent decline of teenagers in the church after college, there is hope of 50 to 60 percent of teenagers keeping the faith, and I believe this is the good news of the gospel of Jesus Christ.[13] While it is true that the spiritual formation of teenagers is a challenge for the twenty-first-century church, within this challenge lies the immense hope that there are teenagers in your midst who love your congregation and its worship practices because they know them, they love the people associated with them, and they want to belong to and participate in your worshiping community with all that they are and all that they have to offer.

12. John D. Witvliet, "Teaching Worship as a Christian Practice," in *For Life Abundant: Practical Theology, Theological Education, and Christian Ministry*, ed. Dorothy C. Bass and Craig Dykstra (Grand Rapids: Eerdmans, 2008), 143–44.

13. See Kara E. Powell and Chap Clark, *Sticky Faith: Everyday Ideas to Build Lasting Faith in Your Kids* (Grand Rapids: Zondervan, 2008), chap. 1.

In the same way, some children, young adults, middle-aged adults, and senior adults have yet to know those teenagers individually, but they love them simply because they are teenagers. Children can't wait to be them, and adults fondly remember when they were them. Whether those children and adults know it or not, those teenagers need them to be all in, 100 percent, worshiping alongside them, reminding them that they are known, loved, and have a purpose. Whether those teenagers know it or not, those children and adults need them to be all in, 100 percent, for the reminder that teenagers bring—namely, that the great God of the universe, who sent his Son incarnate to be born of a virgin teenager and empowered that same Son to preach in the synagogue and call adults to a new way of living and being in the world—is, by the power of the Holy Spirit, still calling the twenty-first-century church to a new way of living and being in the world. May this book inspire all of us to live into our baptismal vocation of loving God with our heart, soul, mind, and strength, and may it remind us to love our teenage neighbors as ourselves.

PART 1

CULTURAL PERSPECTIVES

1

✦ ✦ ✦

Almost Christian

What the Faith of America's Teenagers Is Telling Us about Our Worship

It is time for us to reject the wholesale cynicism of our culture regarding adolescence. Rather than years of undirected and unproductive struggle, these are years of unprecedented opportunity.

—Paul David Tripp, *Age of Opportunity*

Introduction

The twentieth century birthed the study of two fields: adolescence and liturgy. Although both were familiar to individuals through experience, their official study had not yet been formally defined. The study of adolescence began in 1904 when G. Stanley Hall published *Adolescence*, a seminal work he began in the late nineteenth century after studying the second decade of life for five years.[1] In 1944, forty years after Hall's publication, the word *teenager*

The title of this chapter is borrowed from the title of Kenda Creasy Dean's book by the same name. See Kenda Creasy Dean, *Almost Christian: What the Faith of Our Teenagers Is Telling the American Church* (New York: Oxford University Press, 2010).

1. G. Stanley Hall, *Adolescence: Its Psychology and Its Relations to Physiology, Anthropology, Sociology, Sex, Crime, Religion, and Education* (New York: Appleton and Company, 1904). Hall began to use the word *adolescence* in 1898, but his first work cementing the term was published in 1904.

became commonplace in American vocabulary, acknowledging that youth culture was now its "own target market" that possessed its "own rituals, rights, and demands."[2]

A teenager himself as the study of adolescence gained traction, Alexander Schmemann, a Russian Orthodox Christian priest, teacher, administrator, and writer, officially inaugurated the study of liturgy in 1960 with the publication of *Introduction to Liturgical Theology*.[3] Now, in the third decade of the twenty-first century, we know more about teenagers and worship than we have ever known before. Sociologists, psychologists, historians, doctors, executives, think tanks, and other interested parties have produced a substantial amount of information in an effort to define what it means to be a teenager,[4] and this has defined the church's approach to youth ministry in recent decades. Similarly, theologians, historians, musicians, pastors, philosophers, and psychologists have studied and written about the worship practices of the church. The landscape of liturgy has shifted drastically, and so too has its study and practice.

2. Jon Savage, *Teenage: The Creation of Youth Culture* (New York: Penguin, 2007), xv.

3. Alexander Schmemann, *Introduction to Liturgical Theology*, trans. Ashleigh E. Moorehouse (Crestwood, NY: St. Vladimir's Seminary Press, 1966). Schmemann defines previous study of liturgical theology as "a more or less detailed practical study of ecclesiastical rites, combined with certain symbolical explanations of ceremonies and ornaments." He distinguishes his work and liturgical theology as "what is done in worship." See p. 9 of his introduction for his full explanation. To place his work in historical context, see Dwight W. Vogel, ed., *Primary Sources of Liturgical Theology: A Reader* (Collegeville, MN: Liturgical, 2000).

4. While important studies of youth culture and adolescence have been named above, they are by no means the only studies. The most recent examples of this literature are connected with the study of Generation Z. A very small sampling of this literature includes Tim Elmore and Andrew McPeak, *Generation Z Unfiltered: Facing Nine Hidden Challenges of the Most Anxious Population* (Atlanta: Poet Gardner, 2019); Jeff Fromm and Angie Read, *Marketing to Gen Z: The Rules for Reaching This Vast and Very Different Generation of Influencers* (New York: Amacom, 2018); Thomas Hine, *The Rise and Fall of the American Teenager: A New History of the American Adolescent Experience* (New York: Perennial, 2000); Frances E. Jensen and Amy Ellis Nutt, *The Teenage Brain: A Neuroscientist's Survival Guide to Raising Adolescents and Young Adults* (New York: Harper, 2015); Thomas Koulopoulos and Dan Keldsen, *The Gen Z Effect: Six Forces Shaping the Future of Business* (New York: Bibliomotion, 2014); Cynthia Lightfoot, *The Culture of Adolescent Risk-Taking* (New York: Guilford, 1997); Corey Seemiller and Meghan Grace, *Generation Z: A Century in the Making* (New York: Routledge, 2019); Corey Seemiller and Meghan Grace, *Generation Z Goes to College* (San Francisco: Jossey-Bass, 2016); Corey Seemiller and Meghan Grace, *Generation Z Leads: A Guide for Developing the Leadership Capacity of Generation Z Students* (North Charleston, SC: CreateSpace, 2017); Laurence Steinberg, *Age of Opportunity: Lessons from the New Science of Adolescence* (New York: Mariner, 2014); Don Tapscott, *Grown Up Digital: How the Net Generation Is Changing Your World* (New York: McGraw Hill, 2009); Jean M. Twenge, *iGen: Why Today's Super-Connected Kids Are Growing Up Less Rebellious, More Tolerant, Less Happy—and Completely Unprepared for Adulthood; And What That Means for the Rest of Us* (New York: Atria, 2017).

Indeed, the church's way of ministering to teenagers and of worshiping have shifted and evolved. Both might be described as looking and functioning like a shopping mall.[5] Studying either teenagers or worship is like trying to drink from a fire hose; it is nearly impossible to consider everything that has been published. Writing about teenagers or worship is even more challenging. The moment new information is published about teenagers, they have grown up. A new generation of teenagers arises, and the process of studying and writing begins again as culture clamors to learn about the new generational group. What makes it tick? What are its defining characteristics? How does it think? How does it learn? How does it enter the work force? How do we market to this demographic? How do parents adapt their practices? How might businesses adapt? The story of studying and writing about worship is no different than the story of studying and writing about teenagers. As soon as scholars publish work about the latest practices of worship in the Christian church, new trends and traditions emerge, and the process of studying and writing begins again. What new styles have appeared? What worship attracts the most people? How should we think about preaching? How might we incorporate the arts?

The central question here, however, is the relationship between teenagers and worship. How does what we know about teenagers correlate to worship practices in the American church? Despite the numerous research projects, books, articles, and resources that have been published about teenagers in recent years, the role of public Christian worship in adolescent spiritual formation has been only peripherally addressed, if not altogether overlooked.[6] The cumulative effect of neglecting the relationship between worship and teenagers has fostered misperceptions about teenagers and about worship by all ages in the church. The Christian church has long held an innate fear that its children and teenagers will follow in the footsteps of popular artists such as Ed Sheeran, who boasts about learning to sing in church but stopping "at the age of nine."[7]

5. This imagery is borrowed from imagery used in James K. A. Smith, *Desiring the Kingdom: Worship, Worldview, and Cultural Formation* (Grand Rapids: Baker Academic, 2009) and Bryan D. Spinks, *The Worship Mall: Contemporary Responses to Contemporary Culture* (New York: Church Publishing, 2010).

6. This statement is quite generalized, and there are certainly exceptions to it—but not many. As I will show later, worship generally occupies a marginal place in youth ministry literature, and youth ministry generally occupies a marginal place in worship literature. The most prominent exception I can point to is Fred P. Edie, *Book, Bath, Table, and Time: Christian Worship as Source and Resource for Youth Ministry* (Cleveland: Pilgrim, 2007), along with its accompanying resource manual, Brian Hardesty-Crouch, ed., *Holy Things for Youth Ministry: A Guide to "Book, Bath, Table, and Time"* (Cleveland: Pilgrim, 2010). See also the January–March 2014 issue of *Liturgy: Journal of the Liturgical Conference*.

7. Ed Sheeran, vocalist, "Eraser," by Ed Sheeran and Johnny McDaid, Polar Patrol Music, released March 3, 2017, Sony/ATV Music Publishing.

Adults are eager to reach teenagers and often use worship as a means of evangelism to attract and retain young people. In these cases worship is often misunderstood as adults overcompensate by turning worship into a spectacle, a late-night talk show, a series of games, or entertainment. While their intention is worthy, it does not always work. On the flip side, when teenagers try to express their thoughts and opinions about worship to adults, parents, or church leaders, their voices are often dismissed, and it is assumed teenagers will grow out of their thoughts and experiences. In the end, worship suffers. Teenagers perceive worship as irrelevant, entertainment, a show, a ritual, or something to be done alone, outside the worshiping community. If they stay in the church into adulthood, they come to critique present worship practices through the lens of sentimentality, the way they remember worship feeling when they were a teenager, and they fail to exhibit signs of mature spiritual formation and growth, which are perhaps the greatest treasures of public Christian worship.[8]

In recent years, I have come to believe that teenagers in the church want to know, understand, and experience the deep power and possibility inherent in the gathering of God's people for prayer, praise, and proclamation. Teenagers want more than silly gimmicks or hollow routines from the church and its worship practices. They want to know and feel God with their entire beings, make authentic connections with believers of all ages, and be equipped to navigate the world comfortably with the language of faith imprinted on their hearts, minds, and tongues. If we will put worship and teenagers in dialogue and let them speak to each other, I believe that public Christian worship can form the faith of our teenagers, and I believe that teenagers can shape the worship practices of the church for the better. The goal of this chapter, then, is to do just that: to put adolescents in dialogue with the worship of the church to uncover the identity of the worshiping teenager.

Worship is first and foremost about God, but worship is also about the gathered people in the church who worship and the ways that worship equips them for the mission of the church: to be the hands and feet of Christ in the world. With a nod to that three-part liturgical theology, this chapter will be divided into three parts: teenagers and God, teenagers and the church, and teenagers and the world. In each section, I will use studies about teenagers and their relationships to faith from the last twenty years. While some of that literature is now dated, it will help capture themes so that we can paint a picture of the teenager at worship.

8. For more on this larger phenomenon, see Thomas E. Bergler, *The Juvenilization of American Christianity* (Grand Rapids: Eerdmans, 2012); and Thomas E. Bergler, *From Here to Maturity: Overcoming the Juvenilization of American Christianity* (Grand Rapids: Eerdmans, 2014).

Teenagers and God

Encounters with the Transcendent

Though more than twenty years old, the most recent substantial study of teenagers' spiritual lives was conducted between July 2002 and April 2005, when Notre Dame sociologist Christian Smith led a comprehensive study on adolescent spirituality in the United States, known as the NSYR. The findings from this study were initially reported in *Soul Searching: The Religious and Spiritual Lives of American Teenagers*.[9] Smith followed this work with two additional studies, and subsequent research projects and books followed in the paths of his studies.[10] The amount of literature published since 2005 on the faith of America's teenagers is significant and now includes additional cultural studies that focus on specific populations of America's teenagers, such as Catholics, African Americans, Asian Americans, and Latin Americans. It includes literature offering theological perspectives on youth ministry and spiritual formation as well as literature offering pastoral perspectives on ministering to and with America's teenagers.[11]

Smith's study includes key findings about the generation known as Generation Y (Millennials) as teenagers and examines the religious identities and practices of seven groups: conservative Protestants, mainline Protestants, Black Protestants, Catholics, Jews, Latter-day Saints, and nonreligious people. One of the key findings from that study is that more than half of American teenagers report "strong subjective importance and experiences of religious faith in their own lives."[12] In other words, the teenagers interviewed in the NSYR described having powerful encounters or desiring powerful encounters with the living God, which were measured through the importance of faith, their closeness to God, the commitment of their lives to God, the experience of powerful worship, answers to prayer, a lack of religious doubts, and guidance from God.[13] In a more detailed analysis of teenagers who make a personal commitment, have a powerful experience of worship, or receive a definite answer to prayer or what they believe to be a miracle, researchers note

9. Christian Smith and Melinda Denton, *Soul Searching: The Religious and Spiritual Lives of American Teenagers* (New York: Oxford University Press, 2005).

10. Smith's next works included Christian Smith and Patricia Snell, *Souls in Transition: The Religious and Spiritual Lives of Emerging Adults* (New York: Oxford University Press, 2009) and Christian Smith et al., *Lost in Transition: The Dark Side of Emerging Adulthood* (New York: Oxford University Press, 2011).

11. While offering an extensive list is difficult, the body of literature published from 2000 to the present will be the source of this chapter's claims about the worship life of teenagers.

12. Smith and Denton, *Soul Searching*, 68.

13. Smith and Denton, *Soul Searching*, 68.

that "only twenty percent of all U.S. teenagers report not having had any of these four religious experiences."[14] This means that approximately 80 percent of US teenagers who engaged in the NSYR claimed to have had a personal encounter with God, 51 percent of which came through worship that was "very moving and powerful."[15]

In *The McDonaldization of the Church*, sociologist John Drane observes, "We live in a time when the overt search for spiritual meaning has never been more intense than it is now."[16] Teenagers understand this searching more than ever today. They are also attuned to and perhaps even looking for experiences of God anywhere they might find God, and these experiences are becoming as important as, if not more important than, the communal worship of the church. A recent study by the Barna Group found that 59 percent of Generation Z does not attend church because it is not relevant, 48 percent does not attend church because they claim to find God elsewhere, and another 12 percent finds the rituals of church to be empty.[17]

Language for Faith

Generation Z in the United States is the first generation that will have been raised and come to age in a post-Christian context.[18] A recent study by the Barna Group describes Generation Z's worldview as post-Christian, claiming that out of more than sixty-nine million teenagers in Generation Z, only 4 percent have a biblical worldview. Barna also notes that the number of individuals in Generation Z, according to Barna, that identify as atheist is double the number of adults who identify as atheist.[19] Described as "highly inclusive and individualistic," Generation Z, according to Barna, is open minded, empathetic to the feelings and experiences of others, and hesitant to stake claims on whether another's views are right or wrong,[20] implying that their ability to hold convictions about Christianity and other religions is quite limited.

Before Barna's study, the NSYR had revealed that teenagers were unable to speak intelligently about their faith, beliefs, and practices. When asked to

---

14. Smith and Denton, *Soul Searching*, 44. Researchers note that these experiences vary by tradition.

15. Smith and Denton, *Soul Searching*, 45.

16. John Drane, *The McDonaldization of the Church: Consumer Culture and the Church's Future* (London: Darton, Longman & Todd, 2000), 65.

17. The Barna Group, *Gen Z: The Culture, Beliefs, and Motivations Shaping the Next Generation* (Ventura, CA: Barna Group and Impact 360 Institute, 2018), 70.

18. James Emery White, *Meet Generation Z: Understanding and Reaching the New Post-Christian World* (Grand Rapids: Baker Books, 2017), 49.

19. Barna, *Gen Z*, 25.

20. Barna, *Gen Z*, 12.

identify their theological positions, teenagers in the NSYR tended to define themselves by what they and their communities of faith were *not* rather than who they were. Teenagers found it difficult to positively define their theological tenets, but they were "incredibly articulate" on sex, money, family, and relationships.[21] Moreover, the NSYR revealed for the first time that "many teenagers enact and espouse a religious outlook that is distinct from traditional teachings of most world religions."[22] The prevailing religion among America's teenagers is now Moralistic Therapeutic Deism (MTD), which can be summarized by five tenets:

1. A god exists who created and orders the world and watches over life on earth.
2. This god wants people to be good, nice, and fair, as taught in the Bible and most world religions.
3. The central goal of life is to be happy and to feel good about oneself.
4. God is not involved in my life except when I need God to resolve a problem.
5. Good people go to heaven when they die.[23]

MTD has been received with mixed emotions, but Kenda Creasy Dean, professor of youth, church, and culture at Princeton Theological Seminary, offers a condemning word to the church in response. Her summary of the NSYR and the uncovering of MTD is that it reveals "a theological fault line running underneath American churches: an adherence to a do-good, feel-good spirituality that has little to do with the Triune God of Christian tradition and even less to do with loving Jesus Christ enough to follow him into the world."[24]

Dean distills the NSYR findings to illustrate how "teenagers lack a theological language with which to express their faith or interpret their experience of the world,"[25] among other things. While Dean laments the inability of teenagers to speak theologically about God and matters of faith, she rightly blames the American church as a perpetuator "of pseudo-Christian youth activities executed for the sake of good intentions," illustrating how America's congregations and youth ministries have themselves espoused tenets of MTD on a number of levels. "Ski trips and candy sales, performance choirs and martial

21. Smith and Denton, *Soul Searching*, 131.
22. Kenda Creasy Dean, *Almost Christian: What the Faith of Our Teenagers Is Telling the American Church* (New York: Oxford University Press, 2010), 21.
23. Dean, *Almost Christian*, 14.
24. Dean, *Almost Christian*, 4.
25. Dean, *Almost Christian*, 18.

arts teams, confirmation 'statements of faith' and Youth Sundays [have too easily become] opportunities for teenagers to feel good about themselves, or for congregations to feel good about teenagers, or occasions to celebrate middle-class values of achievement, self-expression, and self-determination."[26]

What is more, the church, which was to instill a lasting faith in its teenagers, has failed them. Dean writes, "Most teenagers (three out of five) say they attend worship, and often youth ministry and Christian education programs, regularly." Yet, she observes, "They possess little understanding of historically orthodox Christian doctrine, few religious practices, and virtually no religious language to either critique or construct a worldview informed by . . . Christian faith." The reality facing the church is that "American teenagers may engage in substantial amounts of youth ministry and Christian education, but they do not seem to be spending much time in communities where a language of faith is spoken, or where historically orthodox Christian doctrines and practices are talked about or taught."[27]

Authentic Worship

Like many adults, teenagers long for worship that teaches them the language of faith—namely, the practices of praise, confession, hearing, receiving, and sending. However, in the last century, the church's default evangelism and catechesis has been to reach, attract, and teach young people not through the depth of liturgical experiences and theological tenets but through programmatic worship characterized by cutting-edge styles and quality products. In many cases this has brought teenagers to churches and youth groups in large numbers. This history of worship practices with teenagers illustrates a belief held by the twentieth-century church that new models of worship that borrow presentation methods from popular culture will attract large numbers of young people and keep them in the church. This has birthed new modes of worship, such as choirs at the Billy Graham crusades, the youth musical, Contemporary Christian Music (CCM), and so on. When congregations age and decline in population, their first response is often to change the worship style or engage the latest innovative ministry tactics. This pattern has been utilized by mainline Protestant and Catholic denominations, but it is mainly a product of American Evangelicalism.[28]

The good news for the church is that many of its teenagers want worship that is focused on the right things more than worship that is a particular style,

26. Dean, *Almost Christian*, 110.
27. Dean, *Almost Christian*, 28.
28. This is the topic of chap. 2.

such as traditional or contemporary. Researchers with the NSYR note that teenagers are "mostly oriented toward and engaged in conventional religious traditions and communities."[29] Teenagers who do explore alternative religious or denominational traditions, especially in areas related to worship, most often do so because it is recommended to them by someone else.[30] This is slightly ironic considering the general impression of the American teenager is one of rebellion, nonconformity, wandering, and restless behavior. Contrary to that image, the NSYR proves "that impression is fundamentally wrong."[31] Smith says, "The vast majority of American teenagers are *exceedingly conventional* in their religious identity and practices. Very few are restless, alienated, or rebellious; rather, the majority of U.S. teenagers seem basically content to follow the faith of their families with little questioning."[32] Overall, Barna's studies on Generation Z reach a similar conclusion, suggesting that "perceptions of church are more positive than negative."[33]

In *The Younger Evangelicals*, Robert Webber describes a new era of faith when young people began to react against a strong pragmatic- and entertainment-focused approach to Christianity and worship. His work illustrates how by the end of the twentieth century "evangelical pragmatists emerged as the new religious gurus to create new ministries to appeal to the seekers."[34] The challenge then, he claims, is true now; fostering this kind of overly pragmatic, hyper-entertaining approach to worship can throw the baby out with the bathwater and actually contribute to a decline in church attendance by today's young Christians who are not interested in this approach and may in fact revolt against it. He claims, "The younger evangelical wants to release the historic substance of faith from its twentieth-century enculturation in the Enlightenment and recontextualize it with the new cultural condition of the twenty-first century."[35]

More recently, the Fuller Youth Institute (FYI) published *Growing Young: 6 Essential Strategies to Help Young People Discover and Love Your Church*, which claims that congregations hoping to appeal to young people do not need an "off-the-charts cool quotient," a "big, modern building," a "'contemporary' worship service," a "watered-down teaching style," or a "hyper-entertaining

---

29. Smith and Denton, *Soul Searching*, 27.
30. Smith and Denton, *Soul Searching*, 128.
31. Smith and Denton, *Soul Searching*, 119.
32. Smith and Denton, *Soul Searching*, 120.
33. Barna, *Gen Z*, 70.
34. Robert E. Webber, *The Younger Evangelicals: Facing the Challenges of the New World* (Grand Rapids: Baker Books, 2002), 44.
35. Webber, *Younger Evangelicals*, 17.

ministry program."[36] Rather, congregations wanting to engage young people must focus on one or more of these six practices: unlocking keychain leadership, empathizing with today's young people, taking the message of Christ seriously, fueling warm community, prioritizing young people and families everywhere, and being the best neighbors.[37] In its work, FYI focuses on the power of rituals as "channels through which to answer deep questions of identity, belonging, and purpose with God's response of grace, love, and mission," noting that modern worship is not a "magnet to draw young people."[38] This may require a shift in our thinking about the kind of worship that attracts young people who want worship, a worship that is authentic and conveys a narrative and witness of what it means to follow Christ in the world rather than a programmatic goal of keeping and retaining young people.

Teenagers and the Church

Worship Attendance as Spiritual Practice

Teenagers in America have plenty of communal worship opportunities, as we discussed in the introduction.[39] Teenagers surveyed in the NSYR reported engaging in worship with surprising frequency. Forty percent of them reported participating in religious services once a week or more. This is a minority, but it is a substantial minority. Twelve percent reported attending two or three times per month, 7 percent reported attending once a month, 8 percent reported attending many times a year, and 14 percent reported attending a few times a year. Taken together, this data says that 81 percent of America's teenagers at the time of this study attended worship in their church with some degree of frequency.[40] Attendance at religious services varied across traditions, but teens reported a desire to attend religious services more than they were able to attend.

---

36. Kara Powell, Jake Mulder, and Brad Griffin, *Growing Young: 6 Essential Strategies to Help Young People Discover and Love Your Church* (Grand Rapids: Baker Books, 2016), 25–27. This is part of a larger list, "10 Qualities Your Church Does Not Need in Order to Grow Young," developed by Powell, Mulder, and Griffin in their study focusing on exemplary congregational ministries among fifteen- to twenty-nine-year-olds. While their work was broader than teenagers as defined in this text, their findings are congruent with additional literature focused specifically on teenagers.

37. Powell, Mulder, and Griffin, *Growing Young*. These six themes are the focus of individual chapters in *Growing Young*. They will be referenced in later sections of this book.

38. Powell, Mulder, and Griffin, *Growing Young*, 155.

39. The types of worship practices that teenagers participate in will be described in greater detail in chap. 2.

40. Smith and Denton, *Soul Searching*, 37.

These teens acknowledged factors that prevented them from attending religious services more often, such as academic, athletic, extracurricular, family, and other social commitments and obligations, as well as challenges such as uncooperative parents and transportation issues. But when asked how often they would attend religious services if it were totally up to them, 12 percent of teenagers expressed a desire to attend more frequently. Researchers acknowledged some of this may be "wishful thinking" but added that the "findings provide no evidence supporting the belief that significant numbers of teens would like to stop attending religious services and are only doing otherwise because their parents are forcing them to attend."[41]

The NSYR reported that of teenagers they researched who identified as Christian and engaged in religious services (three-quarters of teenagers surveyed fall into these categories), most reported that these services were important to their spiritual lives. Though their denominational traditions and worship practices are diverse, American teenagers articulated to the NSYR that "religion and spirituality [were] important if not defining features of their lives," and accompanying religious practices such as attending worship, participating in youth group, engaging in prayer, reading Scripture, and serving others were the places where their faith was "activated, practiced, and formed." In fact, the NSYR found these practices to be "crucial to vibrant religious faith."[42] Even the teenagers who identified as "not religious" still described engaging patterns of prayer, church attendance, and other religious activities, leading researchers to make the important distinction that not all the teenagers who might describe themselves as such *acted* "not religious."[43]

A Minority Culture in a Majority of Liturgical Settings

While teenagers worship frequently, more often than not they function as discrete or marginalized worshipers. As we discussed in the introduction, teenagers on the whole are a discreet minority in the worship life of many congregations, and the worship gatherings that teenagers participate in are nearly always the product of adult planning and leadership. Even when teenagers lead the music or speak or play another leadership role in adult or youth worship, teenagers remain influenced by the adults who mentor them and bear responsibility for their actions. It makes sense for adults to lead worship, since teenagers often can't tackle all the planning required. But, leaving teens out of worship may cause them to feel juvenilized. This results in teenagers leaving for college with

41. Smith and Denton, *Soul Searching*, 38.
42. Smith and Denton, *Soul Searching*, 26–29.
43. Smith and Denton, *Soul Searching*, 31.

varying views on the purpose of worship—from thinking it's all about their wants and needs to thinking it's an important rhythm of spiritual formation.

Teenagers and the Worshiping Community

One of today's best observers on how people of faith deal with such challenges in the world is bestselling author Anne Lamott. In her book *Plan B: Some Thoughts on Faith*, she tells of her attempt to teach her teenage son, Sam, the value of a faith community even though Sam doesn't always like to go to church. "Then why do I make him go?" she asks rhetorically.

> Because I want him to. We live in bewildering, drastic times, and a little spiritual guidance never killed anyone. I think it's a fair compromise that every other week he has to come to the place that has been the tap for me: I want him to see the people who loved me when I felt most unlovable, who have loved him since I first told them that I was pregnant, even though he might not want to be with them. I want him to see their faces. . . .
>
> While he lives at my house, he has to do things my way. And there are worse things for kids than to have to spend time with people who love God. Teenagers who do not go to church are adored by God, but they don't get to meet some of the people who love God back. Learning to love back is the hardest part of being alive.[44]

Teenagers want to know and be known by the community in which they worship. In the College Transition Project, FYI searched for a "silver bullet" to help instill in teenagers a faith that would last beyond their high school years. While FYI admitted that spiritual formation in teenagers was more complex than a single factor, they also said that intergenerational worship was the closest their research had come to finding a single silver bullet.[45] This was also a key theme in the NSYR, which found that "cross-generational relational ties" can "help legitimize and reinforce the religious faith and practices of those teens."[46] The NSYR found that 79 percent of teenagers who attend religious services enjoy fruitful relationships with adults who are not family members and who teenagers "enjoy talking with and who give them lots of encouragement." Sixty-one percent of teenagers who attend religious services and do not report this kind of relationship expressed a desire to have one.[47] Overall,

44. Anne Lamott, *Plan B: Further Thoughts on Faith* (New York: Riverhead, 2006), 195–96.
45. Kara E. Powell and Chap Clark, *Sticky Faith: Everyday Ideas to Build Lasting Faith in Your Kids* (Grand Rapids: Zondervan, 2008), 97.
46. Smith and Denton, *Soul Searching*, 61.
47. Smith and Denton, *Soul Searching*, 60.

teenagers see the adults in their congregations as individuals of integrity to whom they can turn for support, advice, and help.

In an overview of ministry practices, the Barna Group's *The State of Youth Ministry* notes that an overwhelming majority of senior pastors (87 percent) and youth pastors (84 percent) describe attending all-church worship services as a youth group activity, meaning they value the presence of teenagers in the worshiping community. In contrast, 65 percent of parents of teenagers describe worship as an activity for all ages in the church, not primarily as a youth ministry activity. Teenagers often still have the opportunity to participate in a worship gathering connected to the youth group throughout the week. Forty-eight percent of youth pastors reported offering large-group worship activities for teenagers as part of their weekly rhythm,[48] though the number of youth pastors who prefer a large-group format with opportunities for youth group worship is 29 percent compared to the 71 percent of youth ministers who prefer small-group discipleship, teaching, and mentoring programs.[49]

Within the worshiping community, parents remain the primary influencers of teenagers' liturgical lives. While relationships with adults who are not parents are important, 66 percent of teenagers said their parents and the family unit were the primary companions for attendance at religious services. They also stated that the family unit serves as the primary nucleus for any kind of liturgical activity beyond the life of the church that might help teenagers connect worship to their everyday lives. This includes talking about God, Scripture, prayer, or other religious and spiritual things. It also includes prayer at mealtimes and opportunities for the teenager to pray out loud or silently with one or more parents at other times.[50] Fifty-four percent of teenagers reported praying with their family at mealtimes, and 41 percent reported praying out loud with their parents at other times.[51] In the end, the importance, or lack of importance, that a teenager's parents place on worship practices will be reflected in the teenager's faith life. In other words, "religion and spirituality are not simply compartmentalized in church, synagogue, mosque, or temple, but are also expressed and shared in the family life of home."[52]

Of particular challenge for parents of today's teenagers is knowing how and when to be involved in their teenagers' spiritual lives. Barna describes the parents of Generation Z as "double-minded," placing them in one of two

48. The Barna Group, *The State of Youth Ministry: How Churches Reach Today's Teens—and What Parents Think About It* (Ventura, CA: Barna Group, 2016), 39–41.

49. Barna, *State of Youth Ministry*, 98.

50. Smith and Denton, *Soul Searching*, 55.

51. Smith and Denton, *Soul Searching*, 54.

52. Smith and Denton, *Soul Searching*, 56.

camps: those who function as overprotective parents (helicopter or lawn-mower parents) and those who function as under-protective. Barna acknowl-edges that most parents are likely a combination of these two traits; they are overprotective in some areas and under-protective in other areas. Barna notes that parents "may be over-involved in many of the wrong ways and too detached in others."[53] Barna does note, however, that parents of Generation Z overwhelmingly say that attending church together is one of the most impor-tant family activities in which they engage.[54] The call for parents, as well as for the entire worshiping community, is to strike a balance in their approach to engaging teenagers inside and outside worship.

Teenagers and the Complexities of the World

According to Pew Research Center, today's teenagers—also known as Gen-eration Z—appear similar to their predecessors, Millennials, on key social and political issues, but this generation is "moving toward adulthood with a liberal set of attitudes and an openness to emerging social trends," such as race, climate, and the role of government in society. For example, mem-bers of Generation Z overwhelmingly believe that individuals who are not white—especially Black people—have been treated unfairly. They also believe climate change is directly linked to human activity, can be controlled, and that other countries are better at taking care of climate change than the United States is.[55] Fifty-four percent of Generation Z, whose members Barna also calls "screen-agers,"[56] believe they spend too much time on their cell phones,[57] and compared to other generations, they view mental health, bullying, drug and alcohol abuse, and school shootings as some of their greatest concerns and challenges.[58] The world today's teenagers inhabit is very diverse, more so than any other generation to date.

53. Barna, *Gen Z*, 34–35.

54. Barna, *Gen Z*, 83

55. Kim Parker, Nikki Graf, and Ruth Igielnik, "Generation Z Looks a Lot Like Millenni-als on Key Social and Political Issues," Pew Research Center, January 17, 2019, https://www .pewsocialtrends.org/2019/01/17/generation-z-looks-a-lot-like-millennials-on-key-social-and -political-issues/.

56. Barna, *Gen Z*, 15.

57. Jingjing Jiang, "How Teens and Parents Navigate Screen Time and Device Distractions," Pew Research Center, August 22, 2018, https://www.pewresearch.org/internet/2018/08/22/how -teens-and-parents-navigate-screen-time-and-device-distractions/.

58. Drew DeSilver, "The Concerns and Challenges of Being a U.S. Teen: What the Data Show," Pew Research Center, February 26, 2019, https://www.pewresearch.org/fact-tank/2019 /02/26/the-concerns-and-challenges-of-being-a-u-s-teen-what-the-data-show/. See also Juliana

In data that mirrors that of the United States Census Bureau, Barna found that Generation Zers are more likely than previous generations to be multiracial, to grow up in multigenerational households, and to be in contact with nonmale and nonwhite people.[59] Teenagers want a worshiping congregation that mirrors the world they inhabit. In fact, Barna stated that a "lack of diversity in a faith community could be a major stumbling block for a generation that has already begun to see church as irrelevant to their lives."[60] Barna also found that "safe spaces" are part of the cultural fabric of today's teenagers, meaning that Generation Z is interested in protecting individuals from "information that could induce or remind one of trauma" and in giving individuals the opportunity to "opt out of discussions that may in any way upset or provoke" them.[61] Barna researchers noted that many teenagers are hesitant to "make declarative statements about anything that could cause offense" and oftentimes struggle to give a definitive answer.[62] "Real safety" is a myth for the teenagers of Generation Z, who do not remember living in a society pre-9/11; they have come of age in a milieu in which war has raged and financial peace is impossible.[63] As this generation prepares to enter adulthood, their first eighteen years have been bookended by tragedy: 9/11 on one end and a global pandemic on the other.[64] Are our worship practices equipping teenagers to navigate the world they experience, care for, and love?

Conclusion

In his autobiography *A Confession*, Leo Tolstoy remembers his anonymous, clever, and truthful friend (someone he calls "a certain-S") who eventually stopped believing in the Christian faith. Tolstoy writes,

Menasce Horowitz and Nikki Graf, "Most U.S. Teens See Anxiety and Depression as a Major Problem among Their Peers," Pew Research Center, February 20, 2019, https://www.pewsocial trends.org/2019/02/20/most-u-s-teens-see-anxiety-and-depression-as-a-major-problem-among -their-peers/; and Nikki Graf, "A Majority of U.S. Teens Fear a Shooting Could Happen at Their School, and Most Parents Share Their Concern," Pew Research Center, April 18, 2018, https://www.pewresearch.org/fact-tank/2018/04/18/a-majority-of-u-s-teens-fear-a-shooting -could-happen-at-their-school-and-most-parents-share-their-concern/.

59. Barna, *Gen Z*, 34.
60. Barna, *Gen Z*, 74.
61. Barna, *Gen Z*, 27.
62. Barna, *Gen Z*, 28.
63. Barna, *Gen Z*, 29.
64. See John Branch and Campbell Robertson, "Meet the Covid Class of 2020," *New York Times*, May 30, 2020, https://www.nytimes.com/interactive/2020/05/30/us/coronavirus-class -of-2020.html.

On a hunting expedition, when [a certain-S] was already twenty-six, he once, at the place where they put up for the night, knelt down in the evening to pray—a habit retained from childhood. His elder brother, who was at the hunt with him, was lying on some hay and watching him. When [the younger man] had finished and was settling down for the night, his brother said to him: "So you still do that?"

They said nothing more to one another. But from that day [he] ceased to say his prayers or go to church. And now he has not prayed, received communion, or gone to church for thirty years. And this not because he knows his brother's convictions and has joined him in them, nor because he has decided anything in his own soul, but simply because the word spoken by his brother was like the push of a finger on a wall that was ready to fall by its own weight.[65]

Research has illustrated that the faith of teenagers across the United States is ready to "fall by its own weight" if the right push removes the right support from a wall that is about to fall. I don't know whether the wall of teenagers' faith is about to fall, but I do know that the God we worship is big enough to support the wall, however shaky or sturdy, that our teenagers are using to prop up their faith.

65. Leo Tolstoy, *A Confession* (1882), Christian Classics Ethereal Library, July 11, 1998, http://www.ccel.org/ccel/tolstoy/confession.html. I am grateful to Melanie Ross, associate professor of liturgical studies at Yale Divinity School and Yale Institute of Sacred Music, for introducing me to this story in 2012. I have used it often to illustrate an incongruence between piety in the adolescent years and piety in the adult years.

2

✦ ✦ ✦

Lessons from the Past

What Our Worship Practices Have Told Our Teenagers

Each people group, each generation, needs to be able to express its sense of
worship in its own voice, in a way that resonates deep in the soul.

—Nicholas Wolterstorff, *The Spirit in Worship—Worship in the Spirit*

Introduction

Although the story is long and complex, Christian worship has moved through
cycles of formation and reformation in nearly all Catholic and Protestant
circles. The narrative is inspiring and intriguing; it is also wrought with scars,
strife, and splits. While history will show that the "vastness of variety in the
Christian experience of worship" makes it difficult to "trace the coherence
that unites the various expressions in time and place," the sheer diversity of
Christian worship over two millennia reminds us "what a lover of variety the
Christian God appears to be."[1]

1. James F. White, *A Brief History of Christian Worship* (Nashville: Abingdon, 1992), 10.
White's text provides a good overview of the history of Christian worship, though it does not

In contrast, the history of youth ministry is much shorter than the history of Christian worship. Despite its own adolescence, youth ministry has run in cyclical patterns that have been defined by innovative ministry approaches that are eventually killed by irrelevance due to societal changes.[2] Like the history of worship ministry, the history of youth ministry is characterized by a mixed narrative of growth and decline, excitement and despair. Yet the overarching story of youth ministry is that through prayer and Scripture, God's people have "expected to experience God's presence during the years of their youth."[3]

Worship with adolescents[4] dates as far back as the earliest history of Christian worship: when young and old worshiped together in the covenantal Old and New Testament communities portrayed in Nehemiah 8 and 1 Corinthians 1. Young people were present for worship with all ages at the tabernacle, temple, synagogue, New Testament house churches, medieval cathedrals and monasteries, Reformation sanctuaries, frontier settlements, charismatic communities, and all the other places God's people have worshiped throughout history. But worship practices with adolescents changed when youth ministry came onto the scene in the late eighteenth and early nineteenth centuries.

To tell the story of adolescent worship is to tell the story of God reaching out to young people and young people reaching back to God. Though neither comprehensive nor exhaustive, this chapter will narrate highlights in the story of adolescent worship practices in the United States. This chapter will use the birth of youth ministry as its starting point and provide snapshots of worship practices with young people from the start of youth ministry until the present day. The hope is that by learning from the past we can inform the future and imagine a path forward for worship practices with teenagers in the remainder of the twenty-first century.

---

adequately tell the history of worship in the evangelical church. Here, a helpful starting place might be White's *Protestant Worship: Traditions in Transition* (Louisville: Westminster John Knox, 1989). White introduced the "Frontier tradition" as a precursor to evangelical worship. Frontier worship is worship that developed on American soil, on the frontier, and often followed a threefold order of music, preaching, and response.

2. Mark H. Senter III, *When God Shows Up: A History of Protestant Youth Ministry in America* (Grand Rapids: Baker Academic, 2010), xiv.

3. Senter, *When God Shows Up*, xi.

4. Here I intentionally use the word *adolescents* rather than *teenagers*. As we will see, youth ministry and its accompanying worship practices began before the word *teenager* was invented. Adolescent worship practices until the mid-twentieth century likely included young people from twelve to the mid-twenties (depending on the era). By the middle of the twentieth century, the age range narrowed to focus primarily on mid-adolescence, or fourteen to eighteen years of age.

A Familiar Pattern: Orientation, Disorientation, and New Orientation

The three-part cycle of orientation, disorientation, and new orientation has been used to describe worship patterns in the United States,[5] patterns of spiritual growth,[6] and patterns in the Psalms.[7] The typical cycle begins with a season of stability and "settled familiarity." When everything is relatively stable, there is "safety in what is known, assurance in the predictable, and ease in the routine." Orientation then moves into a time of disorientation—a time of extreme change when instability emerges from any number of factors, though the ethos is that "the familiar becomes unfamiliar, the settled becomes unsettled, and the comfortable becomes uncomfortable."[8] Over time, disorientation should give way to a new orientation, but this is not guaranteed. New orientation depends on an individual's or a community's willingness to be reoriented by asking questions about the work of God in the world. Moving into new orientation allows "the status quo (the tradition) to be submitted to its full time of testing" so that God can "change us in light of his purposes for the tradition."[9]

The orientation stage could describe worship in early nineteenth century America. Congregations met as intergenerational communities and "supposed the normal worship services to be sufficient for ushering the youth of their church into the presence of God."[10] The patterns of living were comfortable and untested, and people immersed themselves in worship traditions that had begun to provide "great assurance and a sense of well-being."[11] As industrialization and secularization rose, however, the church moved toward a season of disorientation, fearing their initial assumptions would prove flawed and their usual patterns of worship would prove ineffective for young people.

To combat these cultural forces present in the early nineteenth century, "isolated clergy" began experimenting with "gatherings outside the Sunday

5. I am borrowing this pattern from Constance Cherry, "Merging Tradition and Innovation in the Life of the Church: Moving from Style to Encountering God in Worship," in *The Conviction of Things Not Seen: Worship and Ministry in the 21st Century*, ed. Todd E. Johnson (Grand Rapids: Brazos, 2002), 19–32.

6. See James W. Fowler, *Stages of Faith: The Psychology of Human Development and the Quest for Meaning* (San Francisco: Harper & Row, 1981). Fowler uses a model from Piaget that describes movement from equilibrium to dislocation to trust. See also Carolyn Gratton, *The Art of Spiritual Guidance* (New York: Crossroad, 1993).

7. Walter Brueggemann, *The Spirituality of the Psalms* (Minneapolis: Fortress, 2002), viii.

8. Cherry, "Merging Tradition and Innovation," 20.

9. Cherry, "Merging Tradition and Innovation," 21.

10. Senter, *When God Shows Up*, xi.

11. Cherry, "Merging Tradition and Innovation," 20.

morning worship service to engage the rising generation in a quest to know God and live lives in conformity with God's will."[12] Their intent was noble: to enculturate young people in Christian values, promote temperance, teach character, encourage evangelism, and pass down the faith from one generation to the next.[13] While they did not realize the effects their ministry would have on the congregations they pastored or the church at large, their experiments ultimately moved the church into a season of new orientation that included youth ministry and the acknowledgment that adolescents expected to "experience God's presence during the years of their youth."[14] The patterns of orientation, disorientation, and new orientation would repeat themselves in macro and micro ways throughout the late nineteenth and twentieth centuries as youth ministry and worship ministry influenced each other. They would also repeat themselves in local congregations and in the worship lives of adolescents.[15]

The Web of Adolescent Worship

The most important characteristic of adolescent worship is that it comes in varieties, just as people do.[16] It is a complex web that includes a multiplicity of people worshiping in different times and places using varied methods of prayer, preaching, and music, all of which lead to various pieties.[17] James F. White writes, "The primary ingredient of all worship is people, yet rarely do most liturgical studies mention the social realities of what was happening to people in times of liturgical change. *People are the primary liturgical document*."[18]

12. Senter, *When God Shows Up*, xi–xii.
13. Senter, *When God Shows Up*, 104. "Passing down the faith" from one generation to the next is a common expression in youth ministry, but it is also a social construct. See S. N. Eisenstadt, *From Generation to Generation* (London: Free Press of Glencoe, 1956). Here it is also important to note that the age of "young people" then would have been broader than today's definition of teenagers; it would have included those in their twenties and, at times, also children. Chapter 5 in this text outlines a different model: passing *around* the faith.
14. Senter, *When God Shows Up*, xi.
15. How this cycle happens on macro levels is discussed more in chap. 8, which has an entire section on worship and change in congregational contexts.
16. James F. White applies the same principle to Protestant worship. See J. F. White, *Protestant Worship*, 17.
17. Here I am alluding to the method of study used by White (*Protestant Worship*, 16–21). In general, I have tried to use White's schema to examine adolescent worship practices, though it is alluded to implicitly rather than explicitly throughout this chapter.
18. J. F. White, *Protestant Worship*, 16 (emphasis original).

With teenagers as the primary liturgical document, we might start with this question: Where are adolescents familiar with worship—that is, where do they feel a strong sense of stability, of orientation? The answer is most likely inside the walls of the church—namely, all-church worship and youth group worship. Both are known quantities to the average young person participating in the life of the local church through worship ministry, youth ministry, or both. So the next section of this chapter, "Orientation," will provide brief histories of the places that are likely to be the most orienting to the teenager participating in worship inside the local church: the sanctuary, the youth room, and the music room.[19]

A second question might then be asked: Where do adolescents feel unsettled or uncomfortable in worship? The answer might be at a camp, conference, or retreat where they have emptied themselves of technology, family, and friends to focus on their spiritual lives, a place where worship looks different than it does in church. Another answer might be at school, where their friends might see them worship. "Disorientation," a later section in this chapter, will trace snapshots of many worship scenes known to adolescents: worship at camps, retreats, and conferences; worship at school; worship in stadiums; and worship at concerts. While these scenes are familiar to many in the church today, they can be unfamiliar, uncomfortable, and even jarring for teenagers as well as congregations. Yet worship in these locations often provides potential for spiritual growth.[20] In that sense, my use of *disorientation* acknowledges that youth camps, conferences, and retreats have been critical in the spiritual development process of many adolescents, as they were for me in my adolescent years.

Keeping teenagers as our liturgical document, we could ask another question: Might adolescents possess a willingness to be reoriented by asking questions about the work of God in the world, and might the church possess this same spirit? The section of this chapter labeled "New Orientation" will reflect critically on the church's collective learning about teenage worship practices since the dawn of the twenty-first century and ask how we might reorient our worship with teenagers as a result.

This framework is not intended to be a straitjacket, nor is it intended to be a comprehensive work that will use a master key to unlock the door to

19. *Sanctuary* and *youth room* are very broadly defined. By *sanctuary*, I mean all-church worship, the gathering that most in the local congregation attend, overseen by a pastor and/or worship leader. By *youth room*, I mean worship that is probably overseen by a youth minister in the context of the youth group.

20. See Kermit Moss and Jacob Sorenson, "Deep Rhythms of Faith Formation: Separation and Reintegration in Summer Camp and Retreats," in *Cultivating Teen Faith: Insights from the Confirmation Project*, ed. Richard R. Osmer and Katherine M. Douglass (Grand Rapids: Eerdmans, 2018), 67–88.

understanding adolescent worship practices.[21] But if we listen to adolescent worshipers of the past, in all their candor, honesty, pain, joy, and passion, we may find something new as their persistent voices give us a word that turns out to be helpful for worship with teenagers today.

Orientation: Worship Inside the Church

To look at the history of adolescent worship, we must first understand worship inside the church—worship in the sanctuary, worship in the youth room, and worship in the music room—though each of these "rooms" may not exist in every church building. In places where they do exist, they look very different in actual architecture. However they exist, they serve as home base for teenagers at worship, however often they attend, and such rooms provide a level of comfort and familiarity for any adolescent worshiper.

Worship in the sanctuary refers to the primary gatherings of congregations that occur on a weekly basis, usually on Sunday mornings, with all ages, though other times, places, and age factors abound. Worship in the youth room refers to midweek gatherings of teenagers in the context of youth ministry, where worship may occur however explicit or implicit. Historically, this has included models of youth ministry from Great Britain, such as Sunday school associations, temperance movements, and the YMCA, each of which later merged with denominational societies, secular organizations, and youth fellowship groups. Finally, worship in the music room refers to gatherings of teenagers convened by music ministries, such as singing schools, youth choirs, and youth group bands.

Worship in the Sanctuary

When youth ministry began, various Protestant worship traditions were on the scene across the United States. White defines these worship traditions as left wing and right wing by their proximity to late medieval and Roman Catholic worship.[22] As history marched on, the traditions became more relaxed in worship, freeing themselves from the prayer books and

---

21. Brueggemann, *Spirituality of the Psalms*, viii.

22. See J. F. White, *Protestant Worship*, 21–24. White's historical model has proven helpful, but its limitations are in showing Protestant worship now. For instance, two Methodist congregations worshiping down the street from each other may have very different worship practices, each of which have blurred distinctions from the other traditions. See Lester Ruth, "A Rose by Any Other Name," in *The Conviction of Things Not Seen: Worship and Ministry in the 21st Century*, ed. Todd E. Johnson (Grand Rapids: Brazos, 2002), 44–46.

songbooks that had historically guided worship in the Catholic Church. With the exception of the Pentecostal tradition, which developed in the twentieth century, each of these traditions existed in the United States in some fashion when youth ministry emerged in the late eighteenth and early nineteenth centuries. Their continued evolution paralleled the development of youth ministry.

Figure 2.1
History of Worship

	Left Wing	Centrist	Right Wing	
16th Century	Anabaptist	Reformed	Anglican	Lutheran
17th Century	Quaker	Puritan		
18th Century		Methodist		
19th Century	Frontier			
20th Century	Pentecostal			

Adapted from J. F. White, *Protestant Worship*, 23.

In the twentieth century, a number of developments happened in the sanctuary for many congregations. In the years after World War II, many individuals came into the church. Denominational loyalty was highly valued, and family units retained their denominational commitments. The Liturgical Movement began a wave to reclaim the church with several key themes, including reaching for community, increased participation in worship, rediscovery of the early church as a model, rediscovery of Scripture, rediscovery of the Lord's Table, an emphasis on the vernacular in worship, a rediscovery of other Christian traditions, and an emphasis on proclamation and social involvement. In this season, worshipers were committed to the liturgy of the Word and the Table in their worship celebrations with varying degrees of frequency. They were concerned with full, active, and conscious participation, and there was an increased sense that ministers were not the only worshipers: all people contributed to worship.[23]

In the 1960s, church and society experienced a time of extreme social change. In the church, the Charismatic Renewal Movement (post-1950), Vatican II (1962–65), and the Jesus Movement (late 1960s) all occurred. There was an increased concern for the gifts and manifestation of the Holy Spirit in worship, and worship began to be defined by the style of music that was played. Locations for worship were found to enable the gospel to

23. These characteristics are adapted from John Fenwick and Bryan Spinks, *Worship in Transition* (New York: Continuum, 1995), chap. 2.

come to the people—auditoriums, storefront theaters, grocery stores, and beyond. In this season, many churches became more concerned with evangelism and connecting to culture than with connecting to God. The Church Growth Movement, which began in the late 1970s and continued through the 1980s, told people, "Go contemporary, or your church will not survive!" Finally, the twentieth century became overshadowed by postmodernism, a term used as early as 1930 and that reached prominence by the end of the twentieth century. The core of the Postmodern Movement was the refusal to acknowledge absolute truth. Other features became of interest in communities that claimed the loss of a metanarrative to form their identity as a group.

At the risk of being too reductionistic, I will broadly examine worship in the sanctuary through the lenses of evangelicals, mainline Protestants, Black Baptists, and Roman Catholics.[24] The first of these four groups comes from what James F. White refers to as the Frontier tradition, though after setting this tradition in context, I will refer to it as the evangelical tradition. This tradition has influenced adolescent worship in ways too great to cover in this single chapter, yet the other three have also made important contributions. The mainline Protestant and Roman Catholic traditions are each rooted in an ecumenism that comes from the late nineteenth- and early twentieth-century Liturgical Movement, and they influenced each other throughout the twentieth century. Worship practices in Black congregations are as diverse as those of other ethnicities, but Black Baptists birthed the popular Youth Sunday practice, which mainline Protestant and Catholic congregations adopted during the middle and latter part of the twentieth century. In the same way that mainline Protestants adopted Black worship practices, evangelicals and mainline Protestants also adopted practices from Catholicism. Roman Catholic worship renewal served as a precursor to the CCM movement in the evangelical church and the use of folk hymnody in mainline Protestant traditions. Although evangelical worship has at times been at odds with worship in mainline Protestant congregations and Roman Catholic parishes, understanding the fallacies and fruits of evangelical worship may be a path toward new orientation for worship with teenagers today.[25] For that reason,

24. I am examining the sanctuary practices of Black Baptists because Youth Sunday finds its origins in this tradition. It is worth noting that there are Black evangelicals, Protestants, and Catholics, all of whom have experienced unfair treatment in society and in the church. For an examination of racial challenges among Black people and youth ministry, see Montague R. Williams, *Church in Color: Youth Ministry, Race, and the Theology of Martin Luther King, Jr.* (Waco: Baylor University Press, 2020).

25. See Melanie C. Ross, *Evangelical versus Liturgical? Defying a Dichotomy* (Grand Rapids: Eerdmans, 2014).

our journey with worship inside the church will begin with the evangelical approach to worship.

The Sanctuary of Evangelicals

There is much to say about evangelical worship and its relationship to youth ministry, but first it is important to note that this model of worship is not new. As White's historical model alludes, this tradition of worship was birthed on American soil and finds its origins in the work of revivalists such as George Whitefield and Charles Finney, as well as in the nineteenth-century camp meetings of the Frontier tradition. It has influenced virtually every Christian denomination within the United States and beyond, it birthed the megachurch, and it defined the teenage worship experience of many who are now adults in the church. It continues to do the same for many adolescents today.[26]

The study of evangelical worship has flourished in the last two decades as individuals have written about it, though the discourse has been "limited and polemical."[27] Scholars inside the liturgical academy have spoken about evangelical worship with disdain as an ahistorical and therefore invalid form of worship. Evangelicals themselves are often turned off by the study and analysis of their worship practices, believing worship is "more a matter of immediate, unstructured, informal response to God."[28] They have thrown stones at critics, accusing them of "tastelessly [comparing] evangelical . . . worship with the medieval fascination with relics."[29]

Graham Hughes wrote about worship practices among evangelicals and mainline Protestants in his book *Worship as Meaning*. Hughes claims that evangelical worship attempts to make meaning out of the world by "isolating [religious meanings] from the prevalent culture." In other words, evangelical worship establishes "a basic cultural bipolarity in which religious meanings are held antipathetically in relation to the values of the surrounding culture."[30] Hughes believes the evangelical approach to worship is a strong and powerful vehicle of meaning for a large number of individuals for at least two reasons. First, it offers a clarity, simplicity, and accessibility not afforded in the

26. See Thomas E. Bergler, *The Juvenilization of American Christianity* (Grand Rapids: Eerdmans, 2012), introduction, chap. 1.

27. Melanie Ross, "Joseph's Britches Revisited: Reflections on Methodology in Liturgical Theology," *Worship* 80, no. 6 (November 2006): 528.

28. Graham Hughes, *Worship as Meaning: A Liturgical Theology for Late Modernity* (Cambridge: Cambridge University Press, 2003), 234.

29. Rob Redman, *The Great Worship Awakening* (San Francisco: Jossey-Bass, 2002), 91.

30. Hughes, *Worship as Meaning*, 223.

pluralistic society in which we find ourselves.[31] This clarity and simplicity are seen in the music, the sermon, and the response. Through these events, the evangelical approach promotes four prominent values: (1) the importance of the gathered community as disciples of Christ, (2) an insistence on biblicism, (3) an emphasis on making "a personal decision for Jesus Christ," and (4) a call for righteous living.

Second, evangelical worship successfully combines an "inherited or underlying Protestant commitment *to* ordinariness" with a "religious differentiation *from* ordinariness as the sphere of God's self-manifestation."[32] Evangelicals work hard to make God accessible to the mass culture by using vernacular idioms, treating all people—ordained and lay leaders—as equal, emphasizing informality in dress and communication, constructing worship spaces that look like a mall or a stadium, and drawing from popular musical idioms. The overall effect of these efforts "attests a God who is immediately accessible, who does not need priestly or ministerial intermediaries, and who does not stand behind or upon dignity."[33]

Monique Ingalls approaches the study of evangelical worship through the lens of music, which "engages worshipers in a variety of performance spaces that were once distinct, bridging public and private devotional practices, connecting online and offline communities, and bringing competing personal, institutional, and commercial interests into the same domains."[34] Thus, the "sanctuary" in which evangelical worship occurs is loosely defined. As Ingalls has illustrated, evangelicals often worship through music, which may take place in concert, conference, church, public, or online settings, going much further than the traditional weekly gathering of many worshiping communities.[35]

Historian Lester Ruth states that evangelical worship made worship "a tool—not a summit toward which to aspire and not a fount from which great spiritual power is to be drawn—but something to be taken and used for a greater goal." From this pragmatism, Ruth argues, a new type of liturgy has emerged, "one in which *lex orandi*, the Church's rule for prayer, has become dependent upon an evangelistic *lex agendi*, a vision for successful evangelism."[36] We will see that this liturgy is prevalent in historical models of youth ministry, where the *agendi* is attracting young people to church and

---

31. Hughes, *Worship as Meaning*, 241–42.

32. Hughes, *Worship as Meaning*, 242 (emphasis original).

33. Hughes, *Worship as Meaning*, 243.

34. Monique M. Ingalls, *Singing the Congregation: How Contemporary Worship Music Forms Evangelical Identity* (New York: Oxford University Press, 2018), 1.

35. Ingalls, *Singing the Congregation*, 4.

36. Lester Ruth, "*Lex Agendi, Lex Orandi*: Toward an Understanding of Seeker Services as a New Kind of Liturgy, *Worship* 70, no. 5 (September 1996), 403–5.

keeping them in church. For this reason, in *The Worship Mall*, Bryan D. Spinks writes about "youth worship" in his chapter titled "Entertaining Worship or Worship as Entertainment?"[37]

With its values of pragmatism, liturgical freedom, and biblicism and its call to better living—each of which aligns closely with the values youth ministry has historically held—the evangelical tradition of worship became quite successful in helping teenagers make sense of the world. Because of this, many adolescent worship gatherings in the youth room and outside the church adopted in part or in full the ethos and values of the evangelical tradition. No matter where congregations fall on White's liturgical spectrum, the evangelical tradition has infiltrated every Protestant and Catholic youth group in the United States. Even liturgically conservative denominations and congregations have adopted this more progressive model of worship in an effort to engage teenagers.[38] We will see this pattern when we examine worship in the youth room, but for now we turn to the sanctuary of mainline Protestants.

The Sanctuary of Mainline Protestants

If the agenda of the worship gatherings in the evangelical church was to attract and retain young people in the church, then their counterpart occurred in mainline Protestant congregations, whose aim was to teach young people the tradition of their faith and connect them to the broader Christian tradition. Throughout the twentieth century, mainline Protestants used theology, or *lex credendi*, to shape their worship, *lex orandi*.[39] Approaching worship through theology became a classic Protestant approach, first systematized by Geoffrey Wainwright and described well by Maxwell Johnson:

> What we do or don't do in our liturgies forms the community in one way or another. Hence, a [Lutheran] community which celebrates and receives Christ's Body and Blood in the Lord's Supper every Sunday, attends to the rubrical

37. Bryan D. Spinks, *The Worship Mall: Contemporary Responses to Contemporary Culture* (New York: Church Publishing, 2010), 87–88.

38. This is a familiar pattern in worship history. Theologically conservative congregations are generally liturgically progressive; theologically progressive congregations are generally liturgically conservative. See J. F. White, *Protestant Worship*, 22–23. For example, a local Episcopalian youth group, which I observed not long ago, followed a threefold order of singing, sermon, and response. The 2012 gathering of the Evangelical Lutheran Church in America included a number of artists, and many of their prerallies—small, regional gatherings leading up to the large event—also followed this threefold order. See Tom Lyberg, "Singing a New Song: Lutheran Artists at the 2012 Youth Gathering," Living Lutheran, Evangelical Lutheran Church in America, June 20, 2012, https://www.livinglutheran.org/2012/06/singing-new-song/.

39. See Geoffrey Wainwright, *Doxology: The Praise of God in Worship, Doctrine, and Life; A Systematic Theology* (New York: Oxford University Press, 1984).

options and varieties already present in the "authorized" liturgical book(s), faithfully proclaims the lectionary readings, and tenaciously keeps the feasts and seasons of the liturgical year week after week, year after year, will be a different sort of community than one which is continually experimenting with "worship alternatives" and searching for something "better" to meet the so-called "needs" of worshipers and potential seekers alike. And I dare say that the first type of community will, undoubtedly, be more "orthodox," more "Lutheran," in its doctrinal-theological outlook.[40]

On the whole, the mainline Protestant tradition of worship encompasses theologically progressive denominations and congregations whose worship practices are in a literal sanctuary and often utilize prayer books and hymnals, though there are always exceptions to that stereotype.[41] The worship of mainline congregations was rooted in ecumenism throughout much of the twentieth century, endeavoring to "make sense of God by reflecting *from within* its condition in modernity in order to say how and where God may be understood as fitting into this."[42] As the twentieth century progressed, many mainline Protestant congregations adopted the informal worship styles from the evangelical tradition to combat aging congregations and "diminishing resources," but a general characteristic of worship among mainline congregations is still to withdraw from rather than partake in modern culture.[43]

The Sanctuary of Black Baptists and Youth Sunday

While many congregations moved teenagers out of the sanctuary and into the youth room, the Black Baptist church did the opposite during the twentieth century. They integrated teenagers into the overall life of the church, which included a monthly Youth Sunday, where young people planned and led the entire worship service.[44] One of the most prominent examples of Youth Sunday came from First Baptist Church, Capitol Hill, in Nashville, Tennessee, where Rev. Kelly Miller Smith developed programming for all ages and "insisted that all young people stay for the adult worship service."[45]

40. Maxwell Johnson, "Is Anything Normative in Contemporary Lutheran Worship?," in *The Serious Business of Worship: Essays in Honour of Bryan D. Spinks*, ed. Melanie Ross and Simon Jones (London: T&T Clark, 2010), 177.

41. See J. F. White, *Protestant Worship*, 21–22. An example of an exception might be a congregation that worships in an old sanctuary but has a band leading worship because the organ is out of repair or an organist is not available.

42. Hughes, *Worship as Meaning*, 244–45 (emphasis original).

43. Hughes, *Worship as Meaning*, 245.

44. Bergler, *Juvenilization of American Christianity*, 37.

45. Bergler, *Juvenilization of American Christianity*, 103.

Their monthly Youth Sunday included a variety of songs and sermons that emphasized "heroic devotion to Christ and his cause" and contained "comforting reminders of God's help."[46] Throughout the 1950s and 1960s, Youth Sunday, as well as its accompanying Youth Week, in the Black Baptist church would foster important opportunities for the church to call teenagers not only to dedicate themselves to the work of the church but also to organize for social action.[47]

Over time, the practice of Youth Sunday was adopted by many white mainline Protestant congregations as annual, rather than monthly, celebrations where teenagers could "take over" the primary worship service of the church. In these services teenagers replace adults by handing out the bulletins, leading the music, praying the prayers, reading the Scripture, preaching the sermon, collecting the offering, running the soundboard, and doing just about every other job that can be done in worship leadership, with the exception of those liturgical elements that require an ordained minister, such as the celebration of Communion. Many times, Youth Sunday becomes an opportunity for all ages in the church to encourage teenagers, and this can be a positive experience. In its best form, it serves as a symbol to teenagers that their presence as baptized members of the local congregation and larger body of Christ matters. It provides teenagers with an opportunity to understand worship as leaders rather than as participants, and it provides them with an opportunity to practice leadership in the church.

In recent years, Youth Sunday has received more criticism than praise. Criticism has come from the sentiment that having teenagers lead worship once per year is not enough to remind them that they are the church in the present, not the church of the future. In some traditions, it interrupts the liturgical year and other patterns that are familiar to all worshipers.[48] In other instances, Youth Sunday becomes an occasion either to make adult worshipers feel good about the future of Christianity or to deliver a message of guilt for adults who have lost their youthful zeal and passions.[49] The most prominent criticism of Youth Sunday, however, is that it reduces worship to a performance by teenagers, forcing them to do something they are not capable of doing or willing to do. Critics usually encourage congregations to adopt practices

46. Bergler, *Juvenilization of American Christianity*, 104.

47. Bergler, *Juvenilization of American Christianity*, 104.

48. See "Do We Celebrate Youth Sunday?," Evangelical Lutheran Church in America, revised May 2018, https://download.elca.org/ELCA%20Resource%20Repository/Do_we_celebrate _Youth_Sunday.pdf.

49. See Bergler, *Juvenilization of American Christianity*, 103–4; Kenda Creasy Dean, *Almost Christian: What the Faith of Our Teenagers Is Telling the American Church* (New York: Oxford University Press, 2010), 110.

where teenagers contribute to the worship life of the church throughout the year rather than on a single Sunday.

The Sanctuary of Roman Catholics

Worship in the sanctuaries of Protestants and Roman Catholics developed in "almost airtight isolation from each other" for more than four hundred years.[50] As worship ministry and youth ministry found their bearings in the United States, the Roman Catholic Church began to undergo a series of "modern liturgical movement developments," many of which were influenced by Protestant worship.[51] This began in 1833 when Prosper Guéranger of Solesmes in France uncovered a number of practices and ideals from the medieval Mass. This initiated a series of reforms to the Mass, including a Gregorian chant by choirs of boys and men, greater participation by laity, and more frequent Communion. After World War II, the Catholic Church overcame its fear of engagement with the modern world by incorporating modern architecture, increasing the role of Scripture and preaching in the Mass, and incorporating vernacular hymnody.[52]

In this era, young Roman Catholics found themselves growing up "in a world of prayers, candles, holy water, crucifixes, pictures of Jesus and Mary, and countless other devotional objects, with weekly or even daily mass at the center of it all." For some young Catholics the experience of attending Mass could be "suffused with mystery and grandeur."[53] The experience of the Lord's Table "was not cannibalism but its reverse, body taken up in Spirit."[54] For others, the Mass could be "boring" and "scary," requiring little commitment or participation. Thomas Bergler describes young people during the Mass in this era: "Many children and teenagers spent the time daydreaming or examining the statues, paintings, and architecture in their churches. Meanwhile, the altar boys who assisted the priest lived in dread of offending God and the priest by making a mistake, and every child was drilled in how to receive communion and warned not to chew it."[55]

Though Pope Pius XII (1876–1958) attempted to "hold the line for the old ideals of standardized liturgy," change to the Mass eventually came with the Second Vatican Council (1962–65).[56] Vatican II did not occur in isolation

50. J. F. White, *Protestant Worship*, 28.
51. J. F. White, *Protestant Worship*, 32.
52. J. F. White, *Protestant Worship*, 32–33.
53. Bergler, *Juvenilization of American Christianity*, 125.
54. Garry Wills, *Bare Ruined Choirs: Doubt, Prophecy, and Radical Religion* (New York: Doubleday, 1972), 32–37.
55. Bergler, *Juvenilization of American Christianity*, 125.
56. J. F. White, *Protestant Worship*, 32.

but built on earlier papal documents and the swirling Liturgical Movement, which influenced not only the Catholics but also the Protestants.[57] Vatican II ushered in a new era of liturgical change in Roman Catholic worship that brought vernacular liturgy, greater emphasis on the Word of God, and a body of music known as the Folk Mass with contributions by a group of young Jesuit priests with intentions to engage young people.[58]

Many of the changes that came from Vatican II produced ecumenical partnerships between Roman Catholics and mainline Protestants in the latter part of the twentieth century, which included sharing liturgies and music. The effects of Vatican II and the popular Folk Mass ignited a similar movement in Protestant and evangelical circles that "eventually exploded as the multimillion dollar Contemporary Christian Music industry."[59] Yet despite these developments, throughout the twentieth century many Catholic adolescents continued to feel "distant from what happened at mass."[60] Some young people saw the Latin Mass as a "hierarchic dance arranged around the Host, bowings, blessings, kneelings, liftings, displayings, and hidings of it," and young people "told each other scary stories about what happened to those who misused a consecrated communion wafer."[61] Confession "loomed large" and "provoked fears," while popular Marian spirituality sometimes interfered with the work of the church.[62] Like many of their Protestant counterparts, Catholic youth workers began supplementing the daily and weekly Mass in another part of the church, the youth room.

Worship in the Youth Room

As I have already mentioned, youth ministry was born out of a pastoral impulse that believed worship in the sanctuary was not enough to grow the faith of teenagers. When youth ministry began in the early nineteenth century,

57. For more on the Liturgical Movement, see Keith F. Pecklers and Bryan D. Spinks, "The Liturgical Movement," in *The New Westminster Dictionary of Liturgy and Worship*, ed. Paul Bradshaw (Louisville: Westminster John Knox, 2002), 283–89. For specifics of the movement in the United States, see Keith F. Pecklers, *The Unread Vision: The Liturgical Movement in the United States of America, 1926–1955* (Collegeville: Liturgical, 1998). For specifics on music, see Jan Michael Joncas, *From Sacred Song to Ritual Music: Twentieth-Century Understandings of Roman Catholic Worship Music* (Collegeville: Liturgical, 1997).

58. The earliest musical examples include Ray Repp's popular *Mass for Young Americans* (F. E. L. Records, 810F-6403, vinyl, 1966) and the *Hymnal for Young Christians*, vol. 1 (Chicago: F. E. L. Publications, 1967). See Ken Canedo, *Keep the Fire Burning: The Folk Mass Revolution* (Portland, OR: Pastoral Press, 2009).

59. Canedo, *Keep the Fire Burning*, 10.

60. Bergler, *Juvenilization of American Christianity*, 126.

61. Bergler, *Juvenilization of American Christianity*, 125–26.

62. For more on this, see Bergler, *Juvenilization of American Christianity*, 127–29.

it did so by supplementing worship in the sanctuary with worship in the youth room, an age-specific ministry that did not include adults. From the start, worship in the youth room was always different from worship in the sanctuary. At points liturgical activity in the youth room was nonexistent. At other times, youth group gatherings were entirely singing and preaching. Much of the time, worship in the youth room was part worship and part something else—games, fellowship, or skits. Initially teenagers and young adults in their mid-twenties were included; by the 1940s young people would be divided into age groups of early, middle, and late adolescence.

Worship in the youth room has evolved throughout different periods of history. From 1824 to 1870, it was characterized by prayer gatherings that led to the revival of 1857. From 1870 to 1920, it continued to include prayer but also increased activities such as Bible study and teaching and preaching the Word. It continued with prayer and Bible study from the 1920s through the 1960s, but evangelistic efforts that primarily included fellowship opportunities with games and skits were added as key elements of the youth room liturgy. The 1950s and 1960s added music to established rhythms of prayer, Bible study, evangelism, and fellowship. Gradually worship in the youth room evolved into a model of evangelical worship that was born on the frontier and that by the late 1970s would make its way out of the youth room and into the sanctuary as teenagers matured to adults and the American megachurch began to exert its influence.

Worship in Sunday School Associations and the YMCA

In the earliest days of youth ministry, the youth room came in the form of Sunday school associations and the YMCA. Not long after these gatherings of young people began, the revival of 1857–59 broke out as young men associated with the YMCA spent earnest time in supplication to God. These men met during their lunch breaks for prayer, and "the Spirit of God would drive them to repentance and public confession of sin."[63] While the initial revival came from the YMCA, it spread with momentum, and local churches opened their buildings to young people who wanted to gather and pray. The structures of these gatherings were spontaneous, but records show they included singing hymns, reading Scripture, and praying fervently to God for forgiveness, help avoiding temptation, and assistance in living a pure life.[64] Thomas Cuyler, a pastor of a Dutch Reformed congregation that hosted young people in New York, wrote, "It is not too much to say that often there were not less than 8,000

63. Senter, *When God Shows Up*, 111.
64. See Senter, *When God Shows Up*, 111–12; 131–32.

to 10,000 of God's people, who came together at the noon-tide hour with the spirit of supplication and prayer. The flame spread over the city, then leaped to Philadelphia. . . . And so it went on from town to town, and from city to city, over the length and breadth of the land."[65] Cuyler noted how at one point his congregation used every available space in the church building and limited participants to five minutes of prayer so that everyone could pray in the building.

The earliest gatherings of young people in Sunday school associations and at the YMCA included a number of liturgical expressions, and chief among them were singing, prayer, Bible study, and aggressive efforts in evangelism. While these liturgical expressions did exist, worship was not the primary goal of the Sunday school associations, nor other organizations from this period. The primary goal was to teach correct behavior to young people attending church and school, especially those from lower economic classes. This was accomplished by teaching children how to sing and by helping them learn about Scripture; the by-product was well-mannered children who came to faith in Christ.[66]

Worship in Denominational Societies

Following the revival of 1857 and the wide success of Sunday school associations, denominations began to fear the associations' ecumenical influence and moved to eliminate interdenominational fellowship. Nearly every American denomination experienced disagreements among conservative and liberal constituencies between 1870 and World War I,[67] but denominational youth societies were able to function under the watchful eye of local congregations in partnership with global denominations. The first and most well-known society was the Society of Christian Endeavor, a grassroots organization founded by Francis E. Clark, a pastor in Maine. This society included societies from Baptist, Congregational, Presbyterian, Methodist, Reformed, and other Christian churches, and it influenced a number of other denominational societies that emerged during the latter nineteenth and early twentieth centuries.[68]

Clark, concerned about the "problem with youth" in his congregation, formed the Society of Christian Endeavor in 1881. The problem was that

65. Quoted in Senter, *When God Shows Up*, 132.
66. Senter, *When God Shows Up*, 105–11. The intersection of worship and evangelism was born on American soil, and both Great Awakenings were its early precursors. However, the explicit connection between the two came from what White calls "Frontier Worship." See J. F. White, *Protestant Worship*, 171.
67. Senter, *When God Shows Up*, 153.
68. Senter, *When God Shows Up*, 159.

teenagers were worshiping outside the church at the roller-skating rink, the park, the theater, the baseball diamond, and the soda fountain, and he feared the ways of the world were more attractive to them than church. He made multiple attempts to reach teenagers, including an informal prayer meeting "where we shall sit around, talk, ask questions, etc.," but these attempts failed to have the impact he intended due to what Senter calls the "spiritual apathy of parents."[69] Clark decided that teenagers needed more formal parameters to demonstrate their ability to follow through with spiritual commitments. The Christian Endeavor Society provided those parameters through its four "essential features." The first was a pledge that each member signed; the second was regular participation in local church life, the society's weekly prayer meeting, and a monthly roll call "experience meeting" that relied on each attendee giving a testimony of their faith so that "'profitless' members" could be dropped from membership. The third essential feature of the society was systematic, definite, regular committee work; the fourth essential feature was daily prayer and Scripture reading;[70] and the fifth essential feature was denominational loyalty. The society's revised pledge of 1890 read, "Trusting in the Lord Jesus Christ for strength, I promise Him that I will try to do whatever He would have me do; that I will pray to Him and read my Bible every day, and that, just so far as I know how, through my whole life I will try to lead a Christian life."[71]

Weekly gatherings created the rhythm Clark believed young people needed to remain connected to the church and to give evidence that they were living a moral life. These gatherings measured their efficacy by "results of . . . conversion, inspiration, instruction, and sociability."[72] Their liturgies included supper and socialization (the meal was omitted when gatherings reached two hundred or more); a half hour of praise, Scripture reading, and prayer; business, announcements, and planning; a twenty-minute address by a society member; and twenty minutes of testimonies or other devotional activities. The meetings were led by "'home grown talent' so that local society leaders would have their day in the spotlight," though occasionally the society would invite guests to provide variety within the structure to which all gatherings were bound. These strict protocols of organization, time, and management were outlined in various society manuals.[73]

69. Quoted in Senter, *When God Shows Up*, 156.

70. See Senter, *When God Shows Up*, 161–64.

71. Francis E. Clark, *The Children and the Church: and the Young People's Society of Christian Endeavor, as a Means of Bringing Them Together* (Boston: Congregational Sunday School and Publishing Society, 1882), 83. Quoted in Senter, 59.

72. Senter, *When God Shows Up*, 160.

73. Francis E. Clark, *Ways and Means* (Boston: Lothrop, 1900), 257. Referenced in Senter, *When God Shows Up*, 160.

The records of the Society of Christian Endeavor provide some of the most detailed accounts of worship in emerging youth ministries from this era. Through them we learn that the society and others like it characterized a shift in adolescent piety from the nineteenth to the twentieth century. Teenage worshipers who belonged to these societies were expected to faithfully attend worship with all ages in the church, and they were expected to maintain a daily commitment to private worship as part of their piety, which Clark and other adults found lacking.[74] Participant Amos Wells emphasized the reciprocal relationship between the "outer exercises" and the "inner exercises": "It is impossible to maintain in power the outer exercises of religion unless we maintain with fervor this private communion with God, and by course of Bible-study, and by the Quiet Hour pledge of at least fifteen minutes in the early morning for meditation and prayer, . . . the Society is constantly reminding its members that their only strength for any work comes from on high, and must be drawn from reservoirs of prayer."[75] Despite successes by the Society of Christian Endeavor, a strong sense of denominationalism was in place at the turn of the twentieth century. Professional youth workers began creating organizational documents and ministry guidelines, and denominational publishers created materials for the spiritual formation of teenagers. As denominationalism grew, youth group fellowships began to replace denominational societies.

Worship in Youth Group Fellowships

The denominational societies that carried youth ministry into the twentieth century could not compete with the landscape of mainstream education following the Scopes trial of 1925. Around 1936, congregations began adopting new models of youth ministry, known as youth fellowship groups. Composed of twelve- to twenty-four-year-olds, who were often divided into three age groups—intermediates (ages twelve to fourteen), seniors (ages fifteen to seventeen), and older youth (ages eighteen to twenty-four)—youth fellowship groups became the dominant congregational model of youth ministry. Fellowship groups were led by professional ministers in many congregations, while adults served as sponsors.[76] They exhibited diversity, especially across denominations and among those in evangelical congregations and in urban or rural settings.[77]

74. Senter, *When God Shows Up*, 160.
75. Amos R. Wells, *The Officers' Handbook: A Guide for Officers in Young People's Societies, with Chapters on Parliamentary Law and Other Useful Themes*, rev. ed. (Boston: United Society of Christian Endeavor, 1911), 13.
76. Senter, *When God Shows Up*, 182–83.
77. Senter, *When God Shows Up*, 239.

Fellowship groups centered on the youth ministry of congregations, and their goal was fellowship and conversation with Bible study and prayer. Leaders believed that through social interaction with their peers in fellowship groups, teenagers could "experiment with life's experiences and questions without being preached at by their parents' generation."[78] Fellowship groups also provided leadership opportunities for students and opportunities for Christian education and service.

Worship in Catholic Youth Fellowships

As has been said, many teenagers in the Catholic Church failed to connect with Mass and the larger teachings of Catholicism despite the renewal movements of the Second Vatican Council. In response, youth leaders in the Catholic Church developed mechanisms to make both the Mass and the Catholic faith more accessible. These included "special youth masses followed by breakfast and a guest speaker with teen appeal." Catholic youth workers also sponsored national, regional, and local rallies that combined practices of "holy hours, benediction of the Blessed Sacrament, and first Friday devotions" into a single "memorable religious experience." Young Catholics were taught that "the answer to every problem of youth rests in the frequent reception of Holy Communion," but because not all teenagers believed this, adults created "juvenilized versions of these sacramental observances."[79]

Worship in the Music Room

Music in worship comes in many varieties. It can be congregational, choral, instrumental, or solo. It is guitar led in some faith communities and organ led in others. Some churches have professional church musicians, while others rely on amateurs or talented lay members. It is nonexistent in some traditions. While music helps define worship in many traditions, it is important to note that music is not worship; it is a servant to the act of worship. Not only is music a servant to worship, but music is also a servant to youth ministry.

Throughout history, music ministry has played a key role in ministry to teenagers. So to talk about the history of youth worship practices, one must talk about the role music has played in three key areas: the singing school of the eighteenth and nineteenth centuries, the youth choir model that dominated the middle and latter half of the twentieth century, and the youth group

78. Senter, *When God Shows Up*, 198.
79. Bergler, *Juvenilization of American Christianity*, 126.

band that arose in the late 1960s and early 1970s. Versions of each model still survive today.

The Singing School

The earliest form of music ministry as youth ministry began with the singing school in the late seventeenth and early eighteenth centuries. The singing school arose out of a concern for poor congregational singing in the church and attempted to correct it by teaching people how to read music. Ministers or laypersons would hire an itinerant teacher, known as a "singing school master," to teach the basics of music so teenagers could sing better in worship. Students met their teacher two or three times per week for a series of weeks or for an extended weekend to learn psalm tunes and choir anthems. Students arrived with a candle to see by, an instruction book, and a board to hold both. After they learned how to sing music by note, the singers performed a concert to show off "their newfound prowess," and afterward, a local preacher delivered a sermon about sacred music.[80] The influence of the singing school on music, worship, and youth ministry was felt across the nation as different versions came to exist in northern and southern colonies and the growing frontier.[81]

When youth ministry arrived on the scene in the early nineteenth century in the form of the Sunday school association, the American singing school was already teaching young people about proper behavior in worship and proper belief in doctrine by teaching them how to sing. Mark Senter writes, "The significance of singing-schools was that they were essentially parachurch functions in which young men and women could gather in a natural setting and join in a common enterprise. It should be noted that even after youth societies were established later in the nineteenth century, choirs remained in existence by becoming a part of the church's program."[82]

The Youth Choir

The singing school eventually paved the way for the youth choir,[83] following the development of professional music ministries and graded choir programs

---

80. William J. Reynolds and Milburn Price, *A Survey of Christian Hymnody*, 5th ed. (Carol Stream, IL: Hope, 2010), 128. See also Paul Westermeyer, *Te Deum: The Church and Music* (Minneapolis: Augsburg Fortress, 1998), 249–50.

81. See Westermeyer, *Te Deum*, 250–51.

82. Senter, *When God Shows Up*, 103.

83. A portion of this section originally appeared in Eric L. Mathis, "Is It Time to Rethink the 'Conventional Model' of the Youth Choir?," *Choral Journal* 56, no. 11 (June/July 2016): 18–27 (reprinted with permission of the American Choral Directors Association). There I provide alternative models of the youth choir for the twenty-first century.

in many congregations after World War II. Youth choirs became a supplement to the youth fellowship groups that emerged in the middle of the twentieth century. Donald Hustad observes that from 1960 to 1980 "the central focus of the music program in many churches was the youth choir" and that this phenomenon spread beyond Baptist congregations to other mainline Protestant congregations throughout the second half of the twentieth century. [84]

The goal of the youth choir was to attract teenagers and give them a voice in their congregations. [85] In many congregations, the youth choir became a phenomenon with a response that was "overwhelming." Hustad writes, "Young people who had never been interested in traditional music activity, either in the public school or in church, flocked to the choir." [86] The interest in the youth choir stemmed from its model of "adapting popular musical styles of the 1960s and 1970s" that the church was not otherwise engaging until teenagers began showing up, publishing houses began producing youth musicals, and "youth ministries took on a new look." [87] Youth musicals "combined secularly-influenced, youth-type words and music with dramatic action and a certain type of choreography," as well as accompaniment by a band. [88] The musicals were an attempt to appeal to teenagers inside the church and to evangelize teenagers outside the church, reinforcing to both audiences that the Christian life was fun and exciting rather than dull and boring.

The youth musical illustrated a long-held obsession with innovation among church musicians and youth ministers to do whatever would make teenagers stay in youth choir and, hopefully, the church. Though initially built out of concern for education, the youth choir quickly adopted a methodology of pragmatism. While some churches obsessed over the innovative model of youth choir, others ignored it and chose instead to continue with an educational model of youth choir that sang traditional classical repertoire they believed was superior. Musicians espousing the educational model over the pragmatic model of youth choir ministry fought hard against innovation and change, and as a result, two models of youth choir ministry existed side by side: the educational model (largely in mainline Protestant congregations) and the pragmatic model (largely in evangelical congregations). The latter of the two often had professional youth choirs rooted in performance; groups such as

84. Donald P. Hustad, *Jubilate II: Church Music in Worship and Renewal* (Carol Stream, IL: Hope, 1993), 78. Most historians of church music point to the Westminster Choir College as the impetus for these programs.

85. Senter, *When God Shows Up*, 208.

86. Hustad, *Jubilate II*, 434–35.

87. Senter, *When God Shows Up*, 208.

88. Hustad, *Jubilate II*, 434. Usually this accompaniment came as a prerecorded musical track with which the choir would sing.

the Continental Singers and Truth traveled across the country to "highlight what was perceived to be the brighter and more positive aspects of youth culture." These groups were "young, attractive, and energetic, yet, in uniform. . . . A not-so-subtle signal to the establishment that this was neither chaos nor rebellion."[89]

In response to these two models, a third model of youth choir ministry (the pastoral) appeared in the late 1980s and 1990s. It attempted to bridge the educational and pragmatic models of youth choir ministry, which already existed. The pastoral model of youth choir ministry emphasized music education through good choral music and rich texts, but it simultaneously employed elements of pragmatism.[90] This model encouraged teenagers to come to church by placing the youth choir in weekly worship leadership on Sunday mornings or evenings. Participation in rehearsals and worship leadership were rewarded with fellowship opportunities and summer tours, often described as mission trips.

As the church inched toward the worship wars of the 1990s, three models of youth choir ministry coexisted: the educational, the pragmatic, and the pastoral. However, a fourth model of youth choir ministry (the nonexistent youth choir) also emerged as both youth ministry and music ministry began to break down because of shifts in society and the church and the time demands placed on teenagers. Youth choirs disappeared from some congregations because music ministers could not sustain adequate membership, because they could not compete with the praise bands that led worship regularly, or because churches made salary and budget cuts. In other instances, youth ministries and music ministries began to compete for teenagers' time, and the youth choir disappeared due to a lack of collaboration or an inability to find rehearsal time. While the youth choir has waned in some places, it continues to live in many mainline Protestant and evangelical congregations as a model of educational, pragmatic, or pastoral youth music ministry.

The Youth Group Band

In the late 1960s and early 1970s the "music designed and developed for Christian youth groups" birthed the CCM industry, which would later give rise to praise and worship music. It was formed by large-scale youth rallies held

89. Terry York, *America's Worship Wars* (Peabody, MA: Hendrickson, 2003), 27. York also discusses the Up with People singers, a group that is both a secular organization with messages of love, peace, and unity and more characteristic of mainline Protestants.

90. Randy Edwards, *Revealing Riches and Building Lives: Youth Choir Ministry in the New Millennium* (St. Louis: Morningstar, 2000).

by Billy Graham and Youth for Christ, publications such as Britain's *Youth Praise* (1966), and youth musicals such as *Good News* (1967), *Tell It Like It Is* (1969), and *Celebrate Life* (1972).[91] This period also birthed a new form of youth music ministry: the youth group band.[92] The youth group band was composed of local teenage musicians who accompanied the youth musical and provided entertainment for their peers at local youth group functions, rallies, and other events sponsored by the church.

Using the youth group band to entertain at local functions followed a model from Youth for Christ, where director Larry Ballenger hired local teenage groups that could approximate the sound of celebrity musicians. He believed "the 'warm-up music' used at the beginning of his rallies was for entertainment and audience participation, not for spiritual impact."[93] Sometimes this music was religious in content, especially when inspired by CCM, but not always. In its earliest forms, it borrowed from the popular styles of crooners, girl trios, big bands, and jazz.[94] Thus youth group bands developed in a web of culture where rock and folk music had found their way into the life of the church and were validated by the rationale that "young people [enjoyed] performing the new popular music" and were "attracted to the church where they [would] be evangelized and discipled."[95]

Youth group bands became more commonly associated with youth group functions as youth ministers saw how music was used in rallies and other events outside the walls of the church. The earliest iteration of these bands came from David Holmbo, a youth minister and associate music minister at South Park Church in Park Ridge, Illinois, and his ministry partner, Bill Hybels. In 1973 they began midweek youth rallies that used contemporary music in the way that popular youth rallies from earlier decades had done, and these rallies later became Willow Creek Community Church.[96] As word of this effective ministry spread, youth ministers across the nation imitated

91. Greg Scheer, "Shout to the Lord: Praise and Worship from Jesus People to Gen X," in *New Songs of Celebration Render: Congregational Song in the Twenty-First Century*, ed. C. Michael Hawn (Chicago: GIA, 2013), 175–205. See also Pete Ward, *Selling Worship: How What We Sing Has Changed the Church* (Bletchley, UK: Paternoster, 2005), 27.

92. See Spinks, *Worship Mall*, 92. This model of music ministry has many names both past and present. It has been known as the youth praise band, the student worship team, and perhaps other names. Here I have chosen *youth group band* and *youth group worship band* to illustrate this is a group of teenage musicians whose principal function is to provide music for their peers at youth group functions.

93. Bergler, *Juvenilization of American Christianity*, 200.

94. Bergler, *Juvenilization of American Christianity*, 50.

95. Hustad, *Jubilate II*, 30.

96. Senter, *When God Shows Up*, 268–70. Holmbo's church role, part music minister and part youth minister, was common throughout the twentieth century. Many congregations could

the rallies, searching for teenage musicians in their congregations and communities who were capable of entertaining their peers and friends.

As the CCM industry and praise and worship music prospered throughout the 1970s and 1980s and became a mainstay by the early 1990s, the primary function of the youth group band shifted from providing musical entertainment to leading musical worship. The youth group band would become the youth group *worship* band. This shift was largely inspired by parachurch youth gatherings that included times of worship with "youth-generated music, instruments, perspectives, and energy, and freedom from the adults and trappings" of sanctuary worship.[97]

While these services might have made their way to the sanctuary once every three or four months, many youth ministers "obtained permission to conduct youth worship services away from the sanctuary, in the youth building or the basement."[98] In these settings prominent worship band leaders such as David Crowder, Matt Redman, John Mark Brown of Casting Crowns, Martin Smith of Delirious?, and others would get their start, one day growing into adulthood and church leadership.[99] Now, many large evangelical megachurches have youth group worship bands with elaborate audition processes and requirements, as well as remarkable talent.[100]

Disorientation: Worship Outside the Church

Even though specific worship practices varied and morphed over time, youth ministers and music ministers gathered teenagers inside the walls of the church building for worship with the church of all ages, the youth group, and the music and worship ministry, which functioned as a supplement to youth ministry.

---

not afford a full-time youth minister and a full-time music minister, and they combined the positions. See York, *America's Worship Wars*, 24–25.

97. York, *America's Worship Wars*, 26–27.

98. York, *America's Worship Wars*, 27.

99. Brown is a youth minister and worship leader who played in a youth worship band when he was growing up and has started a worship band in every church he has served. His band, Casting Crowns, was formed in 1999 and was the youth group worship band of the congregation he served at the time. Crowder started the David Crowder Band while a student at Baylor University in 1995 and later opened a church with Chris Seay for Baylor students to attend. Smith was twenty-four years old when his song "I Could Sing of Your Love Forever" with Delirious? made it big, and Redman was twenty years old when "The Heart of Worship" became an anthem of contemporary worship music. See Scheer, "Shout to the Lord," 186–94.

100. See, for instance, Ashley Chestnut, "Q&A with the Brook Hills Worship Team," The Church at Brook Hills, March 17, 2015, http://www.brookhills.org/blog/qa-with-the-brook-hills-worship-team/.

Beginning in the early twentieth century, teenagers began to worship with their youth groups outside church walls at camps, conferences, retreats, schools, stadiums, and arenas. Sometimes these gatherings were for worship. Other times these gatherings were concerts, motivational talks, commercials for church attendance, or pep rallies for faith disguised as worship.

Whether large or small, these gatherings outside the church had at least three common characteristics. First, in contrast to worship in the sanctuary, teenagers were the majority and adults the minority. Despite this, adults remained responsible for organizing and implementing the gatherings, no matter how "up front" they were for the actual event. Second, these gatherings gave teenagers opportunities to take a break from the world and focus on their spiritual lives. This was a disorientation for teenagers in its own right. By stepping out of their usual routines of family, school, work, play, and church, many teenagers had the opportunity to experience and commit to God in a new way. Third, these events often created dissonance with worship practices inside the walls of the church. Many teenagers worshiping outside the walls of the church would hear the voice of God, forge a deeper connection with their peers, experience an emotional high, and find it hard to return home, especially when worship in the sanctuary failed to match the standards set by these events. This, too, became disorienting for teenagers, youth ministers, and congregations, who could not or would not change their worship practices quickly enough to match the cravings of teenagers at worship.

Worship at Camps, Retreats, and Conferences

Other than the church walls, Christian camps, retreats, and conferences are one of the most familiar points of worship for youth groups. These events have their origins in late-nineteenth-century New England, though they are products of the camp meeting, urbanization, the fresh air movements, Sunday school associations, the YMCA, the Chautauqua Institution, compulsory education, and the leisure movements.[101] In the late nineteenth century different kinds of camps arose that were sponsored by private organizations, public agencies, and religiously affiliated institutions. The early twentieth century saw the rise of multiple summer camps sponsored by denominational societies, and by the middle of the twentieth century each major Protestant denomination had established Christian summer camps across the country.[102]

---

101. Jacob Sorenson, "A Theological Playground: Christian Summer Camp in Theological Perspective" (PhD thesis, Luther Seminary, 2016), 19–25, https://digitalcommons.luthersem.edu/phd_theses/4/.

102. Sorenson, "Theological Playground," 42.

Many of these denominations acquired land to establish their Christian camp and retreat centers, making the rise of summer camping part of a broader movement toward "specialized ministry with young people."[103]

From 1950 to 1970, Christian camping flourished as denominational camps sprang forth across the nation and evangelicals joined the movement through popular fellowship groups such as Young Life.[104] Though 1970 to 1990 was a tumultuous season for Christian camping, summer camps flourished from 1990 to 2010 and focused on various things. Jacob Sorenson notes that how Christian camps approached Christian education—"as a conversion experience or as Christian nurture"—was an early distinguishing feature of each of these camps, one that continues to divide Christian camps in the present, especially evangelical and mainline camps, and that has implications for each camp's approach to worship.[105] Worship in evangelical summer camps focused on bringing attendees to Christ, and mainline denominational camps became more ecumenical in nature, focusing less on denominational catechesis and more on a "general notion of spirituality."[106]

Historically, camps, retreats, and conferences provided teenagers a place to express their faith away from local congregations, parents, and other social pressures, but they also gave denominations who feared ecumenical and secular influence something they could call their own, as well as a second home.[107] These camps were often located in rural settings and gave teenagers time to grow in their faith tradition through what some came to call a "vacation with Jesus."[108] At summer camps or weekend retreats, teenagers participated in Bible study, outdoor recreation, singing, and worship multiple times per week.[109] Jon Pahl describes worship at Arcadia, a Lutheran camp, in the middle of the twentieth century: "To a degree, the remote setting of the camp had lent itself to theological and practical experimentation right from the start. Worship was held twice a week, on Sunday and Wednesday evenings, but an outdoor chapel and vespers on the beach patio of the camp diffused the location of the sacred in young Lutheran minds beyond the usual church setting."[110]

While the specifics of worship changed over time, worship has been a mainstay at nearly all Christian camps, happening more than a few times a

---

103. Sorenson, "Theological Playground," 25.
104. Sorenson, "Theological Playground," 42–48.
105. Sorenson, "Theological Playground," 26.
106. Sorenson, "Theological Playground," 53.
107. Senter, *When God Shows Up*, 183.
108. Jon Pahl, *Youth Ministry in Modern America: 1930 to the Present* (Peabody, MA: Hendrickson, 2000), 25.
109. Sorenson, "Theological Playground," 29.
110. Pahl, *Youth Ministry in Modern America*, 25.

week, as described by Pahl above. Now, anyone peering into a camp, retreat, or conference is "almost guaranteed to see young people praying as a large group, singing together, worshiping together, and playing group games."[111] In his study of Christian youth camping, Sorenson notes that even those camps with a "low faith emphasis" may still be recognized as camps because they incorporate worship.[112] Even more interesting is that teenagers reported that their overall enjoyment of worship services and music was "strongly correlated with growth in faith."[113]

Worship at School

Acknowledging that "*youth* now meant *teenagers* and that teenagers lived much of their lives shaped by peers in the public high school,"[114] youth ministry shifted to the local high school beginning in the early 1930s. In 1933 Evelyn McCluskey launched a parachurch Bible study for young girls in her congregation. McCluskey's Bible study, the Miracle Book Club, became one of many experiments that tried to incarnate youth ministry in local high schools. The Miracle Book Club focused on Bible study and relational evangelism, and its meetings contained a three-part liturgical structure of music, teaching, and response. In the first fifteen minutes, student officers led singing and "club rituals" and read minutes from the previous meeting. These preliminaries were followed by forty-five minutes of teaching from the Bible using storytelling. An invitation to salvation was "low-key" and "never stated in a manner in which a student might be embarrassed."[115]

One of the best-known teachers in the Miracle Book Club was Jim Rayburn. Rayburn led a Miracle Book Club program in Gainesville, Texas, where he taught and adopted McCluskey's patterns for parachurch high school ministry. However, Rayburn split from the Miracle Book Club and formed Young Life in 1941. Throughout the 1940s and 1950s Young Life became a very distinct parachurch organization that would influence youth ministry and church worship for years to come. First, Rayburn's Young Life approach used gifted adult leaders and communicators rather than students for music and preaching, a departure from McCluskey's program. Second, relationships were cultivated through weekly group meetings as well as small and large group gatherings and rallies, each of which were part worship and part

111. Sorenson, "Theological Playground," 151.
112. Sorenson, "Theological Playground," 156.
113. Sorenson, "Theological Playground," 174.
114. Senter, *When God Shows Up*, 209 (emphasis original).
115. Senter, *When God Shows Up*, 217.

meeting. Third, Young Life gatherings incorporated fun, creating a liturgical pattern that began with fast-paced songs followed by announcements disguised as skits or games, slow songs, a meaningful message, and music with times of prayer.[116] The goal of these meetings was "to make the students as relaxed as possible to 'break down the barriers' and earn 'the right to be heard.'" Rayburn "initiated the transition from the rally model of youth ministry to the group meeting model." He was known for his effective preaching and his conversational approach to ministry in contrast to "the authoritative biblical preaching of the youth rallies." Rayburn was "different from other preachers of his day, neither shouting nor pounding the pulpit. Instead, he just talked."[117]

A sibling to Young Life was Youth for Christ, another parachurch organization that was inspired by the Miracle Book Club. Birthed in 1945 in Kansas City, Missouri, Youth for Christ hosted weekly meetings for its members and Saturday night rallies for members to bring friends who needed to hear the gospel. In contrast to Young Life, Youth for Christ retained the model of student-based leadership it had learned from the Miracle Book Club. The adults' role was to mentor teenagers into leadership roles administrating and emceeing weekly gatherings with guests. Youth for Christ gatherings included special music from traveling artists, sermons from itinerant preachers, skits, and in later iterations, Bible quiz competitions. Students enlisted weekly guests from a large pool of itinerant preachers and musicians "on the circuit" after World War II and used them to attract visitors to their gatherings.[118]

While Young Life and Youth for Christ were flagship after-school programs, they spawned additional school gatherings such as the Fellowship of Christian Athletes and See You at the Pole. The Fellowship of Christian Athletes began in 1945 as an attempt to engage the faith of young athletes and their coaches. Their gatherings—often called huddles—usually included singing, announcements, and a sermon or Bible study by a member or well-known athlete.[119] In the late 1990s a prayer event at middle and high school campuses across the United States was added: See You at the Pole. Millions of teenagers participated in this mid-September gathering at their flagpoles, where they would "pray for their campuses and declare their faith before their watching peers."[120] Many gatherings for See You at the Pole include worship elements

116. Senter, *When God Shows Up*, 219. See also Todd E. Johnson, "Disconnected Rituals: The Origins of the Seeker Service Movement," in *The Conviction of Things Not Seen: Worship and Ministry in the 21st Century*, ed. Todd E. Johnson (Grand Rapids: Brazos, 2002), 57.

117. T. Johnson, "Disconnected Rituals," 57.

118. Senter, *When God Shows Up*, 222.

119. Senter, *When God Shows Up*, 226.

120. Senter, *When God Shows Up*, 87.

such as singing and Scripture reading, and many of these gatherings are preceded by See You at the Pole rallies, where participants worship together to prepare and gain confidence in their leadership abilities.[121]

Worship in the Stadium

As parachurch organizations such as Young Life and Youth for Christ gained momentum in the 1930s and 1940s, Saturday night rallies became an influential means of ministry, especially for Youth for Christ. These rallies "provided the opportunity for public gatherings and painted the picture of a brighter tomorrow through personal faith."[122] For communities across the United States that were reeling from the Great Depression and World War II, the Youth for Christ weekly rallies became religious parties and gained momentum. "Young people, many of whom had never seen old-time religion anywhere but in church, found it exciting to attend rallies in theaters, civic auditoriums, and even stadiums."[123] *Newsweek* covered the story of the forty-five thousand who attended the 1944 Memorial Day Youth for Christ rally at Soldier Field in Chicago, and by the end of 1949 there were an estimated 1,450 rallies happening in cities across the United States, including in St. Louis, Indianapolis, and Minneapolis.[124]

Youth rallies had long been a means of encouraging "greater loyalty to Jesus Christ,"[125] but the rallies had not experienced the fascination of American media in the form of print, radio, and eventually television. However, "for a twenty-year period starting near the end of the Great Depression, various forms of youth rallies captured the attention of the American media and catapulted youthful evangelists into the public eye. While Billy Graham was the most well-known of these evangelists, hundreds of others preached the Christian gospel of personal salvation to the groups who would become known as teenagers."[126]

The rallies borrowed elements of teenage worship that had begun to emerge throughout the nineteenth century, though worship at the rallies could be traced more broadly to a three-part structure consisting of prelimi-

---

121. "Prepare for Your See You at the Pole," See You at the Pole, accessed June 3, 2020, https://syatp.com.

122. T. Johnson, "Disconnected Rituals," 57.

123. Bergler, *Juvenilization of American Christianity*, 50.

124. "Wanted: A Miracle of Good Weather and the 'Youth for Christ' Rally Got It," *Newsweek*, June 11, 1945, 84; "Youth for Christ Now Covers 1,450 Cities," *Minneapolis Star*, February 12, 1949, 8.

125. Senter, *When God Shows Up*, 257.

126. Senter, *When God Shows Up*, 257.

naries, preaching, and response.[127] The rallies catered to radio and television, with multiple testimonies and sermons that varied in length and content so that some could be broadcast on radio and others on television. They relied heavily on music from youth choirs and orchestras or special guests, personal testimonies from athletes or other well-known people, and the hope of a spiritual encounter with Christ that would transform a person from the inside out.[128] The effectiveness of the rallies varied from location to location, but an "army of traveling evangelists and musicians made Youth for Christ rallies their full time work." These individuals served as "rally directors" who were responsible for recruiting and training "teenage musical acts that performed old gospel music favorites in contemporary musical styles."[129] Though many of the preachers assumed biblical authority, for a growing number of people, that authority was "seriously in question."[130] But while arguments over the authority of Scripture were looming for the church, these rallies "defined how the Christian gospel was presented to teenagers" more than "any other single aspect of youth ministry in the middle of the twentieth century."[131]

Weekly rallies disappeared from the youth-ministry scene by the late twentieth century, but other large-scale stadium gatherings eventually took their place. These included large denominational gatherings of teenagers that became supplements to the local youth fellowship groups. These mass gatherings, many of which continue today, were annual, biannual, and triennial conferences held at the national level to bring together teenagers of the same denomination. These types of gatherings include the American Lutheran Church (1979), ELCA Youth Gatherings (1988),[132] the Presbyterian Youth Triennium (PCUSA) (1980),[133] and the Episcopal Youth Event (1982).[134] Each is planned by intergenerational teams and happens in stadium-like settings.

127. T. Johnson, "Disconnected Rituals," 57. This pattern is used for Frontier Worship, characterized by J. F. White and named and defined earlier.

128. Senter, *When God Shows Up*, 258–59.

129. Bergler, *Juvenilization of American Christianity*, 50.

130. T. Johnson, "Disconnected Rituals," 57.

131. Senter, *When God Shows Up*, 271.

132. ELCA Youth Gathering, "The History of the Gathering," Evangelical Lutheran Church of America, August 1, 2019, https://blogs.elca.org/youthgathering/history-of-the-gathering. This gathering was initially a product of the American Lutheran Church (1979, 1982, 1985), though the ELCA gatherings of teenagers started as early as 1961, when Rev. Dr. Martin Luther King Jr. delivered an address to the American Lutheran Church's Luther League.

133. See Deana S., "Presbyterian Youth Triennium," Presbyterian Historical Society, July 14, 2016, https://www.history.pcusa.org/blog/2016/07/presbyterian-youth-triennium.

134. "Episcopal Youth Event," The Episcopal Church, accessed May 31, 2020, https://episcopalchurch.org/episcopal-youth-event.

These gatherings are part camp, part retreat, part conference, and part service, but they all include worship.

These gatherings continue to be products of mainline Protestant and Catholic denominational offices that retain full-time professional youth ministry staff, but they employ pragmatic elements in worship that are in line with nineteenth-century tent revivals and late twentieth-century evangelistic crusades and youth rallies. What is important to note here is that while worship retains certain denominational elements, nearly all of these teenage worship gatherings borrow their look and feel from historical models of youth ministry as well as evangelical worship practices and principles, even though the content of the messages and music might be centered on themes of restorative and reparative justice.[135] The Presbyterian Youth Triennium describes worship as a "traditional Presbyterian and Reformed gathering and storytelling with a . . . twist." The ELCA says in its history, "Youth Gatherings have always been on the cutting edge, challenging young people to do God's most righteous work."[136]

Two other stadium gatherings emerged in the twentieth century from the evangelical ranks: Urbana and Passion. Though each was primarily for college-aged students, both are worth mentioning here because the impact of their work spilled into teenage worship in general, as many college students attended the events and then served as youth small group or church leaders.

The first of the two gatherings mentioned above, Urbana, is sponsored by InterVarsity Christian Fellowship. Urbana was started in 1946 by evangelicals in Toronto, Canada, as a "mighty missionary movement." It was held again in 1948 in Urbana-Champaign, Illinois. It has retained the name Urbana and has been held biannually ever since, now meeting in St. Louis. Urbana is defined as a "sacred space where students find calling and [join] the Lord's global mission whether across campus, zip codes, or the world."[137] Its massive sixteen-thousand-person worship gatherings are characterized by a global tapestry of music, spoken word, and intercessory prayer, and through its live recordings and songbooks, the model of multicultural worship it espouses became a model for the evangelical church throughout the 1970s and beyond.[138] This has become especially true in recent years as three Urbana worship lead-

135. Gretchen Buggeln, "Spaces for Youth in Protestant Churches," in *Making Suburbia: New Histories of Everyday America*, ed. John Archer, Paul J. P. Sandul, and Katherine Solomonson (Minneapolis: University of Minnesota Press, 2015), 228.

136. ELCA Youth Gathering, "History of the Gathering."

137. "About Urbana," Urbana Student Missions Conference, InterVarsity, accessed May 31, 2020, https://urbana.org/about-urbana.

138. "Worship," Urbana Student Missions Conference, InterVarsity, accessed May 31, 2020, https://urbana.org/worship.

ers, Sandra Maria Van Opstal, Josh Davis, and Nikki Lerner, have developed their own teaching and worship ministries.[139]

Passion began in 1997, nearly fifty years after Urbana, with a gathering of two thousand college students in Austin, Texas. Its focus includes mission but is broader than Urbana's. Worship at Passion rallies centers on the statement that "God is most glorified in us when we are most satisfied in him."[140] Passion has since grown to more than sixty-five thousand attendees annually. Beyond its major gathering held each January, the Passion movement now includes a camp, national and international tours, a worship collective, and a congregation.[141] Worship at the Passion conference is known for its "songs of intimate worship, high production standards, and a rock concert setting," all of which create "an emotion-filled worship experience and exhortation to live one's whole life for God." Greg Scheer notes that "Passion also added volume" with sound levels higher than other conferences.[142]

In many ways, Passion is a final rite of passage for many high school seniors as they embark on their journey into young adulthood. While Passion is a gathering for college students ages eighteen to twenty-five, its imprint on teenage worship cannot be underestimated. High school seniors are encouraged to attend Passion with their youth minister, and these students and church leaders return to their youth groups prepared to fan the flame of the gathering among their younger peers, primarily through music.[143] This is why the albums from Passion worship leaders such as David Crowder, Charlie Hall, Matt Redman, and Chris Tomlin became the soundtrack for youth worship in the twenty-first century.[144]

Both Urbana and Passion serve as case studies for what Ingalls describes as "pilgrim congregations."[145] While her work is not specific to other teenage worship gatherings, she acknowledges how denominational and interdenominational rallies and conferences that are "specifically focused on high school

139. See Sandra Maria Van Opstal, *The Next Worship: Glorifying God in a Diverse World* (Downers Grove, IL: InterVarsity, 2016), 9–14; and Josh Davis and Nikki Lerner, *Worship Together in Your Church as in Heaven* (Nashville: Abingdon, 2015). Davis runs a nonprofit worship ministry called Proskuneo.

140. This statement comes from pastor John Piper, a frequent speaker at Passion conferences. See John Piper, *Desiring God: Meditations of a Christian Hedonist*, rev. ed. (Colorado Springs: Multnomah, 2011), 5.

141. "The Story of Passion," Passion Conferences, accessed May 31, 2020, https://passion conferences.com/about.

142. Scheer, "Shout to the Lord," 194–95.

143. "Frequently Asked Questions," Passion 2021, accessed May 31, 2020, https://www .passion2021.com/frequently-asked-questions.

144. Scheer, "Shout to the Lord," 194–95.

145. Ingalls, *Singing the Congregation*, 74.

and college-aged students have become an evangelical mainstay."[146] Ingalls's principles for pilgrim congregations might apply to all teenage worship gatherings in the stadium. She describes them in all their familiarity:

> To experience this transformative encounter, evangelicals do not need to travel to sacred Christian sites in Israel or the Mediterranean, or to important places in US Christian history; rather, they more frequently converge upon sports arenas and stadiums for multi-day conferences generally geared to a specific demographic. As they travel to these conferences on planes, buses, trains, and subways, evangelical pilgrims frequently strike up conversations with strangers who often turn out to be fellow travelers. Downtown hotels in major US cities sell out of rooms as large groups of conference-goers fill their lobbies. In anticipation of the conference's opening session, snaking lines spill out of the doors of the sports stadium in which it will be held. While standing in line, veterans of previous conferences share memories of their past experiences while new attendees describe animatedly the parts of the conference they are looking forward to the most. The atmosphere is both festive and expectant. Although spending time with friends and exploring a new city are certainly draws, most attendees say they have come for a more serious purpose: to "meet God" and to allow God to change their lives through the multifaceted, multi-day conference experience.[147]

As Ingalls notes, the worship practices of youth gatherings in the stadium exerted influence over the worship practices in local congregations large and small. One of the primary areas of influence is the music, which becomes a "souvenir" for the conference pilgrims and serves as "both commodified product and embodied experience." This is how Urbana and Passion were "instrumental in propelling worship music's meteoric rise in popularity."[148]

Worship at Concerts

The 1960s and 1970s birthed the genres of CCM and Contemporary Worship Music (CWM). With them came another form of youth worship: the worship concert. In their earliest days, these new genres of music spread by word of mouth from youth group to youth group, but by the late 1980s and early 1990s, both CCM and CWM were multimillion dollar industries.[149] Like at the youth rallies of the past, young people flocked to arenas for tours

146. Ingalls, *Singing the Congregation*, 75.
147. Ingalls, *Singing the Congregation*, 75.
148. Ingalls, *Singing the Congregation*, 74.
149. Spinks, *Worship Mall*, 92–93.

by their favorite CCM artists or for worship concerts by their favorite CWM artists. Youth groups attended both events together and returned to church expecting the youth group band to put the music they heard to use in the youth room. Both genres relied on young artists barely in their twenties as well as young audience members who would, quite literally, buy into the new music.

Initially, concert tours happened in congregations, cafés, and coffeehouses where young Christian singers and songwriters, such as Larry Norman, performed their music and sold their recordings out of vans.[150] They represented the height of the Jesus Movement (1969–74), where the primary intent was evangelization through "Jesus Music" such as Norman's album the *Everlastin' Living Jesus Concert*.[151] As this movement gained momentum, artists such as Amy Grant, Michael W. Smith, Twila Paris, Steven Curtis Chapman, Sara Groves, TobyMac, Third Day, and Jars of Clay would all sell out arenas, perform their music that had become popular on the radio, and define CCM. The goal of CCM was to "reach the lost in a musical language they could understand" and to give young Christians the sounds of secular music with inspirational messages.[152] This genre moved in waves but eventually capitulated to CWM.[153]

CWM launched in 1974 when Maranatha! Music released the *Maranatha! Praise* album, carving a second distinct path for young worshipers in the arena. This path was represented by publications and recordings that formed the growing corpus of CWM. The purpose of CWM was to exhort believers and to provide new songs for use in corporate worship.[154] Throughout the latter half of the twentieth century, CWM produced Scripture songs, praise choruses, and praise and worship music through well-known individuals such as Karen Lafferty and Rick Founds and through publishing companies such as Maranatha!, Integrity, and Vineyard in the 1980s; Hillsong in the 1990s; former CCM artists in the 2000s; and Elevation, Bethel, and others after 2010. The early part of the twentieth century experienced a crossover between CCM and CWM as former CCM artists such as Michael W. Smith, Third Day, and Sonicflood released worship albums that further blurred the boundaries between worship and entertainment. After 2010 the worship ministries of

---

150. Scheer, "Shout to the Lord," 179.
151. Scheer, "Shout to the Lord," 179.
152. Scheer, "Shout to the Lord," 179.
153. Charlie Peacock, "Charlie Peacock Predicts the Future of Christian Music," *CCM Magazine*, April 1, 2008, https://www.ccmmagazine.com/features/charlie-peacock-predicts-the-future-of-christian-music/.
154. Scheer, "Shout to the Lord," 179.

congregations such as Elevation, Bethel, and Passion City Church influenced the CWM industry.[155]

Soon the concert tour and worship concert strongly resembled each other, making it difficult to distinguish between the two.

> Both have extravagant multimedia and lighting displays, rock band instrumenta-
> tion and amplification, and performer-audience interaction that characterizes
> musical entertainment events, such as cheering and applause. . . . The large
> screens project song lyrics to encourage the audience to sing along. Leaders
> proclaim the words of biblical texts and lead public prayer, while modeling
> devotional gestures such as raising hands and faces as if toward heaven. These
> performative elements help to authenticate the gathering as more than a "mere
> concert" of Christian popular music, but as a congregation gathered for the
> express purpose of worshiping God.[156]

Though the concert tour and worship concert shared many elements, the two were not entirely the same thing. The concert tour was entertainment, and the worship concert was primarily music and prayer with little scripture and preaching. Ingalls carefully distinguishes between the two: "Not just any concert of Christian music is considered 'worship,' and not all artists in the Christian popular music industry are considered 'worship leaders.'"[157] Concert tours by CCM artists included music that was largely understood as personal testimony and used for private devotion, while the worship concert presented music that was sung together and later used in corporate worship.[158] Ingalls admonishes,

> Fans of worship music constantly evaluate worship music artists and events not
> only for their artistic merit but also on grounds of theological accuracy and

---

155. See Scheer, "Shout to the Lord," 171–90. See also Lester Ruth and Swee Hong Lim, *Lovin' on Jesus: A Concise History of Contemporary Worship* (Nashville: Abingdon, 2017). Ruth and Lim's work has filled a gap in the study of this genre of music, along with other publications, many of which are dissertations or theses that focus on the specific contributions of individual groups such as Passion, Urbana, Hillsong, Bethel, and others. For examples, see Monique Marie Ingalls, "Awesome in This Place: Sound, Space, and Identity in Contemporary North American Evangelical Worship" (PhD diss., University of Pennsylvania, 2008); Nelson Cowan, "Liturgical Biography as Liturgical Theology: Co-Constructing Theology at Hillsong Church, New York City" (PhD diss., Boston University School of Theology, 2019); Wen Reagan, "A Beautiful Noise: A History of Contemporary Worship Music" (PhD diss., Duke University, 2015); and Emily Snider Andrews, "Exploring Evangelical Sacramentality: Modern Worship Music and the Possibility of Divine-Human Encounter" (PhD diss., Fuller Theological Seminary, 2020).

156. Ingalls, *Singing the Congregation*, 42–43.

157. Ingalls, *Singing the Congregation*, 42.

158. Ingalls, *Singing the Congregation*, 43.

spiritual efficacy. Concert tours of celebrity worship leaders become proving grounds, where artists, brands, and products are authenticated if they inspire "real worship." While worship concerts draw from preexisting expectations of worship, they do not merely reinforce existing evangelical worship practices. Rather, they promote new songs and styles and, crucially, help to set aesthetic expectations and discipline the worshiping body in particular ways. In the context of a worship concert, participants learn to frame their affective experience as worship and thus experience the concert as congregation as well as an audience of fans.[159]

CCM, CWM, and their accompanying youth culture took on worship in the sanctuary throughout the worship wars of the 1980s and 1990s. Battles were fought "over congregational song, the existence of choirs, the structure of worship, the purpose of worship, and where the line [was] drawn between reform and rejection."[160] In 1999, evangelical magazine *Christianity Today* declared that the fans of worship music had won as "guitars beat out the organ in the worship wars."[161] Worship outside the church walls had won its rightful place inside the church walls as teenagers of the late twentieth century came to adulthood and refused to forget the worship practices of their youth.

Youth Group Worship Moves into the Sanctuary

While twentieth century movements in youth and worship ministry were exciting, the effects of both movements, which aligned so strongly with popular culture, catapulted the larger church into a season of disorientation. This is partly what caused the worship wars of the late twentieth century. Most scholars of worship consider the 1960s to be the time when worship ministry began experiencing the shifts that catapulted it into a challenging season that climaxed with the worship wars of the 1990s. Though the worship wars were not caused by youth ministry alone, youth ministry did play a part. For instance, certain models of evangelical youth ministry inspired the seeker-service model in megachurch congregations such as Willow Creek Community Church and Saddleback Church in the late 1970s and early 1980s.[162] Rayburn's approach to teaching

159. Ingalls, *Singing the Congregation*, 42.
160. York, *America's Worship Wars*, 29.
161. Michael S. Hamilton, "The Triumph of the Praise Songs: How Guitars Beat Out the Organ in the Worship Wars," *Christianity Today*, July 12, 1999, https://www.christianitytoday.com/ct/1999/july12/9t8028.html.
162. See Senter, *When God Shows Up*, 268–70. See also T. Johnson, "Disconnected Rituals," 58–59. Bill Hybels, founding pastor of Willow Creek Community Church in South Barrington,

with Young Life became prevalent in congregations across America throughout the 1970s as the church tried to "sell Jesus" in an increasingly consumer-based culture.[163] These congregations, in turn, began to influence other congregations and to inspire other models of youth ministry across the United States. Out of this influence came what we now call the "contemporary" worship service, a gathering with a liturgical pattern similar to the Young Life model that nearly every youth ministry in America follows: singing, teaching, and response. This type of worship in youth ministry came about because "youth ministry was competing with many other 'products' in an expanding market. The growing tendency was to try to reach youth with the same techniques used . . . on the Pepsi generation: a confluence of message with media in which the two became indistinguishable." Along the way, "the market-driven rituals of evangelism and catechesis provided an entire generation with a new language for God that was not being used in worship. . . . Youth ministry sold Jesus to adolescents because it was relevant, entertaining, and they would 'get something out of it.'"[164]

Though youth ministry's original impetus was to help young people connect their lives to the work of God in the world, this sentiment morphed so that the church began to believe youth ministry existed to solve the problems of the world. In those instances, "adult fears about the fate of America came to rest squarely on the shoulders of young people." While parents, ministers, and "youth leaders believed they were catching the wave of the future and channeling the innate power of young people," it became clear that "they were also building one of the engines that would drive juvenilization in subsequent decades."[165] Bergler summarizes, "By capitalizing on fears about youth and the crisis of civilization, Christian youth leaders and young people were able to launch some much-needed reforms in their churches. Young people pioneered racial integration, created new and exciting methods of evangelism, and gained a new-found sense of their own political power. These changes were at first restricted to youth environments, but they would eventually reshape the lives of adults as well."[166] Youth ministry was driven by innovation and changed and adapted to culture more rapidly than worship ministry. Yet as teenagers found their way out of the youth group and back home in the sanctuary, they began to ask, Now, where will we worship?[167]

Illinois, began the megachurch as a ministry outreach to teenagers. See T. Johnson, "Disconnected Rituals," 57–59.

163. See T. Johnson, "Disconnected Rituals," 57–59.
164. T. Johnson, "Disconnected Rituals," 59.
165. Bergler, *Juvenilization of American Christianity*, 20–21.
166. Bergler, *Juvenilization of American Christianity*, 19–20.
167. Bergler, *Juvenilization of American Christianity*, 59.

The end of the twentieth century and the beginning of the twenty-first century became a time of both gratitude and lament. Since then, scholars and practitioners of youth ministry and worship ministry have given thanks for the fruit born by the past while also writing truthfully about the past. The youth ministry movements and the worship practices that accompanied them met the needs of particular generations and gained support from a number of arenas, not least of which were congregations, church leaders, and a growing middle economic class.[168] A number of visionaries also rose to become the face of various movements, and laypeople, trained and untrained theologians, and the media supported, encouraged, and applauded their efforts. Many times a spirit of revival, the sense that the Spirit of God was blowing fresh winds of faith, ushered these visionaries and the church in a new direction.[169]

Yet as the sun set on the twentieth century, youth ministry found itself in a radically different context and largely in disorientation. Youth for Christ began its decline in the late 1960s, and by the dawn of the 1990s, a shifting culture in high schools across the nation contributed to its further decline. By 1990, it was clear that the approach to youth ministry that had been effective throughout the latter part of the twentieth century had changed.[170] By the last decade of the twentieth century, many youth ministries received criticism for emphasizing programmatic ministry over relational ministry. Two significant criticisms were that youth ministry was "too white" and that it was merely "fun and games."[171] Charles Webb Courtoy summarizes these sentiments when he says, "The weaknesses . . . are legion."[172]

The NSYR findings published in 2005,[173] that young people were leaving the church in droves after high school, was the straw that broke the camel's back for youth ministry, which was already in peril. Kenda Creasy Dean writes, "The hemorrhage of adolescents from mainstream Protestantism began in the late 1950s, and by century's end had swelled to a full-fledged ecclesial crisis." Young people had lost their passion for Christ, which is why many

168. See Senter, *When God Shows Up*, 6–82.
169. Senter, *When God Shows Up*, 82–92.
170. Senter, *When God Shows Up*, 231.
171. Senter, *When God Shows Up*, 306–8.
172. Charles Webb Courtoy, "A Historical Analysis of the Three Eras of Mainline Protestant Youth Work in America as a Basis for Clues to Future Youth Work" (DMin project, Divinity School of Vanderbilt University, 1976), 65–72. Kenda Creasy Dean and others have also been highly critical of this era of youth ministry, as was the World Council of Churches, which in 1965 called for an end to the isolation of teenagers in youth programs and for their integration into the life of the church. See Kenda Creasy Dean, "The New Rhetoric of Youth Ministry," *Journal of Youth and Theology* 2, no. 2 (2003): 9.
173. Christian Smith and Melinda Lundquist Denton, *Soul Searching: The Religious and Spiritual Lives of America's Teenagers* (New York: Oxford, 2005).

of them were not spending significant amounts of time worshiping inside or outside the church walls.[174]

New Orientation: Youth Ministry Calls for Worship Renewal

After worshiping at camps, conferences, retreats, schools, stadiums, and concerts, teenagers return to worship at home where everything is viewed differently. They gauge experiences through the afterglow of worship outside the church walls. If they return home asking "What is God doing?" and "How can I keep my passion for Christ alive at home, church, and school?" they will move into a season of new orientation that allows spiritual growth to come from the season of disorientation. If they fail to ask these questions, transformation may not occur.

Senter acknowledges that a new cycle of Protestant youth ministry emerged in the early 1990s, but in 2010 he noted, "It has taken time for the nature of youth ministry in the twenty-first century to define itself. . . . Clear descriptors of a fourth cycle have yet to emerge."[175] As the sun rose on the twenty-first century, key voices in youth ministry and worship ministry began asking "What is God doing in youth ministry?" and "How can we cooperate with God's initiatives?" Their questions and research moved the church from a season of disorientation to a season of new orientation, especially where teenage worship practices were concerned.

Worship Renewal Centered on Tradition

For many mainline Protestants, a season of new orientation began in the 1990s when the religion division of Lilly Endowment established a number of centers and institutes for youth ministry with youth theological academies. Known collectively as the Lilly Youth Theology Network, they represent "a collaborative effort of Lilly Endowment initiated and inspired Theology Programs for High School Youth located at seminaries, schools of theology, universities, and other church serving organizations across North America." Their mission is to engage high school youth and their adult leaders "in theological thinking about contemporary issues and vocational discernment" as well as "to support youth theology programs in recruiting a cadre of theologically minded youth and adults to become committed Christian leaders

174. Kenda Creasy Dean, *Practicing Passion: Youth and the Quest for a Passionate Church* (Grand Rapids: Eerdmans, 2007), 7.
175. Senter, *When God Shows Up*, xiii.

in church and society."[176] The Lilly Youth Theology Network has, in many ways, single-handedly altered the way the Christian church in the United States thinks about and approaches ministry with teenagers in the twenty-first century.

Many of the centers, institutes, and academies established in the last thirty years sponsor a high school youth theology camp each summer where worship is the most important and central task. These camps name public Christian worship the central practice from which the Christian faith is taught and learned. This philosophy of worship is best represented in the work of Fred P. Edie, founding director of Duke Divinity School's Youth Academy for Christian Formation. He is openly critical of entertainment-based worship, which fails to "provide youth the formative dimensions related to the identity of God or to faithful vocation before God and for the world."[177] Edie contrasts this type of worship with worship in which Scripture, baptism, the Lord's Table, and intentional rhythms of time form teenagers to "live liturgically" in the world. Edie writes, "Worship that fails to induct young people into the truth of the Christian tradition, to effect God's revelation of Jesus Christ through the power of the Spirit (thus setting them on the journey to God's reign), or to connect them to older worship-formed Christian exemplars leaves them doomed to 'the tyranny of their own experience,' as Charles Foster puts it, and without developed resources for deepened liturgical engagement."[178]

Protestants pursued worship renewal with teenagers by viewing worship in community as central to Christian practice, and several evangelical scholars began to call for worship renewal by uncovering the Christian tradition. The best known of these is Robert E. Webber, an evangelical theologian and worship scholar of Wheaton College who published *The Younger Evangelicals: Facing the Challenges of the New World*.[179] There Webber suggests a trend in which younger evangelicals desire "God-centered worship" that includes a genuine encounter with God, genuine community, depth and substance,

176. "Lilly Youth Theology Network," Duke Youth Academy for Christian Formation, October 5, 2015, https://duyouth.duke.edu/518-2.

177. Fred P. Edie, *Book, Bath, Table, and Time: Christian Worship as Source and Resource for Youth Ministry* (Cleveland: Pilgrim, 2007), 36. See the accompaniment to this resource, Brian Hardesty-Crouch, *Holy Things for Youth Ministry: A Guide to "Book, Bath, Table, and Time"* (Cleveland: Pilgrim, 2010).

178. Fred P. Edie, "Liturgy and Adolescents: Introduction," *Liturgy* 29, no. 1 (2014): 2.

179. Robert E. Webber, *The Younger Evangelicals: Facing the Challenges of the New World* (Grand Rapids: Baker Books, 2002). Webber was not the only evangelical to call for worship renewal by uncovering the tradition of the church. See D. H. Williams, *Evangelicals and Tradition: The Formative Influence of the Early Church* (Grand Rapids: Baker Academic, 2005) and former Wheaton professor Dennis Okholm, *Learning Theology through the Church's Worship* (Grand Rapids: Baker Academic, 2018).

more frequent and meaningful experiences of Communion, challenging sermons, more Scripture in worship, participation, creative use of the senses, contemplative music and times for quiet personal reflection, and a focus on the transcendence and otherness of God.[180] Webber's text suggests that young evangelicals at the time had a strong reaction against worship rooted in entertainment and programs and instead desired worship rooted in formation and narrative.

Worship Renewal Centered on Practices

Other voices associated with the Lilly Youth Theology Network also followed a tradition-centric approach to worship renewal, though they were often more nuanced through specific practices that correlated to worship. In 2001, Kenda Creasy Dean, Chap Clark, and Dave Rahn published *Starting Right: Thinking Theologically about Youth Ministry*.[181] This work includes an essay by Mark Yaconelli, a cofounder and former director of the Youth Ministry and Spirituality Project at San Francisco Theological Seminary, who emphasizes that the "context of all Christian practices" is the worshiping community of all ages.[182] Yaconelli outlines a vision for worship with teenagers in which Christianity is a communal faith that "shapes and articulates our practices of faith" through gathering, reading Scripture, proclaiming the gospel, passing the peace, sharing prayers, offering gifts, hearing confessions, celebrating sacraments, and experiencing "the presence of God's spirit." He concludes, "If worship is the fundamental Christian practice, and the worshiping community is the container of all Christian practices, then it follows that adolescent spiritual formation must take place in the worship of God."[183]

Yaconelli later published *Contemplative Youth Ministry*, which focuses on youth ministry through a series of contemplative practices and ancient rituals connected to worship.[184] That same year the director of Youthfront,

180. Webber, *Younger Evangelicals*, 189. Webber's list, taken from a survey of Wheaton College students at the time, closely matches a list of values found in "emerging worship," made more explicit in Eddie Gibbs and Ryan K. Bolger, *Emerging Churches: Creating Christian Community in Postmodern Cultures* (Grand Rapids: Baker Academic, 2005); and Dan Kimball, *Emerging Worship: Creating Worship Gatherings for New Generations* (Grand Rapids: Zondervan, 2004), chaps. 7–8.

181. Kenda Creasy Dean, Chap Clark, and Dave Rahn, eds., *Starting Right: Thinking Theologically about Youth Ministry* (Grand Rapids: Zondervan, 2001).

182. Mark Yaconelli, "Focusing Youth Ministry through Christian Practices," in Dean, Clark, and Rahn, *Starting Right*, 160.

183. Yaconelli, "Focusing Youth Ministry," 161.

184. Mark Yaconelli, *Contemplative Youth Ministry: Practicing the Presence of Jesus* (Grand Rapids: Zondervan, 2006).

Mike King, published *Presence-Centered Youth Ministry*,[185] which calls for a recovery of the tradition of the church, defined as the "living faith of the dead," to connect teenagers to the story of God. This will come, King argues, by introducing teenagers to historic creeds, liturgy, sacraments, and other spiritual practices.[186] While King's and Yaconelli's works focused generally on practices such as contemplative prayer, *lectio divina*, confession, and the Saint Ignatius *Examen*, works in the second decade of the twenty-first century focused more specifically on individual practices such as Sabbath. Examples of these works include *Wrestling with Rest: Inviting Youth to Discover the Gift of Sabbath* by Nathan T. Stucky[187] or *Saying Is Believing: The Necessity of Testimony in Adolescent Spiritual Development* by Amanda Hontz Drury.[188]

Worship Renewal Centered on Congregations and Families

In 2005, findings from the NSYR stated that religious practices such as "habitually worshiping with other believers" were important and even "crucial to vibrant religious faith among American teens." For committed teenagers, religion is "not simply a matter of general identity or affiliation or cognitive belief"; rather, it is something that can be "activated, practiced, and formed through specific religious and spiritual practices."[189] The NSYR also identified the most important worshiper in the pew with teenagers: an adult who exercises "immense influence in the lives of teens," whether for better or worse. It also stated that engaging worship as a worship leader was an influential mode of cultural capital.[190] Finally, the NSYR told the church that worship was not forming teenagers *enough*. Teenagers who participated in public Christian worship espoused Moralistic Therapeutic Deism, a spiritual worldview that was close to, but not quite, Christianity.[191]

Following the publication of the NSYR, additional calls for confession, lament, and renewal came from mainline Protestants and evangelicals. The proposed solutions for worship renewal with teenagers were primarily centered on congregational and familial contexts. The most explicit of these came

185. Mike King, *Presence-Centered Youth Ministry: Guiding Students into Spiritual Formation* (Downers Grove, IL: IVP, 2006).

186. See King, *Presence-Centered Youth Ministry*, 102; see also 103–11.

187. Nathan T. Stucky, *Wrestling with Rest: Inviting Youth to Discover the Gift of Sabbath* (Grand Rapids: Eerdmans, 2019).

188. Amanda Hontz Drury, *Saying Is Believing: The Necessity of Testimony in Adolescent Spiritual Development* (Downers Grove, IL: IVP Academic, 2015).

189. Smith and Denton, *Soul Searching*, 27.

190. Smith and Denton, *Soul Searching*, 245.

191. Smith and Denton, *Soul Searching*, 162–71.

from Dean in her book *Almost Christian*. There Dean claims the solution to the "lackadaisical faith" of America's teenagers in the twenty-first century "lies not in beefing up congregational youth programs or making worship more 'cool' and attractive." Rather, it is to come from "modeling the kind of mature, passionate faith we say we want young people to have."[192] For Dean, this comes through helping teenagers discover a creed, a community, a call, and a hope, each of which has implications for worship with teenagers that will be explored later in this text.[193]

Coming alongside Dean's proposed solution was the work of FYI at Fuller Theological Seminary in Pasadena, California. Initially led by Chap Clark and later Kara E. Powell, FYI has prompted the renewal of worship with teenagers in congregational and familial contexts. Initially FYI called for the primacy of intergenerational worship as the single most important factor that determined whether a teenager's faith would last beyond high school and into college.[194] FYI also emphasized the role that parents, family, and rituals played in "reinforcing identity."[195] A later publication, *Growing Young*, assured congregations that they did not need a "'contemporary' worship service," a "watered-down teaching style," or a "hyper-entertaining ministry program" to attract teenagers and young adults to congregational work and worship.[196] Rather, congregations needed to have six priorities with implications for worship: unlock keychain leadership, empathize with today's young people, take Jesus's message seriously, fuel a warm community, prioritize young people and families everywhere, and be the best neighbors.[197]

Conclusion

In many ways, youth ministry was born with a deeply sacramental mindset that held profound liturgical implications. Teenagers' desire to encounter God has been realized throughout history as youth ministry has grown, and congregations across the United States have accepted the reality that teenagers need and desire more opportunities to practice and grow their faith.

192. Dean, *Almost Christian*, 4.
193. Dean, *Almost Christian*, 60.
194. Kara E. Powell and Chap Clark, *Sticky Faith: Everyday Ideas to Build Lasting Faith in Your Kids* (Grand Rapids: Zondervan, 2008), 113–19.
195. Powell and Clark, *Sticky Faith*, 60–62. See also Mark DeVries, *Family-Based Youth Ministry*, rev. ed. (Downers Grove, IL: InterVarsity, 2004).
196. Kara Powell, Jake Mulder, and Brad Griffin, *Growing Young: 6 Essential Strategies to Help Young People Discover and Love Your Church* (Grand Rapids: Baker Books, 2016).
197. Powell, Mulder, and Griffin, *Growing Young*, 42–43.

Teenagers worship not only in faith communities but also in youth groups; at camps, conferences, and retreats; on local and global mission trips; at schools, rallies, and concerts; and through individual and communal prayer, Scripture study, community fellowship, and music. On one hand, our worship efforts with teenagers have been deeply formative spiritually. On the other hand, the dominant historical pattern has been to focus on the medium of worship over the message of worship to attract and keep teenagers. Yet having teenagers show up to worship is not enough if they are not growing spiritually and finding faith and worship meaningful enough to last beyond high school. The church needs to reframe its approach to worship with teenagers by asking, Who do we want our teenagers to be as a result of the worship practices they engage? This question is the topic of the next chapter.

3

✦ ✦ ✦

Worship with Teenagers

Beginning with the End in Mind

To begin with the end in mind means to start with a clear understanding of your destination. It means to know where you're going so that you better understand where you are now and so that the steps you take are always in the right direction.

—Stephen Covey, *The Seven Habits of Highly Effective People*

Beginning with the End: A Telos for Teenagers

An important leadership lesson is to always start with the end in mind. Sadly, we rarely begin with the end in mind for our teenagers. If we did, the outcome of the NSYR might have been different. We might be celebrating its findings rather than lamenting and correcting them. The truth is that teenagers are not entirely capable of prescribing who they want to be when they grow up. Part of the church's vocation is to prescribe what it means for teenagers to grow into the faith. If we fail to paint a picture of the teenager at the end of her time in the youth group, how do we know what our worship practices with her and her friends need to look like?

An underwhelming vision for worship that forms teenagers into beloved children of God is a challenge of teenage worship practices today. Our inability to imagine who we want our teenagers to be makes worship a routine act, something the church does week in and week out like a sprint rather than the long marathon that it actually is. Worship examined in the short term without a nod toward the long term is bound to present an incongruent vision of the Triune God, God's people, and their call to be the hands and feet of Christ in the world.

A better approach to worship with teenagers, then, is to start with these questions: Who do we pray teenagers might be on the eve of their twentieth birthdays? How do we hope the worship practices they have engaged during their teenage years have formed them? This chapter will begin with my own prayer for who I hope the teenagers in my life might become by the time they are twenty, and it will invite you to pray that prayer with me. As we paint this picture for who we hope teenagers will be on the eve of their twentieth birthdays, it will help us ask and answer our next logical question: How might we shape our worship practices to help our teenagers live into that vision?

Here is the prayer, which will become the overarching outline of this chapter.

God, we pray that our teenagers will be captivated by an encounter with the living God and connect their passion to the passion of Christ. We pray that the God story will be told to them in their community of faith through its rhythms, songs, prayers, creeds, confessions, pardons, Scriptures, sermons, testimonies, table fellowship, offerings, and blessings so that over time the repetition of these things might capture their imagination for the kingdom and infect the body of Christ. We pray that they might become salt and light in civil society where they flourish while practicing patience waiting for the King. Amen.

Desiring the Kingdom: A Worshiping Disciple

Called

What does it mean to pray that our teenagers will be captivated by an encounter with the living God and connect their passion to the passion of Christ? The place to start is with a captivating encounter with the living God. Before the teenager is anything, the teenager is called. The calling must be captivating enough that it prompts teenagers to tether themselves to the life of Christ as Christ's disciples, because to worship the Triune God is to be in relationship with that God, through Christ, by the power of the Holy Spirit.[1]

1. I am aware of the messiness of this statement. It begs the question of whether a relationship with God is a prerequisite for worshiping God and exhibiting the traits of a disciple. This

After being called, the disciple becomes a pupil or a learner, but learning the way of Jesus was not easy for Jesus's disciples. It demanded a radical conversion for all the disciples, just as it does for us. In the same way the act of following Jesus remains sacrificial for us. Being a disciple "means learning a way of life that embodies particular dispositions, attitudes, and practices that place the disciple in relationship to, and as a participant in, God's mission to serve and transform the world."[2] Many individuals have their own definitions of what it means to identify with the life of Christ and to learn as his disciple, but Kathleen A. Cahalan identifies disciples by a set of seven characteristics that can be connected to the broader Christian tradition: being a follower, a worshiper, a witness, a neighbor, a forgiver, a prophet, and a steward. Construed as practices, these identities become following, worshiping, witnessing, neighboring, forgiving, speaking, and caring.[3]

The disciple is a follower. First and foremost, the disciple is called to be a follower of Jesus Christ. As a follower, the disciple is baptized into the Christian family and "enters into a lifelong process of learning from Jesus, to come to know who and what Jesus is and what Jesus is claiming about God's call to relationship, communion, and mission."[4] One of the earliest markers of our Christian witness is baptism. As children and teenagers come to faith,[5] they are apprenticed first in the way of Christ by passing through the waters of baptism, where they are buried with Christ and raised to walk in newness of life, signed and sealed with the promise of God. Baptism serves as a macrosymbol of the fact that walking the path of Christ will mean continually cycling through patterns of life, death, and resurrection.

is perhaps a topic for a later book. Without getting into the particulars of baptism, confirmation, and different congregational traditions, I will say that at some point teenagers need to be captivated enough by Christ to lean into this vision of Christ through their own agency, especially if their faith is going to last throughout their teenage years. For more, see Stephen R. Holmes, "Trinitarian Missiology: Towards a Theology of God as Missionary," *International Journal of Systematic Theology* 8, no. 1 (2006): 89.

2. Kathleen A. Cahalan, *Introducing the Practice of Ministry* (Collegeville, MN: Liturgical, 2010), 4. Cahalan also illustrates these themes in her text *The Stories We Live: Finding God's Calling All around Us* (Grand Rapids: Eerdmans, 2017).

3. Cahalan, *Introducing the Practice of Ministry*, 4. Cahalan also illustrates these themes in her text *Stories We Live* and connects them to the practice of ministry. Though not the subject of this book, they have bearings for teenage worship leaders who may be called to Christian ministry. The identities and practices converted to a ministry framework mean that the disciple becomes a minister characterized by the practices of teaching, preaching, worship, pastoral care, social ministry, and administration. See Cahalan, *Introducing the Practice of Ministry*, 55.

4. Cahalan, *Introducing the Practice of Ministry*, 5.

5. I will not go into the many ways that children and teenagers come to faith or into the complexities of baptism and confirmation among different Christian traditions.

The disciple is a worshiper. Throughout his ministry, Jesus engaged in liturgical actions and invited his disciples to do the same. The Gospel of Luke portrays Jesus as a "man of prayer" throughout his life. He prays "entering his ministry, during ministry, setting out for Jerusalem, facing his death, and hanging on the cross," and he teaches his disciples how to pray and worship by example.[6] In John 4:23, he foreshadows how true worship will be worship that follows the spirit of the Christ event in "spirit" and in "truth." Then, during his most difficult moments, Jesus turns to God in prayer, witnessing that conversation with God "demands total trust and dependence on God, even in the darkest hour when only lament rises to our lips."[7] Jesus was the perfect worshiper and, through the Christ event, becomes the object and the mediator of our worship. To be a worshiper as Christ was is to assume doxology, or praise, as a way of offering one's life. Romans 12 connects our worship to our living. "Once we fathom that *everything* is created for the glory of God and not necessarily for our own consumption, this changes how we relate to the totality of the universe."[8] Disciples, then, are those individuals who join with the body of Christ in Christ's prayer, "a prayer of obedient love, a prayer of a servant, of one who will follow, taking the cup and following the way of the cross."[9]

The disciple is a witness. Following and worshiping Christ is not enough; disciples must also "offer a testimony, to proclaim and announce a message."[10] This includes speaking truth about those things they see and hear. Scripture is laden with witnesses from the Old Testament to the New Testament: Moses, Joshua, the prophets, Jesus himself, and certainly the disciples, who were eyewitnesses of the life, death, and resurrection of Christ. Being a witness has liturgical implications in the form of testimony, which is an external expression of our internal belief that is intended to point "to the truth of God in human frailty as well as strength in order that each individual life becomes bound to a common story."[11]

The disciple is a neighbor. The central role of neighbor formed the Great Commandment, which connects the love of God to the love of people. In

6. Cahalan, *Introducing the Practice of Ministry*, 6.

7. Cahalan, *Introducing the Practice of Ministry*, 7.

8. Catherine Mowry LaCugna, *God for Us: The Trinity and Christian Life* (San Francisco: Harper & Row, 1991), 342ff. Quoted in Cahalan, *Introducing the Practice of Ministry*, 8.

9. Cahalan, *Introducing the Practice of Ministry*, 8.

10. Cahalan, *Introducing the Practice of Ministry*, 9.

11. Cahalan, *Introducing the Practice of Ministry*, 10. Amanda Drury has done a significant amount of work on the role of testimony in the lives of teenagers. This will be explored more fully in later chapters. See Amanda Hontz Drury, *Saying Is Believing: The Necessity of Testimony in Adolescent Spiritual Development* (Downers Grove, IL: IVP Academic, 2015).

declaring this commandment, Jesus established a new hierarchy for following Christ that demoted "all forms of temple sacrifice and worship." Christ's own model of table fellowship with the neglected of society demonstrated his uncompromising witness to neighboring in "a radical display of who God considers to be neighbor." The definition of *neighbor* was made even more radical when Jesus commanded disciples to preach the good news to the ends of the earth, which meant that they were bound to travel "into neighborhoods beyond Israel where Gentiles abide." In other words, to be a neighbor is to welcome all, not to discriminate against "people or groups based on social categories." This kind of indiscriminate ministry characterized the ministry of Jesus, who engaged individuals though they were sick, hated, neglected, poor, unclean, or unworthy. He envisioned people sharing food together and rejoicing together when things lost were found.[12]

The disciple is a forgiver. The disciple is also one who learns how to forgive self and others. The act of forgiveness is "one of the most complicated acts of discipleship," for it requires a disciple to come "face-to-face with their wrongdoings as well as the hurts and wounds born from others' actions, emotional as well as physical."[13] Engaging in forgiveness involves engaging in reconciliation; it requires "admitting failure and sin and seeking forgiveness, and forgiving another's sin."[14] Cahalan writes that "forgiveness is grounded in the recognition that God's love conquers all sin, a love that empowers disciples to seek and grant forgiveness in the face of much pain and hurt. Neighbor love proceeds neighbor forgiveness in the Christian story."[15]

The disciple is a prophet. "Prophets," Cahalan writes, "are a witness with a keen perception for what harms a neighbor: scorn, hatred, disobedience, hubris, unbelief, greed, and selfishness." As neighbors, they "give witness to neighbor relations that become distorted, forgotten, and abused."[16] The prophet calls all people everywhere to embody and pursue restorative and reparative justice, the process of righting wrongs. As disciples take seriously the call to follow Jesus, they engage in the whole of discipleship, "calling fellow members to the fullness of life in Christ." In this process, the role of the prophet is twofold: to condemn the faults of the community and to announce the "good news about God's mission."[17]

12. Cahalan, *Introducing the Practice of Ministry*, 12.
13. Cahalan, *Introducing the Practice of Ministry*, 12–13.
14. Cahalan, *Introducing the Practice of Ministry*, 13.
15. Cahalan, *Introducing the Practice of Ministry*, 14.
16. Cahalan, *Introducing the Practice of Ministry*, 17.
17. Cahalan, *Introducing the Practice of Ministry*, 19.

The disciple is a steward. The principle of stewardship is grounded in the understanding that God created the world and human beings as good. God was the first steward in the creation of the world, and God extended that responsibility to humanity when God created them. In this sense, stewardship applies to the whole order of creation, which extends to neighbors, and includes keeping, tilling, serving, preserving, and cultivating the gifts of the earth. Through the ministry of Christ, disciples are called to be stewards of the mission of God, and in Paul's writings, they are called to steward the whole "economy of salvation" by proclaiming the mysteries of faith. Finally, disciples of Christ must be stewards of vocation, "the gifts received for service in the community."[18]

Combined, these seven traits serve as a starting place for understanding the identity to which teenagers are called when they worship with the gathered church, a community of disciples whose witness in worship gives witness to the claim "Jesus Christ is Lord."

Selfless

All four Gospels frame Jesus's calling of the disciples in two parts. In the first part, the disciples are taught how to follow Jesus, and in the second, they continue following Jesus despite hardship, difficulty, and persecution. Following Christ demands some kind of sacrifice. The Gospel writers never tell us all the agony, challenges, and hardships that come from leaving behind families, jobs, and homes, though Jesus himself does emphasize that nothing should get in the way of being a follower of the Way.

Following Christ requires a radical conversion that may well lead to death, whether metaphorically or through martyrdom. In many ways, however, this is what teenagers want: a love worth dying for.[19] Indeed the youthful "ultimatums" that we often hear from our teenagers are something like, "Please tell me someone loves me this much and won't let me go. . . . Please show me a God who loves me this much—and who is worth loving passionately in return. Because if Jesus isn't worth dying for, then he's not worth living for, either."[20] For a teenager, being called to follow Jesus involves courage, bravery, sacrifice, and the wherewithal to embrace and endure hardships and

18. Cahalan, *Introducing the Practice of Ministry*, 21, 22.

19. Recently, young Christians have lost their lives while attempting to take the gospel to the literal ends of the earth. News accounts have shown that those young missionaries knowingly put themselves in harm's way. This statement does not advocate that kind of behavior, which sadly, may be characterized as irresponsible evangelism.

20. Kenda Creasy Dean, *Practicing Passion: Youth and the Quest for a Passionate Church* (Grand Rapids: Eerdmans, 2007), 32.

to keep following even when the path is difficult. It is passion that helps them persevere in the face of challenges.

Passionate

As a disciple, the teenager is a called pupil who embraces Christ's identity even to the point of sacrifice. But the teenager is not just any pupil; the teenager is a passionate pupil whose love is directed toward Jesus Christ, the object of our worship and the object of the teenager's passion. Passion is one of the most unique characteristics of adolescence, though it is not always viewed positively. On the one hand, we appreciate that teenagers are passionate about their desires and causes, especially when those desires and causes connect to faith. On the other hand, we chastise teenagers when their passions get the best of them and cause them to act uncontrollably. This is why we often segregate them from adults in worship; we worry they will act out or mess things up for the rest of us.

Yet the passion of teenagers cannot be reduced to a token expression of adolescence. Being passionate is at the very heart of being a disciple of Jesus. The earliest disciples, we are told, *immediately* left everything and followed (Mark 1:17–18); in some way they were captivated by the life and ministry of Christ. They connected their own lives to the life of Christ, an act that was sacrificial but that also reached out toward other people. This kind of passion, the kind that reaches out toward God and others, is learned primarily through praise.[21] Catherine LaCugna writes, "Praise is the creature's mode of ecstasis, its own self-transcendence, its disinclination to remain self-contained. The creature's doxology is evoked by God's ecstasis, God's glorification in the economy. Praise is the mode of return, 'matching' God's movement of exodus. God creates out of glory, for glory. The return is part of the rhythm of life from God to God. In that communion of love is gathered all religious endeavor."[22]

In the act of offering God thanks and praise, the worshiper focuses on a singular object set against all other objects. Teenagers who direct their passion toward praise of God "attain a differentiated unity" that "unites the fragments of their existence around a god who matters most, who stands 'beyond' all other gods, and who is therefore worthy of praise." When young people offer God their praise, they are making a movement linked with the passion of Christ by imitating "God's ecstatic movement toward them by reaching back toward God."[23] The passionate teenage disciple who has been captivated by

21. Dean, *Practicing Passion*, 113.
22. LaCugna, *God for Us*, 350.
23. Dean, *Practicing Passion*, 114.

the message of Christ and is willing to follow Jesus at all costs, even to the point of death, has much to learn from but also much to teach the church.

If our own idolatries of youthfulness have taught us anything, it is that the church cannot rely only on the teenager's passion to infect the church. First, the worship of the church must capture the imagination of the teenager in the way it proclaims the message that Christ is alive. This message must be infectious in its own right if it is to become incarnate in the lives of teenagers by meeting them where they are and moving them to a place of desiring the kingdom. We now turn to the second part of our prayer for teenagers: that the God story will be told to them in the community of faith through its rhythms, songs, prayers, creeds, confessions, pardons, Scriptures, sermons, testimonies, table fellowship, offerings, and blessings, and that the repetition of these things might capture their imagination for the kingdom and infect the body of Christ.

Imagining the Kingdom: A Worshiping Member

A teenage disciple of Christ has had a passionate encounter with the living God and has joined their life to the passion of Christ. Yet disciples cannot function outside the context of community, and the Christian community cannot function without dedicated disciples. Disciples are members of the body of Christ, and in that body, they enact and share the God story, rehearsing its past, present, and future. In doing so, they focus on the reign of God, which was active in history, is active in the present, and will establish a new reign in a kingdom not bound to the world that teenagers inhabit.

The Christian community as we know it was born out of Jesus's calling of the first disciples. As they journeyed with Christ, these disciples developed a way of being in the world that included particular words, signs, symbols, and gestures. Because of their way of communicating with one another, Luke refers to them as people of "the Way" (Acts 9:2). People of the Way were the Jews who followed the ministry and message of Christ. They were first called Christians in Acts 11:26, and they were known for their baptism both in water and in the Holy Spirit. Over time, people of the Way were characterized by their rhythms, songs, prayers, creeds, confessions, pardons, Scriptures, sermons, testimonies, table fellowship, offerings, and blessings. These elements of worship served to form the community's identity and reinforce that each member of the community belonged and had purpose.

Following Christ presented a conundrum for some of the earliest disciples who would deny that they knew Christ or that they were part of the body of

Christ. That same conundrum exists for teenagers in the United States today, who must consistently wonder whether it is "more valuable to learn how to stand tall as a capable individual or to learn how to recognize [their] need for others and [others'] need for [them]."[24] Our culture prizes individuals and encourages individuals to express themselves from the inside out; rarely does our culture place value on individuals who work to fit into communities of faith where they are formed from the outside in. Yet the history of humanity has shown that we are in need of one another, and "none of us can ever hope to live up to the rhetorical expectations of independence and solitude that we have been trained to pursue, even if we wanted to."[25] When teenagers join the body of Christ, they are linked to a community of faith where belonging is fostered through relationships and all ages in the church become dependent on one another.

Infectious

Christianity is a movement that was born out of infectious excitement from the pronouncement that Christ was not in the tomb, pronounced most prominently when Mary met Jesus and ran to tell the others, "I have seen the Lord" (John 20:18). Like *passion*, words such as *contagious* and *infectious* have negative associations with diseases, pandemics, epidemics, and other threats to society. But if you have ever been around someone who has an electrifying energy, you know that energy can spread to others in the room; it is contagious.

That said, when teenagers are excited about something, it is difficult to contain their spirit, and young and old want to participate in their moment of ecstasy. The goal is for teenagers to experience a deep connectedness to the local and global body of Christ in worship so that the infectious nature of that community spreads to them. This will happen as teenagers experience the true belonging that comes because they know their presence in the community and their participation in its worship make a difference. A young entrepreneur understands this well. "I believe that we're all contagious," she writes. "Any time that we walk into a room, there's an impact we have. We can't control what's happening in that room, or how people receive us, but we can control how we show up to make that impact the best possible. Even if we blow it, or have unintended impact, we can recover faster by rebooting our intentions, energy, and presence. How we show up matters and has a

24. Chap Clark, *Hurt 2.0: Inside the World of Today's Teenagers* (Grand Rapids: Baker Academic, 2011), 182.
  25. Clark, *Hurt 2.0*, 183.

profound influence on our results. Know that, and we'll all be better off for it."[26] Making the best impact possible comes about through belonging with those we love and having agency to impact the community.

Faithful

When teenagers experience the community as a place where they belong and also have an impact, they develop a faithful commitment to the worshiping community that prompts them to return week after week. This is fidelity, or the ability to be faithful. It is the strength behind teenagers' passion, and it is what provides teenagers with the capacity to cling to a person or an idea. In the act of being faithful to the worshiping community, the teenager participates in the familiar, repetitive, and formative patterns of worship.

Through fidelity to formative worship, teenagers learn eight key "vertical habits" of Christian worship. John D. Witvliet of the Calvin Institute of Christian Worship identifies these eight habits as a means of expanding our worship vocabulary so that we can connect the words we speak in worship to the words we speak in the world.[27] The vertical habits are rooted in the Psalms, and they are central to a biblical understanding of worship. In their simplest form, these habits are expressed in the following ways: "Love you." "I'm sorry." "Why?" "I'm listening." "Help." "Thank you." "What can I do?" And "Bless you." Spoken liturgically, these are words of praise, confession, lament, illumination, petition, thanksgiving, service, and blessing. These eight habits align with the seven traits of disciples presented earlier. The worshiper speaks praise by saying, "Love you." The trespasser offers a word of confession with "I'm sorry." The prophet laments with "Why, Lord?" The witness prays for illumination before saying, "I'm listening." The neighbor petitions, "Help, Lord." The steward says a prayer of thanksgiving: "Thank you." Finally, the follower, before leaving to follow God in the world, says, "Bless you."

Through these vertical habits we are reminded that Christianity is first and foremost a relationship, mediated through Jesus Christ by the power

---

26. Paul Spiegelman, "You're Contagious, and That's a Good Thing," *Forbes*, December 12, 2018, https://www.forbes.com/sites/paulspiegelman/2018/12/12/youre-contagious-and-thats-a-good-thing/.

27. The theme of "vertical habits" was developed by the Calvin Institute of Christian Worship in the early 2000s. Much of what is used here comes from their online repository but is found most explicitly in John D. Witvliet, "Vertical Habits: Missional Churches at Worship" (presentation, Calvin Symposium on Christian Worship, Grand Rapids, January 2006), https://storage.googleapis.com/cicw/microsites/worshipsymposiumorg/files/2006/witvliet.pdf. See also Betty Grit, "Vertical Habits: Worship and Our Faith Vocabulary," Calvin Institute of Christian Worship, January 10, 2012, https://worship.calvin.edu/resources/resource-library/vertical-habits-worship-and-our-faith-vocabulary/.

of the Holy Spirit, between the individual who is called to be a disciple and God. As a means of practicing faith, the individual participates in a community of worshipers with the understanding and expectation that worship is a dialogical encounter in which God talks to us and we talk to God. To that end, worship must be understood as the "enactment of a divine-human relationship"[28] that has been in place since the Old Testament, when God says in Deuteronomy 4:10, "Assemble the people for me, and I will let them hear my words, so that they may learn to fear me as long as they live on the earth, and may teach their children so."[29] This passage from Deuteronomy reminds us of an important point. If a worshiper is to possess fidelity to the Christian tradition, Scripture reading and prayer must be central. We must allow opportunities for God to speak and listen to us, as well as opportunities for us to speak and listen to God. The conversation should be two-sided.

One of the beautiful things about these habits is their ability to "help each of us express our particular experience" as well as "practice forms of speech we're still growing into." At the same time, Witvliet reminds us that worship "challenges us to practice forms of faithful speech to God that we are not likely to try on our own."[30] While we can use the words above to express our thoughts and feelings to God, we should also presume that worship will be formative and teach us new words and ways of expressing ourselves. In other words, "worship doesn't just reflect where we are. It moves us further along as we grow in the life of faith."[31] We deepen our walks as disciples by practicing the language of discipleship in much the same way a pianist practices scales or a baseball player practices throwing a curveball.

Yet fidelity cannot happen without a mutuality that enables teenagers to be "for" something, so long as that something is "for" the teenager first.[32] Here we see again the reciprocal nature of the worshiping community for the teenager. The teenager, as a disciple of Christ, participates in worship with the body of Christ, offering contributions to that body, not the least of which is a unique penchant for sacrifice and passion, which are infectious to the worshiping community. But the church must learn to be there for the teenager, primarily through relationships with other worshipers, especially adults. Fidelity is a

28. Witvliet, "Vertical Habits," 3.

29. Witvliet, "Vertical Habits," 3. Witvliet outlines this theme more explicitly in John D. Witvliet, *The Biblical Psalms in Christian Worship: A Brief Introduction and Guide to Resources* (Grand Rapids: Eerdmans, 2007).

30. Witvliet, "Vertical Habits," 2.

31. Witvliet, "Vertical Habits," 3.

32. Dean, *Practicing Passion*, 76.

mandate that belongs to the Christian *community*, not just to any individual or group of individuals. Fidelity is practiced by congregations "who [reveal] their passion for young people in practices and policies that risked on their behalf."[33] This happens inside as well as outside worship.

Imaginative

In the community of disciples, exercising imagination is a prerequisite. Disciples must dare to believe that an invisible God created the world out of nothing; that the same God was abstinent yet sent a baby, God's son, to be born to a virgin teenager, rise from the dead, and ascend into heaven with a promised victorious return; and that the same protective God sent an invisible ghost of sorts through wind and fire to be with God's people as an animating Spirit while they wait for the King to return. As Walter Brueggemann has shown, the formation of disciples happened in an alternative community that stood in a lineage of alternative communities that harked back to Moses.[34] The primary purpose of alternative communities was to form an "alternative consciousness" so that "the dominant community may be criticized and finally dismantled."[35] For Brueggemann the task of prophetic ministry, then, is to "nurture, nourish, and evoke a consciousness and perception alternative to the consciousness and perception of the dominant culture around us."[36] Worship invokes this alternative consciousness in the faith community by helping the community imagine the kingdom of God. The imagination creates a liminal experience where worshipers have one foot in one world and the other foot in another world; imagination allows worshipers to live in both worlds simultaneously, like the book of Revelation invites readers to do. Richard Bauckham writes,

> One of the functions of Revelation [or of worship] was to purge and to refurbish the Christian imagination. It tackles people's imaginative response to the world, which is at least as deep and influential as their intellectual convictions. It recognizes the way a dominant culture, with its images and ideals, constructs the world for us, so that we perceive and respond to the world in its terms. Moreover, it unmasks this dominant construction of the world as an ideology of the powerful which serves to maintain their power. In its place, Revelation offers a different way of perceiving the world which leads people to resist and

33. Dean, *Practicing Passion*, 91.
34. Walter Brueggemann, *The Prophetic Imagination*, 40th anniv. ed. (Minneapolis: Fortress, 2018), 101.
35. Brueggemann, *Prophetic Imagination*, 101.
36. Brueggemann, *Prophetic Imagination*, 3.

to challenge the effects of the dominant ideology. Moreover, since this different way of perceiving the world is fundamentally to open it to transcendence it resists any absolutizing power or structures or ideals within this world. . . . This is the most fundamental way in which the church is called always to be counter-cultural.[37]

This is best illustrated if we think about worship primarily as play or as a game—with no disrespect intended. Games have their own rules, customs, boundaries, and etiquettes. They suspend our normal patterns of being in the world and invite us into a controlled space and time. Generally, games are undertaken for their own sake as leisure activities, but they are useful tools for training because they are relatively safe, which means there is freedom to take risks, experiment, fail, and discover. The more often that individuals play a game, the better they will become at playing it, and whether they win or lose, they will likely develop new habits and new skills. Worship is a game that instills in us new habits and new skills that we will need in the kingdom of God, and this is critical for thinking about worship with teenagers.[38]

Thinking about worship as play may be uncomfortable for some in our faith community, but using the analogy can also be transformational because play calls teenagers outside of themselves and into something different—similar to how they worship while living in the secular world yet belonging to another kingdom. Kenda Creasy Dean writes, "Playful worship is re-creational—which is not the same thing as saying it is trivial, light-hearted, or even exciting. Youth have their fill of frivolity elsewhere, and the church neither can nor should out-entertain the entertainment industry. Playing in worship means relinquishing control to God, who transports us into a new reality regardless of the 'style' of the service."[39]

Teenagers—and their faith communities—are transformed over time in worship so that they are characterized by virtues of the kingdom such as patience, perseverance, courage, and self-control. As disciples who rehearse the values of the kingdom in worship, they also begin to develop a series of virtues that Robert C. Roberts has referred to as "Christian emotion-virtues."[40] These are contrition, joy, gratitude, hope, peace, and compassion. Like the words *passion* and *infectious*, the word *emotion* often conveys mixed mean-

37. Richard Bauckham, *The Theology of the Book of Revelation* (Cambridge: Cambridge University Press, 1993), 159–60.
38. See Bernhard Lang, *Sacred Games: A History of Christian Worship* (New Haven: Yale University Press, 1998).
39. Dean, *Practicing Passion*, 214.
40. Robert C. Roberts, *Spiritual Emotions: A Psychology of Christian Virtues* (Grand Rapids: Eerdmans, 2007), 9.

ings and has been dismissed by some altogether. But "emotions are a primary means for our being in touch with our world."[41] For teenagers, who are emotional beings, as Erik Erickson has taught us, developing Christian emotion-virtues is immensely important. In the same way that we want their cognitive understanding of faith to be "right theology," we want their affective understanding of the faith to be "right psychology." The emotions of contrition, joy, gratitude, hope, peace, and compassion connect with a disciple's identity as forgiver, worshiper, steward, witness, neighbor, and prophet, respectively.

This happens as teenagers suspend life in the world and participate in an exercise that imagines the kingdom of God by re-storying the biblical narratives of creation, fall, incarnation, redemption, salvation, and restoration. As teenagers willingly participate in worship that resembles the reign of God, their imaginations, wills, feelings, minds, and bodies are rehearsed into new stories that manifest Christlike ways of being. Each time they leave worship, they are more prepared to embody these values outside the walls of worship, among those they work, study, and play with. With that thought, we now turn to the third part of our prayer: that teenagers might become salt and light in civil society as they flourish and practice patience while waiting for the King.

Awaiting the King: A Worshiping Citizen

A Citizen

Teenagers are citizens of the world, and the NSYR demonstrated that religion is important to teenagers, as it is important to many Americans. The challenge is that the religion we have encouraged teenagers to practice is not necessarily the religion we want them to confess. Now, they want a God who meets their needs in the world where they can get good service. They want a friendly God who will bless them as they do good and pursue comfort, money, and success. Like many Americans, the objects of their attention have become their gods, and fulfilling their desires has become their religion.[42]

Yet "it is the worship of the church as institute that *forms* those who will be the rays of light in civil society." Worship teaches teenagers how to be salt and light in the world, the "norms for flourishing," and also "how to wait"

41. Mark Johnson, *The Meaning of the Body: Aesthetics of Human Understanding* (Chicago: University of Chicago Press, 2007), 65.
42. Juan M. Floyd-Thomas, Stacey M. Floyd-Thomas, and Mark G. Toulouse, *The Altars Where We Worship: The Religious Significance of Popular Culture* (Louisville: Westminster John Knox, 2016), 1–3.

with patience for the King.[43] As disciples, teenagers are called to connect the practices of discipleship rehearsed in worship with their role as citizens in society. In society they may function as sons or daughters, brothers or sisters, grandchildren, students, friends, athletes, musicians, mentors, mentees, employees, or any other identity the world assigns them. But because they are trained to be something different in worship, these identities of the world become secondary to their identity as Christ followers who practice, speak, and embody the way of the kingdom.

Flourishing

Our culture has a penchant for milking life for all it's worth, so to speak. We try to satisfy ourselves and those we love most in all areas of work and play. A recent project called God and Human Flourishing was funded by a Templeton grant under which scholars and practitioners were to study joy, adolescent faith, and flourishing, especially in the context of youth ministry. It included theological research on joy and the good life among teenagers, including those things that both cause human flourishing and tamper with it. Interestingly, the word *joy* became a regular substitute for the phrase *human flourishing* in this project. Researchers noted that "a joyful human is a thriving one," but they also noted that joy was closer to adolescents' descriptions of what they actually desire. "While lives of faith and human flourishing are the goals of our ministries with young people, joy is not an *outcome* of this ministry—it is the *condition* for it."[44] A logical question follows: What, then, is joy? Dean defines it this way: "Joy is more than a fleeting emotional response to circumstance. Just as my experience of a joyful church stood in contrast to a prolonged period of spiritual 'hemorrhaging,' adolescents inevitably describe joy in the context of an experience of loss or suffering. In fact, it became clear that the vulnerability that accompanies suffering was, in fact, a condition for joy as well. But it was a particular kind of vulnerability, emanating not from a place of weakness but from a place of self-chosen, self-giving love."[45]

It strikes me as unique that adolescents' experience of joy includes loss and suffering. This is the experience of the psalmist throughout the Psalter: "Joy precedes and follows sorrow, and as often as not, joy exists alongside

43. James K. A. Smith, *Awaiting the King: Reforming Public Theology* (Grand Rapids: Baker Academic, 2017), 88–89.

44. Kenda Creasy Dean, "Losing Our Scales: The Adolescent Experience of Joy," in *Delighted: What Teenagers Are Teaching the Church about Joy*, by Kenda Creasy Dean et al. (Grand Rapids: Eerdmans, 2020), 4–5.

45. Dean, "Losing Our Scales," 5.

sorrow."[46] Perhaps this is why Dietrich Bonhoeffer wrote, "The joy of God has been through the poverty of the manger and the affliction of the cross; therefore, it is indestructible, irrefutable. It does not deny affliction when it is there, but it finds in the very midst of distress that God is there; it does not argue that sin is not grievous, but in that very place of sin is found forgiveness; it looks death in the face and it is just there that it finds life."[47] For teenagers to flourish while they wait for the King, then, they must participate in the world with its fullness of joy and sorrow and "rejoice insofar as [they] are sharing Christ's sufferings, so that [they] may also be glad and shout for joy when his glory is revealed" (1 Pet. 4:13).

Interrupting

After a memorable experience with Kirk Franklin's song "Revolution" during a summer-camp dance party, it became a staple song of a youth group I pastored. I will spare you the details, but for months after the dance party, whenever a teenager would play or start singing "Revolution," and if two or more teenagers from our congregation were gathered together, singing and dancing would break out as though we were back on the dance floor at summer camp. We really did dance as though no one was watching, so says another song.

When something in the world captures their attention through imagination, teenagers develop the courage to share it. Think about the teenage climate activist Greta Thunberg and the raucous response she caused around the world when she chastised the United Nations summit for caring more about "fairy-tales of eternal economic growth" than dying ecosystems, mass extinctions, and people suffering from climate change.[48] Elizabeth Corrie, director of the high school Youth Theology Initiative (YTI) at Candler School of Theology, writes about a group of teenagers who, as a result of formation in this program, possessed the courage to protest the execution of Troy Davis in 2011 during a public liturgy. Corrie describes the act:

> In defiance of the liturgy of the mall, young people donned decidedly unflattering 'I am Troy Davis' T-shirts and took public transportation down to an inner-city

46. W. David O. Taylor, *Open and Unafraid: The Psalms as a Guide to Life* (Nashville: Nelson, 2020), 100.

47. Dietrich Bonhoeffer, *My Soul Finds Rest in God Alone*, trans. and ed. Edwin Robertson (Grand Rapids: Zondervan, 2002), 109.

48. Kalhan Rosenblatt, "Teen Climate Activist Greta Thunberg Delivers Scathing Speech at U.N.," NBC News, September 23, 2019, https://www.nbcnews.com/news/world/teen-climate-activist-greta-thunberg-delivers-scathing-speech-u-n-n1057621.

park, where they stood alongside homeless and working-class people to hear speeches and to sing songs. In defiance of the liturgy of the athletic stadium, young people cheered on—and became—courageous speakers who were critical of the government and state violence and carried signs that spoke of restorative rather than retributive justice. In defiance of the liturgy of the frat house, young people activated their social networks to organize their peers to help someone they had never met, for a cause that would never gain them personal wealth or position.[49]

Protest liturgies like this one remind us that Christian worship is a public act, but it is also a political act, a way of speaking against things that are not right in the world. When teenagers' worship spills into the world, it creates a momentary interruption in the normal patterns and behaviors of not only society and their lives but also the lives of their families and friends. Bernd Wannenwetsch describes how "worship again and again interrupts the course of the world. Through worship the Christian community testifies that the world is not on its own. And this also means that it is not kept alive by politics, as the business of politics, which knows no sabbath, would have us believe. This is why the celebration of worship is not directed simply against this or that totalitarian regime; it is directed against the totalization of political existence in general."[50]

While much time has been dedicated to talking about the liturgies of the world, time can also be spent talking about the politics of the liturgy. Liturgy is political in that it helps teenagers declare an ultimate allegiance to God and to the peace, or shalom, found in the kingdom of God, which is a more hopeful vision of peace than that which comes from the world. Because teenagers are called to reflect on this experience in congregational worship, their testimony and witness will become infectious to the children who might think the teenagers are doing something right, to the senior adults who wish they had the courage and energy to do what the teenagers are doing, to the middle-aged adults who remember a time when they did similar things, and even to those quiet observers in the faith community who believe the teenagers' actions are disruptive but acceptable because "they are just teenagers."

Waiting

We live in a culture where waiting is nearly unacceptable. Waiting in line. Waiting for a concert to begin. Waiting for a movie to release. To be educated

---

49. Elizabeth W. Corrie, "Christian Liturgy Spilling Out into the World: Youth as Public Theologians," *Liturgy* 29, no. 1 (January–March 2014): 17–18.

50. Bernd Wannenwetsch, *Political Worship* (New York: Oxford University Press, 2009), 127.

by the culture in which teenagers reside is to be used to getting things quickly—immediately, in fact. For a generation of people who can accomplish most tasks with the push of a button or the swipe of a finger, waiting or having patience is generally not considered positive. And yet here we are, waiting for the reign of the King to break into our midst and bring shalom.

James K. A. Smith writes, "Worship is not a rehearsal of a 'natural law' that can be known by reason or conscience; it is the restor(y)ing of a renewed humanity who are liturgically schooled. The index and criterion for justice and the right ordering of society is not some generic, universal, or 'natural' canon but rather the revealed, biblical story unfolded in God's covenant relationship with Israel and the church."[51]

Worship in Waiting

As teenagers experience the liminality of adolescence and live in a world that they are not of, they learn to practice patience in the rhythms of the seasons that follow the life of Christ and the work and mission of the church in the world, all the while waiting for the return of the King. And as they wait, they worship by playing with the world's material goods of water, wine, candles, ashes, fire, and branches; inspiring people with clapping, shouts of praise, dancing, and postures of humility; and participating in the table of the Lord, which dramatically tells the story of how Christ has died, Christ is risen, and Christ will come again. As they do these things, their sights are aimed on "the holy city, the new Jerusalem, coming down out of heaven from God, prepared as a bride adorned for her husband" (Rev. 21:2). Andy Crouch writes, "Play and pain—feasting and fasting—these are the calling, not just of the Christian artist, but of the Christian. We bend our lives toward the recognition of Christ's body, beautiful and broken, at play and in pain. The real challenge for the church . . . is to discover Christ taking, blessing, breaking, giving. To become just slightly more the kind of people who could be like Christ and take, bless, break, and give where we are."[52] May this vision inspire us to dream better for our teenagers and engage them in worship that forms them to be the hands and the feet of Christ.

---

51. Smith, *Awaiting the King*, 60.
52. Andy Crouch, "How Is Art a Gift, a Calling, and an Obedience?," in *For the Beauty of the Church: Casting a Vision for the Arts*, ed. W. David O. Taylor (Grand Rapids: Baker Books, 2010), 42.

PART 2

LITURGICAL PERSPECTIVES

4

✦ ✦ ✦

Linking God's Story with Teenagers' Stories

The Role of Christian Worship

People in our society know in their bones that they are made to reflect God's image; but they feel exiled, futile, and stale; so they go in for tired and shoddy celebration, seen only too clearly in the forced frivolity of television programmes over Christmas and New Year.

—N. T. Wright, *For All God's Worth*

Drowsy Worship: Two Scenarios

It was Wednesday night, and hundreds of teenagers were gathering in the youth wing of a large Southern Baptist congregation in Texas. I was there as a participant-observer, and it seemed the teenagers were rushing from the entire metropolitan area to connect with their faith community through worship and small groups. Most of the teenagers had ended their school day with all the extracurricular activities teenagers participate in after school: sports practices, marching-band drills, speech and debate club, foreign language club, and so on. I suppose a few of them had time to run home for a change of clothes and dinner, but the smell of teenage perspiration in the room suggested otherwise, and I'm sure the cool church building was a haven from the Texas heat that plagued the afternoon.

No doubt, most of the teenagers in this congregation had a life that many would label "privileged." Their lives mirrored what the American Psychological Association has said about the teenage years—namely, that "the picture of adolescents today is largely a very positive one." Many adolescents "succeed in school, are attached to their families and their communities, and emerge from their teen years without experiencing serious problems such as substance abuse or involvement with violence."[1]

That fall Wednesday evening in Texas, the room was electrified with youthful energy, and as the lights in the room dimmed to light the stage, the college-aged worship leader stepped to the microphone and said, "Hey, everybody. We are here to worship, so just set all your worries aside as you come in the door and focus directly on God."

These teenagers were privileged to be sure. Yet even the most privileged of teenagers can have lives that are complex, filled with worries and anxieties. Was the worship leader telling these teenagers that worship is a form of escapism that involves putting the complexities of their lives to sleep?

Contrast that scenario with one that occurred on Wednesday, February 14, 2018, which was both Valentine's Day and Ash Wednesday. On that day, an armed nineteen-year-old walked into Marjory Stoneman Douglas High School in Parkland, Florida, killed seventeen people, and injured fourteen more in one of the deadliest school shootings in our nation's history. I watched this unfold on news channels and in internet stories. By the end of the day, I found myself on a group text with three teenagers who I had encountered one year prior. This was their text: "You may not know, but we're about forty-five miles from Parkland, where the school shooting happened. We've been asked to help lead a prayer service at our high school. What songs do you sing at a vigil for a high school shooting?"

I paused in my tracks. Was this text message a mistake?

That night I attended an Ash Wednesday service in my community. This service, designed to be an act of penitence, did not acknowledge the events in Parkland, Florida. Many families attended this service, and I counted several dozen teenage worshipers who walked forward to receive the sign of the cross in ash on their foreheads. As I counted them, I wondered about their experience. Were they also thinking about Parkland? Did they connect the words

---

1. Andrea Solarz, *Developing Adolescents: A Reference for Professionals* (Washington, DC: American Psychological Association, 2002), 3. This study was part of the American Psychological Association's Healthy Adolescents Project.

of Ash Wednesday to the tragedy in Parkland? Or were they also living in a spiritual slumber?

I have often entered worship spaces and heard a worship leader give an invitation to worship akin to the one the first group of teenagers received that Wednesday evening: "Put all your troubles down; set your worries aside for this hour and *just* worship." It is common rhetoric in worship gatherings of all ages. Like the second group of teenagers, I can count a number of times when tragic events have happened in our world and have not been addressed in worship. Is it right to ask teenagers—or worshipers of any age—to set aside the world they inhabit every day when they enter the doors of the church?

As the introduction to this book suggested, worship is about God, the church, and the world. This means that on a fundamental level worship should connect God's story with our story. Worship requires us to give God all that we are, including our worries, troubles, anxious thoughts, and fears, and it reminds us that the life, death, and resurrection of Jesus Christ hold our stories with the promise that in the end God will make all things well. Yet these worship gatherings made me wonder if Mark Labberton was right when he said, "The church is asleep. Not dead. Not necessarily having trouble breathing. But asleep . . . to God's heart for a world filled with injustice."[2] Have we lulled our teenagers to sleep?

An Outer Shell and an Inner Reality: The World of Teenagers

In *Hurt 2.0: Inside the World of Today's Teenagers*, Chap Clark writes about his experience as a participant-observer at Crescenta Valley High School, a public high school in Los Angeles County. He engaged, studied, and documented the teenagers there with whom he interacted over an academic year using social-scientific research and ethnographic principles. His goal was to understand and subsequently care for these teenagers. His final analysis was that "adolescence is a fundamentally different thing than it was even thirty years ago."[3] Adults who dismiss today's teenagers as "a more spoiled breed of us when we were young" are fundamentally wrong.[4] The "defining issue" for adolescents, according to Clark, is abandonment—in other words, "a longing that parents, teachers, and other adults have ceased as a community

2. Mark Labberton, *The Dangerous Act of Worship: Living God's Call to Justice* (Downers Grove, IL: IVP, 2007), 14.

3. Chap Clark, *Hurt 2.0: Inside the World of Today's Teenagers* (Grand Rapids: Baker Academic, 2011), 7.

4. Clark, *Hurt 2.0*, 5.

to fulfill."[5] In response to this longing, American adolescents "have been forced by a personal sense of abandonment to band together and create their own world—separate, semisecret, and vastly different from the world around them."[6]

As they navigate their daily lives, teenagers experience a conflict between the "outer shell" and the "inner reality."[7] The outer shell is the external picture that many teenagers, especially mid-adolescents, present to "adapt to the expectations of those who control the world in which they live."[8] This outer shell, which is projected by adolescents as an identity, sounds strikingly similar to the identities of adolescents of previous generations. Current adolescents "enjoy their home life, find security and comfort in their peer relationships, and approach life as a grand challenge to be conquered."[9] While the ones who control their world may be adults, they may also be friends, family, and any other person to whom teenagers present one of their "multiple selves," none of which may be their true self.[10] The true self lies in the inner reality that privately exists in "the world beneath," which is "more like an underground society: sophisticated, pervasive, and not meant to be seen."[11] It is where teenagers hold fast to friendships and a few caring adults they might dare to let inside. This has led to a pervasive loneliness among teenagers that can be traced to a fear of abandonment, which has caused teenagers to "dive underneath the observable surface of the adult world, even while adapting to the shifting and often oppressive expectations of our external and performance-driven culture."[12]

The ways in which mid-adolescents "make decisions about issues such as ethics, sex, busyness and stress, family, alcohol, gaming, and internet use" are not unlike that of the vaudevillian plate spinner. This showman has the unique ability to get multiple plates spinning in the air at once and make it look easy to the audience, all the while being aware internally that the entire show could fall apart in one step. Madeline Levine summarizes this act for teenagers adequately: "Not only are many of these kids expected to perform at the highest levels; they are also expected to make it look easy. Heavily dependent on their 'public' success for a sense of self, many of these youngsters

5. Clark, *Hurt 2.0*, 27–28.
6. Clark, *Hurt 2.0*, 28.
7. Clark, *Hurt 2.0*, 53–56.
8. Clark, *Hurt 2.0*, 52. The term *mid-adolescence* appeared in the 1990s and includes grades nine through twelve, ages fifteen to eighteen. See Clark, *Hurt 2.0*, 17, for more on this definition.
9. Clark, *Hurt 2.0*, 57.
10. Clark, *Hurt 2.0*, 2.
11. Clark, *Hurt 2.0*, 44.
12. Clark, *Hurt 2.0*, 57.

have little in the way of authentic purpose in their lives, leaving a void where conscience, generosity, and connection should be."[13]

Clark is not the only author who has tackled the troubling world in which many adolescents find themselves today. A group of practical theologians published a collection of essays with the question "Have you seen God?" graffitied on the cover.[14] Andrew Root has written about the pain adolescents experience when their parents divorce.[15] Amy Jacober has described ministry among youth with disabilities.[16] Many individuals have written about the plight of young Catholics in America.[17] Hak Joon Lee has described the challenges inherent in the spiritual and moral lives of young Asian Americans,[18] and Almeda Wright has done the same for young African Americans.[19]

The texts above represent the real and legitimate pain that young people experience in the world. These, however, do not include the issues in the world about which today's teenagers are passionately concerned and of which they are also deeply terrified. A long but not exhaustive list of these issues includes personal safety, income security, mental health, income inequality, human sexuality, climate control, marriage, gun control, racial injustice, sex, abortion, science, technology, sports, communal safety, big business, and politics.[20] Indeed, these are the larger issues with which today's young people concern themselves. While there are themes of hope in these texts, other dominant themes describing America's teenagers emerge in each: they are hurt, scared, terrified, yearning, isolated, reforming their identities, socially endangered,

13. Madeline Levine, *The Price of Privilege: How Parental Pressure and Material Advantage Are Creating a Generation of Disconnected and Unhappy Kids* (New York: Harper Perennial, 2008), 35.

14. Mary Elizabeth Moore and Almeda M. Wright, eds., *Children, Youth, and Spirituality in a Troubling World* (St. Louis: Chalice, 2008).

15. Andrew Root, *The Children of Divorce: The Loss of Family as the Loss of Being* (Grand Rapids: Baker Books, 2010).

16. Amy E. Jacober, *Redefining Perfect: The Interplay between Theology and Disability* (Eugene, OR: Cascade, 2017).

17. Christian Smith, Kyle Longest, Jonathan Hill, and Kari Christoffersen, eds., *Young Catholic America: Emerging Adults in, out of, and Gone from the Church* (New York: Oxford University Press, 2014). See also Hosffman Ospino, ed., *Our Catholic Children: Ministry with Hispanic Youth and Young Adults* (Huntington, IN: Our Sunday Visitor Institute, 2018).

18. Hak Joon Lee, ed., *Intersecting Realities: Race, Identity, and Culture in the Spiritual-Moral Life of Young Asian Americans* (Eugene, OR: Cascade, 2018).

19. Almeda M. Wright, *The Spiritual Lives of Young African Americans* (New York: Oxford University Press, 2017).

20. For an explicit overview of these global issues and teenagers' relationship to them, see Jean M. Twenge, *iGen: Why Today's Super-Connected Kids Are Growing Up Less Rebellious, More Tolerant, Less Happy—and Completely Unprepared for Adulthood; And What That Means for the Rest of Us* (New York: Atria, 2017).

and in need of public witness. When was the last time the church proclaimed this reality in worship?

Forgotten Narratives

The Distancing of God

In *Ancient-Future Worship*, Robert Webber claims that Christianity has lost the story of God in worship.[21] This was not a new thought for Webber. He had long suggested that Christian worship, especially evangelical worship, had lost its ability to proclaim and enact the narrative of God and God's people. *Ancient-Future Worship* uses five historical paradigms to show how this occurred over the centuries in different churches: ancient, medieval, Reformation, modern, and contemporary. The ancient church understood the remembrance and anticipation of God's story, but the medieval period reduced it to Christ's sacrifice for sin. The Reformation church placed more attention on the individual's condition before God, while the modern church reduced worship to education and experience. Then, the contemporary church reduced worship to evangelism and atheological principles.

Webber traces this loss of God's story to a number of issues but primarily to the church not reading Scripture holistically, as "God's whole story." Webber suggests that Christians are primarily interested in being "New Testament Christians rather than Bible Christians." In particular, Webber notes that we fail to "connect the creation liturgy with God's purposes for the world," and as a result, we fail to "pay attention to how God is working in history to redeem and rescue the whole world and fulfill his creation vision."[22] The result is that our worship practices become fragmented, emphasizing one part of the God story over and above another part. For instance, if worship focuses on God as father, it misses the themes of incarnation, redemption, and eschatology. Conversely, if worship focuses only on Christ's ministry, death, and resurrection, it misses the incarnation and creation story. When worship succumbs to fragmentation, "God's whole story is reduced to individualism. God saves this or that individual, but he does not save and restore the whole world."[23]

While Webber is intentionally critical of the evangelical church, the criticism also applies to other Christian traditions. For instance, Roman Catholic

---

21. Robert E. Webber, *Ancient-Future Worship: Proclaiming and Enacting God's Narrative* (Grand Rapids: Baker Books, 2008).

22. Webber, *Ancient-Future Worship*, 67.

23. Webber, *Ancient-Future Worship*, 42.

sacramental theologian Bernard Cooke makes a similar argument in *The Distancing of God*.[24] A historical documentation of the church's theology of presence, Cooke's work focuses on symbols' role in either making the saving love of God present for people or distancing the divine reality from people's awareness. Cooke understands symbols broadly as signs, words, and gestures. He also understands humanity's existence symbolically. He traces these symbols in Christian thought and ritual beginning with the earliest Christians influenced by the Easter experience on through modernity, science, and religion. Thus, the earliest Christians understood the *real presence* of Christ because they had encountered Christ. This real presence changed to sacramentality, which later became moralism. Then, modern Christianity "moved God out, . . . put God at a distance in people's imagination."[25] Cooke concludes that symbols used in worship *distance* God rather than make God more present.

In different ways, both Webber and Cooke label a crisis in our worship, particularly in content and form. If worship is intended to find its roots in the gospel of Jesus Christ, then "when worship fails to proclaim, sing, and enact at the Table the Good News that God not only saves sinners but also narrates the whole world, it is not only worship that becomes corrupted by the culture, it is also the gospel."[26] Thus the goal for us is to recover the cosmic story of God, God's good news for the whole world, so that we can recover the fullness of worship, which gathers the church to "sing, tell, and enact God's story of the world from its beginning to its end."[27] Both Cooke and Webber call upon public Christian worship to reclaim the narrative of God and the intersection of that narrative with God's people. Before we look at the ways worship might provide a corrective to proclaiming the story of God, we must first examine the story of God's people, which leads to an important question: If worship has lost the story of God, has worship also lost the story of God's people?

The Distancing of God's People

Thomas Long talks about the disconnect between our Sunday-morning experience and our Saturday-night or Monday-afternoon experience. Most of the time, the two are not congruent with each other. One experience represents our faith and religion, while the other represents our meager attempts at trying to be human. "We go to worship, and we sing the hymns, pray the

24. Bernard J. Cooke, *The Distancing of God: The Ambiguity of Symbol in History and Theology* (Minneapolis: Augsburg Fortress, 1990).
25. Cooke, *Distancing of God*, 238.
26. Webber, *Ancient-Future Worship*, 40.
27. Webber, *Ancient-Future Worship*, 40.

prayers, listen to the sermons, and then we go back out into the real world, where we have to deal with the mundane realities of life and make compromises and hard choices."[28]

Put another way, our experience is a series of liturgies that form us to be people of the world. We are formed by our participation in liturgies at the football field, shopping mall, gym, workplace, grocery store, restaurant, and so forth. While we are called to be God's people, worship on the Lord's Day usually lasts ninety minutes on average, and "this is not much time to enact counter-measures to the secular liturgies in which we are immersed the rest of the week!"[29] James K. A. Smith goes on to ask, "Wouldn't this explain why Christian worship just doesn't seem to 'work'? . . . Isn't it the case that, though many Christians in North America gather for worship week in and week out, we don't seem to look very peculiar? That is, we don't seem to be a people that looks very different from our neighbors, *except* that we go to church on Sunday mornings while they're home reading the paper."[30]

There is a disconnect between how we live, act, and breathe in the world and how we live, act, and breathe at church. Our liturgies of the world do not call us to be Christ followers, yet at the same time, our liturgies of worship do not always acknowledge the reality of living in the world we inhabit. The two are fragmented.

While it is easy to see how the liturgies of the world do not call us to be Christ followers, it is more difficult to see how our liturgies fail to account for the way we live in the world. In *Mighty Stories, Dangerous Rituals*, Herbert Anderson and Edward Foley help illuminate this gap by suggesting that our worship practices have lost *our* stories, the stories of God's people.[31] Ultimately, this is an issue of pastoral care and concern that has long gone unaddressed by Christians and Christian leaders around the globe. They claim this has happened in at least six ways:

1. failing to construct ritual models for significant moments of crisis or transition,
2. conducting standard public rituals in churches as "ceremonies without stories,"

28. Thomas G. Long, *Testimony: Talking Ourselves into Being Christian* (San Francisco: Jossey-Bass, 2004), 39.
29. James K. A. Smith, *Desiring the Kingdom: Worship, Worldview, and Cultural Formation* (Grand Rapids: Baker Academic, 2009), 207.
30. Smith, *Desiring the Kingdom*, 208.
31. Herbert Anderson and Edward Foley, *Mighty Stories, Dangerous Rituals: Weaving Together the Human and the Divine* (San Francisco: Jossey-Bass, 1998), 17–18.

3. not rethinking standard rituals that have radically new contexts,

4. failing to unite our social structures and support healthy patterns of living,

5. presuming faith communities know the biblical narrative, and

6. fragmenting our ministries and creating congregations that are "living communal webs made up of interdependent parts."[32]

Anderson and Foley claim that we, as the church, have spent time concealing, ignoring, or lying about the stories of God's people to the detriment of individual and communal faith. We conceal truths about ourselves and our faith community. "Our storytelling is used only as a tool to develop an identity and offer a respectable self-interpretation of ourselves for ourselves."[33] We ignore stories and are thus silent on circumstances that may need pastoral attention. This is a method of secret keeping, and it is fraught with ethical dilemmas. Anderson and Foley write, "When communities such as families or parishes keep secrets, the consequences are extensive both for the individuals and the communities. . . . As a result the community is stuck in fixed patterns of interaction, roles are rigidly defined, and stories are closely monitored in order to keep the secret safe. Such secret keeping is deceptively mythic: prematurely announcing that reconciliation is possible without allowing participants in the story to name that which needs to be reconciled."[34] We fib by telling stories that are too big. We call attention to "larger than life" stories and situations in worship and people feel disconnected. All the while, worshipers "hunger for illustrative materials that more accurately reflect life as they actually know and experience it."[35] Anderson and Foley claim that any of these fallacies create deceit in our worship gatherings: "Worship is in danger of succumbing to deceit whenever it promotes the divine narrative to the detriment or denigration of the individual and collective stories of the gathered community. The implication of this one-sided storytelling is that human narration is unimportant, except as it reiterates or interprets the divine narrative. It is equally problematic, however, if human stories are promoted and emphasized at the expense of telling the stories of God."[36]

The church misses opportunities to connect the story of God to the story of teenagers in many ways. The church misses an opportunity when it ignores

32. Anderson and Foley, *Mighty Stories, Dangerous Rituals*, ix–xi.

33. Anderson and Foley, *Mighty Stories, Dangerous Rituals*, 9.

34. Anderson and Foley, *Mighty Stories, Dangerous Rituals*, 16–17.

35. Leonora Tubbs Tisdale, *Preaching as Local Theology and Folk Art* (Minneapolis: Fortress, 1997), 130.

36. Anderson and Foley, *Mighty Stories, Dangerous Rituals*, 43.

teenagers' stories and the realities of the local and global world they inhabit. Here, worship fails to equip them to speak to God about the world, and it misses the opportunity to help teenagers speak to God on behalf of the world. The church misses an opportunity when it promotes passive rather than active participation in worship. This happens in both evangelical and mainline Protestant congregations. On the one hand, teenagers are fully engaged at youth rallies, camps, and conferences; on the other hand, they slump in boredom through rituals that are dull, hollow, and meaningless. The church also misses an opportunity to connect teenagers' stories to God's story when it asks them to stay on the sidelines while visiting the local soup kitchen or worshiping with Indigenous peoples in Kenya.

The message teenagers receive, however implicit or explicit, is that God is not concerned about the world they inhabit—and presumably that God is not concerned about them. It is no wonder teenagers are drowsy worshipers by the time they graduate from college and are ready to move on to something else. Why would they wake from their slumber on a Sunday morning if the church is just going to give them an invitation to go back to bed?

Trying Another Way

Woke Worship

Anyone who has worked in youth ministry knows the challenge it is to get teenagers to go to sleep. They ask to stay up for thirty more minutes at their friend's slumber party. They talk with their friends into the wee hours of the morning at church camp. Victoriously, they stay awake through the whole night at church lock-ins. It is hard to put teenagers to sleep when they have energy and are wide awake to the causes about which they care, and they care about the world they inhabit. It keeps them awake at night.

The good news is that teenagers are open to and interested in worship gatherings that are "woke," to use an expression from my friends Sandra Maria Van Opstal and David Bailey. Both Sandra and David imply that "woke worship" is worship that fully acknowledges injustices in the world, laments the hurt they have caused, and calls the church to pursue justice.[37] I believe

37. I have borrowed this term, *woke worship*, from Sandra Maria Van Opstal and David Bailey, who used it on two separate occasions. Van Opstal has long spoken about worship that addresses the realities of the world, especially different ethnic groups. As an example, see Sandra Maria Van Opstal, "Your Woke-ness Is Not Worship," interview by Sarah Bessey and Jeff Chu, *Evolving Faith* podcast, August 12, 2020, https://evolving-faith.libsyn.com/your-woke-ness-is-not-worship-with-sandra-maria-van-opstal. Her theories and book *The Next*

teenagers desire woke worship because they live with the realities of these injustices every day in the hallways at school, and they want the church to help them make sense of it all by connecting their story to God's story. I have seen them energized by worship that speaks directly to injustices locally and globally. Moreover, FYI has found that interest in "the centrality of Jesus" and the message he proclaimed "offers congregational leaders both clarity and hope." They write, "Jesus is compelling, and the vast majority of young people in churches growing young want to talk about him."[38] Calling all congregations to rectify the gap between divine and human stories, Anderson and Foley write, "The future of faith communities depends on their capacity to foster an environment in which human and divine narratives regularly intersect. More specifically, the future of Christian communities requires that they enable the weaving together of the divine and human in the image of Jesus Christ."[39]

What would it look like to let our teenagers lead us in the cause to connect teenagers' stories with God's story? Jesus knew that God wanted to bring "the state of flourishing in all dimensions of one's existence: in one's relation to God, in one's relation to one's fellow human beings, in one's relation to nature, and in one's relation to oneself." So our worship must then be connected to setting things right in the world, articulating that "God's love for each and every one of God's human creatures takes the form of God desiring the *shalom* of each and every one."[40]

Learning from Jesus

One of the earliest ministry scenes of Jesus offers a picture of him practicing woke worship, articulating a vision for human flourishing (Luke 4:14–30). We don't know all the details, but I imagine that worship in the synagogue was going on as usual. The typical liturgical elements were probably in place. But on this day, there was a guest preacher, Jesus. He had returned to his hometown of Nazareth, where he had once been a teenager, to participate

---

Worship: Glorifying God in a Diverse World (Downers Grove, IL: InterVarsity, 2016) will be examined more in chapter 6. My friend and colleague David Bailey of Arrabon Ministries in Richmond, Virginia, used the term *woke worship* in a panel conversation I facilitated in 2018. His definition suggests woke worship is worship that honestly acknowledges the injustices of the world, specifically those toward Black people in the United States of America.

38. Kara Powell, Jake Mulder, and Brad Griffin, *Growing Young: Six Essential Strategies to Help Young People Discover and Love Your Church* (Grand Rapids: Baker Books, 2016), 138.

39. Anderson and Foley, *Mighty Stories*, 42.

40. Nicholas Wolterstorff, "The Contours of Justice: An Ancient Call for Shalom," in *God and the Victim: Theological Reflections on Evil, Victimization, Justice, and Forgiveness*, ed. Lisa Barnes Lampman and Michelle D. Shattuck (Grand Rapids: Eerdmans, 1999), 113 (emphasis original).

in the familiar liturgy. He had been empowered by the Spirit at his baptism, fasted forty days in the wilderness, and begun his ministry in the Galilee region, where people were talking about his work favorably. When the time came, Jesus got up, opened the scroll to the Isaiah passage, read it, gave the scroll back to the attendant, and sat down to teach.

Here the story begins to get a little more dramatic. Luke inserts one of those long, pregnant pauses to tell us that all eyes were fixed on Jesus, the preacher, the once young man now grown and back visiting his family. I don't know what thoughts were going through their heads in that moment, but I can imagine some were proud that Mary and Joseph's boy had come back to town. This village helped raise this promising young man, and they probably wanted to claim some of his fame for themselves since some people in the region were saying that there were no prophets from Galilee. What did they expect Jesus to say, or what did they want Jesus to say? If they believed he was a prophet, they may have wanted him to assure them that the Scriptures were "promises of God's exclusive covenant with them."[41] They may have wanted Jesus to set them free from their oppressors. And they must have had certain liturgical expectations for Jesus in that moment, and they must have known, like we know, that the words we say or don't say, the symbols we use or don't use, the gestures we make or don't make actually say something about who we are and who we aren't, about who God is and who God is not.

If they had certain expectations like we have certain expectations when the church gathers for worship, it is easy to see how their eyes might have opened a bit wider when Jesus got to the point in his sermon that suggested God's understanding of the Isaiah passage was different from theirs. I can see how they might have begun to shift in their seats, cross their arms, talk to one another, and question Jesus's identity when he proclaimed that liberation was coming to the whole world—all those who were poor and oppressed—not just to the Jews. It's no wonder they shut Jesus up, dragged him out of town, and tried to throw him off a cliff when he used the public platform of worship to advocate for the radical nature of the gospel, which is the heartbeat of life in the kingdom of God. They had not heard this message before. Jesus changed worship for them, and honestly, they didn't want anybody tampering with the worship practices they had come to know and love, just like we don't want anyone tampering with the worship practices we have come to know and love.

Meltdown may have happened in the Nazareth synagogue that day. But it didn't happen for reasons we are familiar with; it wasn't because Jesus favored

---

41. R. Alan Culpepper, "Luke," in *The New Interpreter's Bible Commentary*, ed. Leander E. Keck, vol. 9, *Luke–John* (Nashville: Abingdon, 1996), 108.

contemporary music instead of traditional music or used projection while teaching, because the pews were uncomfortable, because the sermon was too long, or because of any other grievances we name as if our personal preferences really are the most important criteria for appraising worship. Meltdown happened because Jesus issued the wake-up call that he issued throughout his public ministry: that the Spirit of the Lord had anointed him to bring good news to the poor, to proclaim release to the captives and recovery of sight to the blind, and to let the oppressed go free (Luke 4:18).

Jesus articulated the Isaiah passage in the context of the Jewish liturgy because Jesus knew that worship was about waking people up. Jesus knew that worship was about questioning dominant paradigms and asking whether worshipers were "bowing before reality or falsehood, before God or idols."[42] Jesus woke worshipers up to the harsh reality that God's purpose in and for the world was much more cosmic than their individual and "jealous motives."[43] He exposed the biases and prejudices they held individually and communally. He proved that "their commitment to their own [communal] boundaries took precedence over their joy that God had sent a prophet among them."[44] Jesus announced the *missio Dei*, and he announced it in worship.

This suggests that worship is to create lives "fully attentive to reality as God sees it."[45] And the reality Jesus paints in Luke 4 is an all-encompassing mission that is "never subject to the limitations and boundaries of any nation, church, group, or race."[46] Proclaiming and enacting the mission of God is the dangerous act of worship. This was and continues to be the work of Jesus, who even today "sends his people as he was sent: to be light to the world, to give healing and hope to the ill and the weak and the uneducated; to suffer, perhaps unjustly, on behalf of others."[47]

Linking God's Story to Teenagers' Stories

Remembering God's Work in the Past for the Present and Future

Linking God's story to teenagers' stories begins with a pattern of worship that situates worship in the story that it calls to mind. For Webber, this

42. Labberton, *Dangerous Act of Worship*, 20.
43. Culpepper, "Luke," 106.
44. Culpepper, "Luke," 108.
45. Labberton, *Dangerous Act of Worship*, 19.
46. Culpepper, "Luke," 108.
47. Andrew Walls, "The Old Age of the Missionary Movement," *International Review of Mission* 77 (1987): 26.

is a biblical pattern of worship that "remembers God's work in the past, anticipates God's rule over all creation, and actualizes both past and future in the present to transform persons, communities, and the world."[48] Worship remembers God's work in the past through "historical recitation" and "dramatic reenactment."[49] Historical recitation involves naming and remembering the acts of God throughout Scripture and history through preaching, creeds, and song. Dramatic reenactment "draws the worshiper into the action, not as an observer, but as a participant."[50] This occurs through the Lord's Table, the Christian Passover (Easter), and the Christian way of marking time.

Remembering the past, however, is not enough; worship should also connect the past with the future by anticipating the future that God has for the world. Ultimately, this is "God's rescue of the entire created order and the establishment of his rule over all heaven and earth. The eschatological nature of worship has to do with that place and time when God's rule is being done on earth as it is in heaven."[51] Worship that anticipates the future "holds up God's vision of a new heaven and earth and an eternal community of God's people living in fellowship with God, doing God's will on earth, walking in God's ways, and fulfilling the vision of creation."[52]

Connecting Sunday with Monday

Worship that connects past, present, and future brings together worship and "holy living." It "shapes the ethical behavior of God's people to reflect kingdom ethics here on earth. Consequently, the ethical life of the church is an eschatological witness to the world of how people should be living and how the world will be under the reign of God."[53] This combination of worship, spirituality, and ethics reminds worshipers they are "a chosen race, a royal priesthood, a holy nation, God's own people, in order that [they] may proclaim the mighty acts of him who called [them] out of darkness into his marvelous light" (1 Pet. 2:9).

While a central role of worship is to call teenagers *from* the noisiness of the liturgies of the world to focus and name priorities, it is equally true that a second role of worship is to form disciples of all ages who are better equipped to follow Christ faithfully *in* the world. If worship regularly invites teenagers to escape from the world and recharge their spiritual batteries, it

48. Webber, *Ancient-Future Worship*, 43.
49. Webber, *Ancient-Future Worship*, 48.
50. Webber, *Ancient-Future Worship*, 51.
51. Webber, *Ancient-Future Worship*, 57–58.
52. Webber, *Ancient-Future Worship*, 61.
53. Webber, *Ancient-Future Worship*, 66.

promotes a partial view of God's story and a partial view of their stories. For teenagers, this imbalance is ultimately an issue of honesty. In the words of a young evangelical, this kind of worship is inauthentic:

> Worship is where we as individuals leave our other loves and come together to share our common first love. We leave things that we are doing, to honor [God] in his house with his children. It doesn't have to be complicated or cluttered. We have an hour to an hour and a half of focusing and praising God together, and yet I get a sense we are squeezing God out and sticking more of us in. We are having trouble emptying ourselves of our gifts and of what we do to come before the Lord and worship Him together.[54]

Cultivating a Consequential, Storied Faith

So, through worship, how might we best cultivate a generative, consequential faith that is rooted in the story of God, nurtured by Christian community, and important enough to extend beyond adolescence? In her research on teenagers, Kenda Creasy Dean asks how the church can better connect teenagers to the God story in which they participate for a faith that is generative and consequential.[55] Dean says that the church should learn from the group identified as "religiously devoted teens" in the NSYR. These teenagers account for 8 percent of all teenagers. They have resisted Moralistic Therapeutic Deism, and their identities are grounded in four theological accents:

- *Creed*. They confess their tradition's God story.
- *Community*. They belong to a community that regularly enacts the God story.
- *Purpose*. They feel called by this story to pursue a larger purpose in life.
- *Hope*. They have hope for the future promised by the God story that is told to them.[56]

Beyond their grounding in creed, community, purpose, and hope, religiously devoted teens are connected to congregations who regularly engage them in an intergenerational community that intentionally exercises three faith practices "so infused with desire for God and love for others that it becomes

---

54. Testimony from Ashley Olsen. See Robert E. Webber, *The Younger Evangelicals: Facing the Challenges of the New World* (Grand Rapids: Baker Books, 2003), 194.

55. Kenda Creasy Dean, *Almost Christian: What the Faith of Our Teenagers Is Telling the American Church* (New York: Oxford University Press, 2010), 22.

56. Dean, *Almost Christian*, 49.

generative."[57] In other words, the community's faith practices help faith stick with America's teens. Dean defines the three faith practices in this way:

- Translation: "handing on" the lived faith from one generation to the next
- Testimony: helping teens articulate/confess their Christian identity to others
- Detachment: decentering and cultivating empathy as they focus on Christ rather than themselves[58]

Dean says that these four theological accents and their three accompanying faith practices become tools churches can use for building a consequential faith in Christ "that matters enough to issue in a distinctive identity and way of life."[59] For our purposes, we might ask how these theological accents and faith practices measure up when examined through the lens of our worship practices with teenagers. How might our worship practices help our teenagers make meaning of God and the world they inhabit? How might the evangelical approach distort our teenagers' understanding of God and the world they inhabit? Using Dean's theological accents and faith practices as a guide, we will hold a mirror up to our worship practices by asking four questions. I will offer two responses to each question; the first will note a strength, and the second will expose an area for growth.

Creed: Confessing the God Story

How well do our worship practices promote teenagers' understanding of the God story and their faith tradition through translation and testimony? Perhaps the most positive feature of worship with teenagers is making central tenets of the Christian faith clear and accessible. While the tenets of clarity and accessibility match particular models of liturgical inculturation that are to be valued, this comes with a warning: clarity and accessibility must not be mistaken for simplicity and dumbing down the faith. Rather, a message presented with clarity and simplicity is a message presented within the boundaries of teenagers' faith development. In favor of appealing to teenagers, many faith communities have watered down or rejected wholesale the Christian tradition, and this is perhaps the greatest challenge to helping teenagers understand the God story and their faith tradition. As one example, there is sometimes little room for traditional hymnody in many of our worship practices, yet this

57. Dean, *Almost Christian*, 22.
58. Dean, *Almost Christian*, 22.
59. Dean, *Almost Christian*, 21.

body of congregational songs is one of our greatest repositories of the faith tradition. Perhaps choosing music for theological variety rather than musical style is a place to begin. Worship that links God's story to teenagers' stories needs to maintain a sense of the faith tradition while maintaining its cultural relevance, and the reality is that our teenagers need both.[60]

Belonging to a Community That Enacts the God Story

How well do our worship practices give teenagers the sense that they belong to a community that regularly enacts the God story through translation and testimony? Worship promotes the visible, gathered community, and this has the potential to create a place of involvement and connection for teenagers. This is important because, as any youth minister will say, teenagers are asking three questions: Who am I? Do I matter? Do I belong? Evangelical worship leader Darlene Zschech of Hillsong says, "My heart and the culture of our church are committed to people's knowing that they are valued for more than what they can do, for who they are. In the church in Acts a strong community had one heart, one mind, great power—a great awakening of the Spirit—a united team, a sense of belonging, and a commitment to each other's success."[61]

The challenge posed by many worship gatherings among teenagers today is that teenagers are isolated from the rest of the church. Teenagers worship as a group of teenagers rather than with the church of all ages. For a faith tradition so grounded in Scripture, generationally segregated worship has no roots in Scripture; in fact, as later chapters will demonstrate, intergenerational worship is the standard model of worship that Scripture gives us. Moreover, from research we know that teenagers learn from watching others, particularly their parents. This becomes a problem if teenagers never have the opportunity to see other ages worship.[62]

Pursuing a Larger Purpose in Life

Do our worship practices give our teenagers a sense of their larger purpose in life: to imitate the life and work of Christ in the world they inhabit?

---

60. For the role of testimony in helping teenagers articulate the gospel through the lens of their lives, see Amanda Hontz Drury, *Saying Is Believing: The Necessity of Testimony in Adolescent Spiritual Development* (Downers Grove, IL: InterVarsity Academic, 2015).

61. Darlene Zschech, "The Role of the Holy Spirit in Worship," in *The Spirit in Worship—Worship in the Spirit*, ed. Teresa Berger and Bryan D. Spinks (Collegeville, MN: Liturgical), 288–89.

62. Kara E. Powell and Chap Clark, *Sticky Faith: Everyday Ideas to Build Lasting Faith in Your Kids* (Grand Rapids: Zondervan, 2008), 23–24.

Historically, worship gatherings with teenagers have placed a strong emphasis on cultivating a personal relationship with Christ and being morally responsible, but there are two problems with this: (1) the personal relationship is often seen as a one-time decision rather than a process, and (2) Christian living is often described as moral responsibility. In other words, the church often gives teenagers a list of dos and don'ts, teaching them "a gospel of sin management" rather than what it means to trust and follow Christ. Kara Powell and Chap Clark have suggested that this is the reason teenagers often stare blankly when asked to describe their faith.[63] And one has to ask whether following Christ means spending hundreds of thousands of dollars on light shows and technology to make faith relevant to teenagers. It is not insignificant that the God of the universe, who could have sent Jesus into the world whenever God wanted, chose an epoch before there was even electricity.

Perhaps the best way our worship practices can cultivate purpose among our teenagers is by reducing the rift between accepting and rejecting culture. One youth group I know did this by reducing their worship technology budget by half and giving the remainder to those in need: local orphanages, prisons, hospitals, and nursing homes. Besides, as Sally Morgenthaler writes,

> Great musical performances, thought-provoking drama, touching testimonies, relevant messages, and apologetics about God and faith are wonderful tools God can use. . . . However, . . . their operation does not hinge on any sort of movement or response from those in attendance. They are all examples of presentation, and presentation does not require people to give anything of themselves back to God. . . .
> Most often, presentation inspires people to think about God and themselves. . . . But we need to be careful. . . . Inspiration and worship are not synonymous.[64]

Finding Hope in the God Story Promised to Them

Do our worship practices give teenagers hope for the future, as promised by the God story that is told to them? The greatest way our worship practices can offer hope is through their ability to clarify our Christian identity. Although teenagers live in a changing and seemingly distorted world, worship consistently reminds them that they are rooted in the Christian community and in Christ. Negatively, however, worship practices can overshadow trusting the hope promised in Christ by emphasizing self-preservation. I learned from one teenager that her congregation's worship practices never incorporate

63. Powell and Clark, *Sticky Faith*, 33–34.
64. Sally Morgenthaler, *Worship Evangelism: Inviting Unbelievers into the Presence of God* (Grand Rapids: Zondervan, 1999), 48.

celebrations of baptism and the Lord's Supper. Instead, they emphasize self-preservation through forty-five-minute sermons each week. Contrast that with another congregation that regularly engages their teenagers in celebrating rites of passage with the entire congregation. They regularly acknowledge freshmen entering high school by putting them in a Bible study group and praying that God will use that group to give them strength throughout high school. They offer a spiritual gifts class for their sophomores to discover their natural giftings and celebrate them in a worship gathering. Juniors go on two spiritual retreats to begin thinking about their life after high school, and seniors are commissioned before the whole church.[65]

Conclusion

Teenagers are awake to the realities of the world. This is both bad news and good news for the church. The bad news is that the story of teenagers is a story of young men and women who are hurting, anxious, and afraid. Putting a fine point on what worship is and who worship is for is very important. The good news is that through gathering, singing, praying, proclaiming, responding, giving, and going forth into the world, we have the opportunity to instill in teenagers a language of faith that grows over time, tells the God story, instills the narrative of the Christ event, and cultivates within them a love for the gathered church of all ages. More importantly, this language gives them the tools they need to talk about their Sunday faith in the hallway on Monday.

At the same time, the language of worship reminds teenagers that while worship is connected to the rhythms and routines of our lives, it is anything but routine. One of the best examples of an encounter with God happens in Isaiah 6:1–8. Here the story of Isaiah is connected to the story of God. Isaiah is called into the presence of God, and his life is centered. The same is true with teenagers. When they are called into the presence of God through worship, their lives should be centered, their attention should be refocused, they should be reminded who God is, and they should be reminded that God has a purpose for them in the world. Then they should be sent out into the complex world to become the hands and feet of God. Labberton writes, "Waking up is the dangerous act of worship. It's dangerous because worship is meant to

65. Steven Johnson, "Milestones of Faith: Creating Rhythms through Rites of Passage," Fuller Youth Institute, accessed February 19, 2013, http://www.studyinglifelongfaith.com/uploads/5/2/4/6/5246709/milestones_of_faith_creating_rhythms_through_rites_of_passage__sticky_faith.pdf.

produce lives fully attentive to reality as God sees it, and that's more than most of us want to deal with."[66]

When we take the stories of teenagers and carefully weave them into God's story, we remind ourselves that the lives we lead are anything but normal and ordinary—because of the work of the Triune God in our midst. We remind ourselves that worship is a disturbing event, for God is present among us, challenging us to recognize sin, embrace our enemies, transform our lives, and proclaim that the full story of God is still working its way into our midst.

66. Labberton, *Dangerous Act of Worship*, 19–20.

5

✦ ✦ ✦

From Intergenerational to Adoptive Worship

Embracing Teenagers in the Church of All Ages

Even those who can't, don't, or won't fit in end up creating communities of misfits.

—Meredith Gould, *Transcending Generations*

A Multi-table Mentality

A Weekly Segregation

A large congregation in my community represents a multi-table mentality. The church campus has multiple buildings, all identified by the age group to whom the building belongs. They have a children's building, a youth building, an adult building, and a senior-adult building. On Sunday mornings, parents drive by one building to drop their young children off for children's church, then they drive across campus to drop their teenagers off in the youth building. Then they park in front of the main sanctuary where their own activities are held. In their respective buildings, each age group participates in and enjoys age-specific programming. Children participate in games and activities designed especially for them, teenagers hang out with their friends and sing the most recently recorded worship music, parents worship without the interruption of their children, and senior adults enjoy music, prayer, and preaching that is familiar and comfortable to them.

On the one hand, this model of ministry makes sense. It is easy and a win-win situation for everyone involved. Children can exert their energy without a stare from a senior adult, teenagers can worship with their peers, adults can sing freely without distractions from children, and senior adults can hear a sermon without the noise that comes from children ruffling papers or speaking above a whisper. Church staff can prepare content and programming that can be easily packaged, prepared, disseminated, and understood. Community is readily developed among people of the same age. Families are reunited following the experience to share about their morning activities over lunch before moving on with the rest of their day. However, while a family might go to church together, they do not attend church together. They do not actually see one another read Scripture, pray, sing, or respond to the spoken Word. Because families are so busy, they may not even connect in the car or over lunch to share their church experiences with one another.

Given the positive factors for age-specific worship programs and ministries, it may be difficult to see any adverse effects of these ministries. However, if history has taught us anything, it is that a once-innovative approach to doing ministry will eventually proliferate its own set of problems. Chapter 2 taught us that the creation of youth ministries in the twentieth century met a specific need, but when teenagers who had completed youth ministries became bored with church as their parents once knew it, the church was ill-equipped for the mass exodus of young adults from their parents' churches to the megachurches, which would eventually occur during the latter half of the twentieth century. These are the large congregations that have developed models of generationally driven worship practices that are clean, well executed, and well intentioned. But are they effective?

Collective critical reflection from the last twenty years has presented a particular dissonance among ministries that are siloed by specific age groups. Regarding teenagers, this has meant that "while many of us in the church have been busy doing all things necessary to keep the numbers up and keep the people happy, we have also successfully raised a generation or more of younger people who now expect worship to be catered especially to them and their needs."[1] This has also had an adverse effect on other ages in the church; for example, adults are now "scratching their heads wondering where

---

1. Randall Bradley, "Desegregating Worship," *Creator*, September 9, 2013, https://creator magazine.com/desegregating-worship.

the younger adults are and why they're not returning to the church after high school and college. Somehow, the cold hard reality that younger people are doing exactly as they've been raised to do has not yet occurred to the congregation or the clergy."[2]

An Annual Segregation

A different kind of ministry silo exists in the annual practice of Youth Sunday. I recently visited a congregation down the road from my house that was celebrating this annual ritual. It, too, is familiar to many congregations across the United States. Youth Sunday is the one Sunday of the year when teenagers lead the entire worship service for all ages in the church. As is the custom in many congregations, the whole worship gathering in this congregation was planned and led by teenagers who sang, prayed, read Scripture, preached, collected the offering, and prepared all other elements of worship. In this particular congregation, the teenagers did really well. At the end of worship, the pastor stood up and said, "Well done, teenagers! You are the future of the church." As the church applauded, I couldn't help but wonder why teenagers were the future rather than a present part of the church. I couldn't help but wonder if on that day, worship had been reduced to a performance by teenagers rather than worship with teenagers. This story is another example of generational segregation in the United States, though in this instance the segregation occurs annually rather than weekly.

A Larger Phenomenon

Stereotyping Generational Cohorts

Both practices pertain to a larger phenomenon that exists in the American church: generational segregation that promotes unhealthy attitudes toward generational cohorts in the church. Too often the church fails to acknowledge the strengths that can come from the contributions of each generation. We treat children and teenagers as though they will contribute to the life of the church when they reach a certain age. We communicate to single twenty-somethings that their contribution will be greater when they are married. We communicate to those in their thirties that their contribution will be greater when they have children. As individuals reach their forties and fifties, we joke that they are not able to run, work, and play with the energy they once

2. Bradley, "Desegregating Worship."

possessed. Then, as church members reach retirement, we treat them and all senior adults as though their finest contributions are in the past.

In some congregations, generational cohorts assume that everything done in youth worship gatherings is shallow, sentimental, and therefore to be looked down upon. Alternatively, other congregations maintain a youth-centric approach to worship that throws time, money, and preference toward entertainment-driven models of worship and mountaintop experiences so that children and teenagers stay in church. Yet when these young adults turn twenty, they leave church because church is no longer focused on them. In a reverse discrimination, when a church's worship leader turns sixty, he is too old to be a worship leader and must retire or find another occupation. These and other generational assumptions are magnified when viewed through the lens of a single generation such as adolescence, and when viewed as a whole, intergenerational considerations require us to address a massive cultural issue.[3]

The Convenience of Multigenerational Worship

It is no surprise that congregations across the United States have espoused models of age-specific worship ministry; it is very convenient. Furthermore, many would likely not describe their models as segregated, because of the negative connotations that accompany that term. In fact, most of these congregations are very well intentioned and lean into a pastoral approach of meeting church members where they are in all stages of life. From the work of James Fowler, we know there are unique stages of faith development that run from the infant to the senior adult.[4] Approaches to Christian spiritual formation throughout the twentieth century have been largely age specific, and they have been very fruitful.

Despite this, a number of practical theologians and church leaders have recently called the church to examine this age-specific approach to determine how new models of ministry could combine age groups for fruitful interaction.[5] The reality is that to truly engage models of intergenerational ministry

3. A number of authors illustrate the necessity and the complexity of naming the unique qualities each generation has to offer the church. See Kathleen A. Cahalan and Bonnie J. Miller-McLemore, *Calling All Years Good: Christian Vocation throughout Life's Seasons* (Grand Rapids: Eerdmans, 2017). See also Kathleen A. Cahalan, *The Stories We Live: Finding God's Calling All around Us* (Grand Rapids: Eerdmans, 2017).

4. James W. Fowler, *Stages of Faith: The Psychology of Human Development and the Quest for Meaning* (San Francisco: Harper & Row, 1981).

5. See, for example, Andrew Root, *Faith Formation in a Secular Age: Responding to the Church's Obsession with Youthfulness* (Grand Rapids: Baker Academic, 2017).

and intergenerational worship is to intentionally change and recalibrate, and that can become messy. This is why there is a body of literature addressing the challenges of multiple generations existing simultaneously in any congregation. The titles found in that literature are enough to be daunting—for example, *Anxious Church, Anxious People*;[6] *Bridging Divided Worlds*;[7] and *One Church, Four Generations*.[8]

Actually, many congregations think they are intergenerational when they are really multigenerational, and there is a difference between the two.[9] *Multi*generational congregations include the church of all ages but have not pursued the arduous task of moving from independent, siloed forms of ministry by age to collaborative, integrated forms of ministry organized by other frameworks. To truly move toward intergenerational ministry, congregations will need to change their behavior, values, and attitudes through processes of experimentation and learning. These will "challenge us to embark on a journey to a land we do not currently know."[10] Using the distinction between *multi*generational and *inter*generational, we might say that multigenerational worship is more common than intergenerational worship because the latter is more difficult than the former. Indeed, true intergenerational worship is messy.

Blessing All Ages

The church has yet to solve this problem, but engaging the topic of intergenerational worship provides the hope of a different way for the church of all ages through blessing all generations in the community. Moreover, it offers hope for providing agency to teenagers by loving them and affirming them while also teaching them a rhetoric of wisdom, discipline, and responsibility that is rooted in the Christian tradition. The long-term impact of engaging in meaningful intergenerational worship practices is the promotion of full, active, conscious participation in worship life from all ages in the church. More importantly, intergenerational ministries have the potential to cultivate

6. Jack Shitama, *Anxious Church, Anxious People: How to Lead Change in an Age of Anxiety* (Earleville, MD: Charis Works, 2018).

7. Jackson W. Carroll and Wade Clark Roof, *Bridging Divided Worlds: Generational Cultures in Congregations* (San Francisco: Jossey-Bass, 2002).

8. Gary L. McIntosh, *One Church, Four Generations: Understanding and Reaching All Ages in Your Church* (Grand Rapids: Baker Books, 2002).

9. For definitions and distinctions between *inter*generational and *multi*generational, see Cory Seibel, "From *Multi*generational to *Inter*generational," in *Intergenerate: Transforming Churches through Intergenerational Ministry*, ed. Holly Catterton Allen (Abilene, TX: Abilene Christian University Press, 2018), 18.

10. Seibel, "From *Multi*generational to *Inter*generational," 89.

the capacity to respect and understand worship in all its fullness from the perspective of all ages.

In congregations where teenagers are engaged in the worship life as participants and as leaders, the conversation of youth ministry and worship ministry moves from a fear-based approach—which argues, "We must invent new worship styles to keep teenagers in the church"—to an approach that says, "By engaging the broad tradition of Christian worship through gatherings that provide teenagers with opportunities to connect to all ages in the church, we can foster the full, active, conscious participation of teenagers in the worship life of the church now and in the future." If congregations are willing to cultivate an understanding, a vision, and empathy toward the promises and challenges of all generational cohorts—especially adolescents—the church will find itself raising a generation of worshipers who later contribute to the renewal of the church at large.

Intergenerational Worship

A New Issue for a New Day

Intergenerational worship has become a "new issue for a new day."[11] Howard Vanderwell identifies three factors that explain why intergenerational worship has particular challenges in this epoch. The first is the increasing longevity of life, which creates a significant age difference between the youngest and the oldest members of the congregation. The second is the diversity that exists among all generations, including everything from familial expectations to working environments to familiarity with technology to increasingly pronounced expectations on the church and its worship. The third and final factor that Vanderwell names is the diversity of ministry practices that exists within all congregations across North America. Niche programming became the basis for teaching worshipers to shop for congregations to meet their needs, and this caused worshipers to think first of their individual needs and second of the needs of the church of all ages. Vanderwell writes that despite these challenges "each generation has the same significance before the face of God and in the worshiping congregation. Each and all are made in the image of God. Each and all have worth."[12]

11. Howard Vanderwell, "A New Issue for a New Day," in *The Church of All Ages: Generations Worshiping Together*, ed. Howard Vanderwell (Herndon, VA: Alban Institute, 2008), 1; see also chap. 1 above.
12. Vanderwell, "New Issue," 4–10.

A Case for Intergenerational Worship

In 2008, Vanderwell predicted that "the importance of [intergenerational worship] will only increase in the years ahead as congregations grapple with the development of effective ministries."[13] Vanderwell was right: the importance of understanding, preparing, and practicing intergenerational worship has become more important than ever before, especially where teenagers are concerned. Three years after Vanderwell penned those words, research from FYI demonstrated that while there is no "silver bullet" to building a generative faith with teenagers that is strong enough to last beyond high school and into college, "the closest our research has come to that definitive silver bullet is . . . that for high school and college students, there is a relationship between attendance at churchwide worship services and Sticky Faith."[14] All ages need intergenerational worship. Vanderwell is right: "While there is no greater privilege than the Christian practice of worshiping God, we believe there is no better way to [worship God] than as an intergenerational community in which all are important, all celebrate, all communicate, and all encourage and nurture the faith of others. As pilgrims on a journey, we travel together."[15]

Worshiping with the church of all ages instills particular faith practices in teenagers, and it is also biblical. Scripture presents a compelling vision for this kind of intergenerational community. The Old Testament is rich with imagery about faith lived in the context of intergenerational community. Passages like Genesis 17, Deuteronomy 6, Isaiah 11, and 1 Timothy 4 remind us of the importance of all ages in a covenant community. God promises in Genesis 17:7 to establish a covenant with Abraham and his offspring. Deuteronomy 6:6–9 is a stark admonishment for adults to pass down faith to younger generations, and other Old Testament passages, such as Nehemiah 8, present pictures of all generations worshiping together. Pictures of household baptisms in Acts 16:15, 31–34 and 1 Corinthians 1:16 remind us of liturgies that occurred in the context of intergenerational family.

In her book *Transcending Generations*, Meredith Gould has written that no one can deal with the complexities of life alone. Gould writes that intergenerational relationships are necessary for the longevity and well-being of the church and its congregants, and those relationships are not as difficult to achieve if people shake off stereotypes and see "at a core level, that what

13. Vanderwell, "New Issue," 11.
14. Kara E. Powell and Chap Clark, *Sticky Faith: Everyday Ideas to Build Lasting Faith in Your Kids* (Grand Rapids: Zondervan, 2008), 97.
15. Howard Vanderwell, ed. *The Church of All Ages: Generations Worshiping Together* (Herndon, VA: Alban Institute, 2008), xxii.

unites our generations is more significant than anything dividing us."[16] After all, as Barna reminds us,

> When Daniel, Ezekiel and other Hebrew elites were taken forcibly to Babylon, their view of the world was utterly changed. In order to remain faithful to their calling as the people of God, they had to adjust to a new reality. They had to reimagine what it meant to practice Judaism in a world where the Temple—the epicenter of their religious practice—no longer existed. They had to rethink their own story, to reexamine their understanding of their place in the world and in God's intentions for creation. In response to a worldview-shifting calamity, prophets arose to equip God's people with a new way of living in a new world.[17]

Is God calling all ages in the church to be pilgrims who equip one another to live in a new world through the prayers we pray and the songs we sing as the people of God with the people of God? While research and Scripture are important, no adult can convince a teenager they need to be in worship with their family by citing Scripture or quoting research. This is the predicament in which we find ourselves, especially when we teach teenagers to view worship through the lens of our stylistic preferences.

To uphold intergenerational worship is to help our teenagers worry less about personal stylistic preferences and the need to have individual needs met in worship. To uphold intergenerational worship is to help our teenagers see that God is faithful throughout all of life. Intergenerational worship that is faithful to Scripture exhibits the message that teenagers need—namely, that they can trust in God for the duration of their lives, no matter what it looks like.

The Challenge of Intergenerational Worship

Intergenerational worship brings all ages together under one roof for worship, but in doing so, it must account for the diversity of ages in the planning and implementation of worship. Intergenerational worship is messy because on any given week it risks not meeting the needs of one generation for the sake of meeting the needs of another generation.

Intergenerational worship also moves toward a model of formative worship more than a model of expressive worship. Establishing a pattern of intergenerational worship means embracing adolescent spiritual formation through patterns of worshiping with all ages throughout their adolescence. These

16. Meredith Gould, *Transcending Generations: A Field Guide to Collaboration in Church* (Collegeville, MN: Liturgical, 2017), xiv.

17. The Barna Group, *Gen Z: The Culture, Beliefs, and Motivations Shaping the Next Generation* (Ventura, CA: Barna Group and Impact 360 Institute, 2018), 9.

events are important for teenagers, and they are not to be dismissed. This is why weekly all-church worship is critical to the spiritual formation of teenagers. It is also why the church suffers when young people are disconnected or absent during the main Sunday morning worship service.

One of the most significant threats to intergenerational worship is the season of life that any generational cohort might find itself in on any given Lord's Day. The church has always worshiped through times of change, but the fast-paced change of our current culture poses a significant challenge for Christians of all ages. Older Christians often feel as though they are practicing a Christianity that is very different from what they once knew, and younger Christians often find themselves grappling with versions of Christianity they have yet to know or, worse yet, know but don't want to know. While the church has always navigated the challenges posed by different generational cultures, intergenerational worship requires the church of all ages to implement consistent worship practices that are prepared to meet the challenges of the real-life situations all of us find ourselves in, no matter the season of life.

Psalm 137, a hymn expressing the yearnings of the Jewish people in exile following the Babylonian conquest of Jerusalem in 587 BCE, seems to express the plight of Christians of all ages who find themselves wondering, "How can we sing the songs of the Lord while in a foreign land?" Sometimes older Christians find teenagers' "songs of the Lord" to be strange songs that were not part of their own Christian heritage. But teenagers find it odd to sing a song and embrace a faith heritage that looks vastly different from their Monday to Saturday world. Worshiping in the midst of clashing cultures was the struggle for our heroes in the Old Testament who found themselves under a new set of challenges stemming from the imperial power of Babylon, and they worked tirelessly to maintain their local faith traditions. Walter Brueggemann claims that the plight of the Jewish community was not unlike the plight of "contemporary Christians who must live agilely in the midst of the deeply problematic power" that is in the world.[18]

A Digital Babylon

In their research on Generation Z, the Barna Group labeled our current cultural context "digital Babylon." Illustrating how, not too long ago, North America felt to many Christians the same way Jerusalem felt to ancient Judeans, Barna writes that living in North America was much like living in Jerusalem. Both were once culturally homogenous and religiously comfortable.

18. Walter Brueggemann, *Out of Babylon* (Nashville: Abingdon, 2010), 1.

As cultural change accelerated, both places left individuals feeling like exiles in their homes. In the United States, many older American Christians have begun to feel like exiles in their home country, and like the Hebrew exiles of the Old Testament, they feel they are living in a place very different from the land of their "tribe."[19]

Barna demonstrates how components of society have shifted for all generations by looking at Generation Z through the lenses of security, well-being, politics, family, technology, and relationships. For instance, "Millennials were between the ages of 5 and 20 when the 9/11 terrorist attacks shook the nation, and many were old enough to comprehend the historical significance of that moment, while most members of Gen Z have little or no memory of the event. Millennials also grew up in the shadow of the wars in Iraq and Afghanistan, which sharpened broader views of the parties and contributed to the intense political polarization that shapes the current political environment."[20] Now "Gen Z has come of age in a post-9/11 nation reeling from the 2008 recession and is incredibly anxious about their future. Their goals revolve around professional success and financial security, and a majority says their ultimate aim is 'to be happy'—which a plurality defines as financial success."[21] Politically, "most Millennials were between 12 and 27 during the 2008 election, where the force of the youth vote became part of the political conversation and helped elect the first black president."[22]

Technology complicates this picture even more. "Technology, in particular the rapid evolution of how people communicate and interact, is another generation-shaping consideration. Baby Boomers grew up as television expanded dramatically, changing their lifestyles and connection to the world in fundamental ways. Generation X grew up as the computer revolution was taking hold, and Millennials came of age during the internet explosion."[23] Now, "the internet is at the core of Generation Z's development. It has a uniquely powerful influence on their worldview, mental health, daily schedule, sleep patterns, relationships, and more."[24] Looking at the religious identity of each of these generations, one notes that the percentage of Generation Z that identifies as atheist is more than double that of US adults.[25]

19. Barna, *Gen Z*, 9.
20. Michael Dimock, "Defining Generations: Where Millennials End and Post-Millennials Begin," Pew Research Center, January 17, 2019, http://www.pewresearch.org/fact-tank/2018/03/01/defining-generations-where-millennials-end-and-post-millennials-begin/.
21. Barna, *Gen Z*, 12.
22. Dimock, "Defining Generations."
23. Dimock, "Defining Generations."
24. Barna, *Gen Z*, 12.
25. Barna, *Gen Z*, 25.

Generational Approaches to Worship

The contrast between generations becomes starker when we compare them through the lens of worship. Those born before 1960 likely remember a time when all worshipers worshiped the same way. They "attended worship services on Sunday at 11:00 am. They listened to the swell of a pipe organ as they quietly awaited the beginning of the worship service. They followed a planned order of worship, written on a bulletin. They sang familiar congregational hymns that they knew and loved. They thrilled to the sound of a choir singing a powerful anthem. They heard a sermon from the Bible on how to love and trust God. Then they dismissed at noon to beat the Methodists to the cafeteria!"[26] Generation X and Millennials probably resonate more with a world where people shop for worship: "The mall is open on Sundays and competes with the Church, and people have to make a choice. . . . Worship styles too represent a mall, offered by different churches to suit your personal taste or spirituality, all enticing in different ways, and in competition with one another. Who are they for? Who do they appeal to?"[27] Generation Z will most resonate with Barbara Brown Taylor, who writes,

> People are usually trying to tell me that they have a sense of the divine depths of things. . . . They know there is more to life than what meets the eye. They have drawn close to this 'More' in nature, in love, in art, in grief. They would be happy for someone to teach them how to spend more time in the presence of this deeper reality, but when they visit the places where such knowledge is supposed to be found, they often find the rituals hollow and the language antique. . . . Where is the secret hidden? Who has the key to the treasure box of More?[28]

One Step Further

Adoptive Worship

Increasingly, I have become concerned with worship practices where the only goal is to be intergenerational, because I believe it misses the mark. As

26. Paul Basden, "Something Old, Something New: Worship Styles in the Nineties," in *Ties That Bind: Life Together in the Baptist Vision*, ed. Gary A. Furr and Curtis W. Freeman (Macon, GA: Smyth and Helwys, 1994), 171.

27. Bryan D. Spinks, *The Worship Mall: Contemporary Responses to Contemporary Culture* (New York: Church Publishing, 2010), xxiii.

28. Barbara Brown Taylor, *An Altar in the World: A Geography of Faith* (New York: HarperOne, 2009), xv–xvi.

has been shown, to worship together as a church of all ages is important (*multi*generational), but we must also integrate the church of all ages (*inter*generational). Even then, *inter*generational worship also misses addressing segregation in other areas. It misses the opportunity to provide connection points where all ages *know* one another and teenagers experience a deep sense of community that they know and love. How do we integrate the church of Jesus Christ, where everyone is welcome at the table, no matter their age, ethnicity, gender, sexual identity, political persuasion, socioeconomic status, or any other label one might use? How do we show teenagers that worship with the church of all ages is participation in a community where they are known, loved, and cared for? How do we uphold an ecclesiology with our teenagers that they can feel in their bones?

Segregation of any kind is going to be one of the greatest detractors to any teenager who lives in a complex and integrated world outside the walls of the church. Our goal is to do more than integrate our worship practices generationally. It is to teach teenagers to love the *whole* church and to connect them "to all the other people in this congregation who are ready and willing to love and care for them."[29] Chap Clark writes, "It's not enough to invite kids to faith and to discipleship if we do not encourage and equip them to find themselves as part of God's household through history."[30]

Worship practices that adopt teenagers into the family of faith are more in line with an ecclesiology that invites teenagers into the living body of Christ and teaches them not only how to worship but also how to extend hospitality to one another.[31] Liturgical hospitality invites teenagers to adopt the faith that has nourished other generations by singing the great songs of faith, praying the prayers of their brothers and sisters locally and globally, making space for the living Word of God that speaks to the community, and responding on behalf of the community. At the same time, hospitality invites all other ages in the church to do the same for teenagers, adopting them into the worshiping community by singing their songs, praying their prayers, making space for the Word they need to hear, and responding on their behalf.

We can worship together at the same table, but unless we pass food and drink around the table and feel comfortable in conversation with one another,

29. Chap Clark, *Adoptive Church: Creating an Environment Where Emerging Generations Belong* (Grand Rapids: Baker Academic, 2018), 31.

30. Clark, *Adoptive Church*, 32.

31. I am grateful to Brad M. Griffin, senior director of content for the Fuller Youth Institute, who first introduced me to the metaphor of adoption in youth ministry during a consultation at Samford University on January 13, 2014. It, along with Chap Clark's *Adoptive Church*, became the genesis for my thinking about "adoptive worship."

we are merely eating, not dining, and worship is meant to be dining. Worship is meant to be a banquet where the church feasts on the riches of the goodness of God and the goodness of the gathered community. Teenagers need to be brought into that community, and they need to know the roots of that community. At the same time, they also need to understand—with the rest of us—that coming to the table as members of a family means relinquishing some of their own needs, wants, and desires to receive the gifts that others in the community have to offer. Once they learn to relinquish and receive, then teenagers can learn to reciprocate.[32]

Passing Down the Faith

The congregation where I most recently served was founded in 1920, and it is a hybrid between what Jackson Carroll and Wade Clark Roof call an "inherited-tradition" congregation and a "blended" or "mixed" congregation. While the former can "ignore" or "downplay" generational cultures,[33] the latter works to "appeal to the different generations it encompasses."[34] The leadership regularly evaluates worship and ministry practices through the lenses of multiple generations, and it is not uncommon to find teenagers interacting with children, college students, middle-aged adults, and senior adults.

In recent years, this congregation has begun to describe itself as a "family of faith" with congregational practices where every generation is considered valuable and important. In some instances, the families that attend represent fourth- and fifth-generational cultures, where the fourth and fifth generations of a particular family have all worshiped at this church. When asked about the significance of this dynamic in the congregation at worship, their music and worship pastor said, "There's this legacy piece to the fabric of our congregation that says, 'This is what we do as a family—we worship, we serve, and we do it together.'"[35] It is true that the family metaphor can be problematic in some arenas, especially for teenagers who engage congregational life with a nontraditional family structure or without a family at all, but the metaphor of adoption still reminds us that the goal is not to simply worship and coexist but to treat every person in the church as a sibling adopted through God in Christ by the power of the Holy Spirit. Indeed, "the goal of

32. See Kelley Nikondeha, *Adopted: The Sacrament of Belonging in a Fractured World* (Grand Rapids: Eerdmans, 2017).
33. Carroll and Roof, *Bridging Divided Worlds*, 109.
34. Carroll and Roof, *Bridging Divided Worlds*, 140.
35. John S. Woods (music and worship pastor, Dawson Memorial Baptist Church, Birmingham, Alabama), interview with Charles E. Stokes, October 2017.

adoptive ministry is that everything we think, do, and plan should enhance those familial relationships."[36]

Historically, the Christian church has approached spiritual formation using the language of "passing down the faith." This metaphor has been common in youth ministry rhetoric for some time now, and scores of books, articles, sermons, curricula, and other literature have helped congregations understand how our faith is passed down from one generation to the next. While well intended, conversations about intergenerational worship show us precisely how this metaphor is now well worn and also incomplete. We need to help older members pass *down* the faith, yes, but we also need to help younger members in our congregations pass *up* the faith to older members. Adoptive worship takes the metaphor one step further and suggests we pass *around* the faith.

Passing around the Faith

Returning to a culinary metaphor, we might think about a home-cooked meal where all ages are gathered at the family dining table. A father helps a child take a scoop of mashed potatoes before passing along the dish to his mother, the matriarch of the family. She takes a scoop for herself, then passes the dish along to her grandson telling him how her own mother used to make that dish for her. Although he is not sure he wants a scoop, he takes one anyway because he loves and trusts his grandmother. Passing around the faith is the most accurate biblical model. Worship rooted in the rich metaphor of adoption is less about passing down the faith and more about passing around the faith.

When a congregation employs intentional strategies to engage all ages, especially teenagers, in all-church worship and is also intentional about providing teenagers with multiple pathways to explore worship, what is the end result? A vibrant energy in worship and in congregational life where teenagers pass their faith around to children, and teenagers and children together pass their faith around to older adults. Teenagers help the church know how to pass the faith around. Here, I am willing to go so far as to say that children and teenagers, more than any other age group, are poised to cross ministry and generational bridges in the church. They are catalysts for activity, participation, and change in worship. At the same time, teenagers need the church of all ages to call out and support their gifts and to help them realize their baptismal vocation and identity, clothe themselves with Christ, and surround themselves with faithful disciples of all ages at the table of the Lord.

36. Clark, *Adoptive Church*, 8.

Whether made up mostly of young adults, midlife families, or retirees, worship that includes all the ages of the church living together as an adoptive community is unquestionably the most fertile soil for nourishing worshiping teens.[37] When teenagers are intentionally adopted into the worshiping community, children observe and live into teens' love for the church. Middle-aged adults are reminded of the vibrant faith they may have possessed as a teenager and are drawn further into the worshiping community. Senior adults are refreshed by the youthful expressions of faith and the hope of a spiritual legacy of worship.

Adoptive Congregations

More than Style

Adoptive worship is not about the perfect style of worship.[38] The key is for people of every age to feel included and important in all-church worship gatherings. Changing all-church worship to accommodate young people while distancing senior adults will not produce good fruit and neither will blending styles while disconnecting worship from all ages equally. And though segregating worship by age groups will alleviate an immediate, practical need to please everyone, it creates a series of long-term problems, especially for teenagers.

Instead of focusing on style as a gauge for the health of adoptive worship, congregations might instead consider the following: First, which worship service is considered the "main" service, the one that most members would "count" as having gone to church? For most churches, a Sunday morning service has the most symbolic power. Second, do all ages, including teenagers, feel included and important in this main service? If the answer is an enthusiastic yes, then this is good news. If the answer is a more tentative yes or even a no, congregations should consider which ages are left out and which life stages are not fully engaged.

If teenagers (or any age group) do not feel included or important in all-church worship, there is a need for change. For most congregations, changing the main service is challenging, even contentious, work and thinking about

37. Although my focus is different, here I echo sentiments outlined in Kara Powell, Jake Mulder, and Brad Griffin, *Growing Young: Six Essential Strategies to Help Young People Discover and Love Your Church* (Grand Rapids: Baker Books, 2016), see esp. "10 Qualities Your Church Doesn't Need in Order to Grow Young," 25–27.

38. My former colleague Charles E. Stokes was instrumental in helping me develop the material here and in the next section on becoming an adoptive congregation.

such change causes many youth ministers, worship leaders, or pastors to begin skeptically shaking their heads. In congregations where all-church worship may be a challenging place to start, leaders could instead look to age-specific ministries, such as graded Sunday school, youth group, or youth choir, which can serve as fantastic arenas for making gradual change. All-church worship will benefit slowly but surely as these ministries look for opportunities to engage in intergenerational activities that might yield good fruit in the main worship service.

With all generations, it is necessary to avoid what could be a very big mistake: tokenism. Tokenism is putting any age group on display during worship as a sort of self-congratulatory exercise that says, "We are an adoptive congregation"—when, in fact, this is not the case.

Becoming Adoptive

Nurturing Habits

Congregations come in all shapes and sizes, and so, too, do their worship practices. However, not all practices are effective at drawing all ages into the worship and life of the church. Adoptive congregations, where teenagers are flourishing as worshipers and worship leaders, demonstrate one or more of the following nurturing habits. They

1. decide to actively engage all ages in the worship life of their congregation;
2. teach all ages about worship;
3. foster formal and informal conversations about worship with all ages;
4. mentor worship leaders of all ages, especially children and teenagers;
5. choose collaborative over isolated ministries;
6. inventory the gifts of those who are interested in worship leadership;
7. invite all ages into worship leadership;
8. balance excellence with multiple opportunities to lead and experience worship;
9. equip families to have conversations about worship; and
10. engage all of the arts in worship.

This list of habits is more of a packing list than a recipe. We pack differently for different trips, but order is very important in most recipes. Put another way, if a model tells churches where they are and helps them determine where they would like to go next, then the list above can help them start packing for the journey that is best for their context. The habits above are grouped into three stages—start, sustain, and stretch—each corresponding to a different stage in the process of becoming an intentional congregation.

A Place to Start Adoptive Worship

1. Decide to actively engage all ages in the worship life of the congregation.
2. Teach all ages about worship.
3. Foster formal and informal conversations about worship with all ages.

Sometimes the hardest part of engaging all ages in worship and worship leadership is simply getting started. Fortunately, the starting stage of becoming an adoptive congregation is something nearly every church can do. Most congregational life, especially worship, is driven by habit and momentum. Once a pattern has been established, it is easy to keep it going. This tendency is a blessing for keeping things stable, but it is the curse of change making. Moreover, when unexpected good things happen, we often don't know why. Some seeds blossom while others wither, and we feel as if there is little we can do. When a congregation has decided to engage all ages in worship, has found ways to include all ages in discussions about worship, and has begun teaching all ages about worship, it has made a great start, and good fruit will already be emerging. The start stage is not easy, and often it is not most congregations' number one priority. This stage can be boosted by the hope and excitement that accompany most new undertakings, but it is important to also think about future crops.

A Way to Sustain Adoptive Worship

4. Mentor worship leaders of all ages, especially children and teenagers.
5. Choose collaborative over isolated ministries.
6. Inventory the gifts of those who are interested in worship leadership.
7. Invite all ages into worship leadership.

These next four habits are indicative of congregations that are able to sustain healthy, truly adoptive worship. The real test of the "soil" is whether it can continue to produce a good crop for years to come. Creating sustainable change involves staying alert, making sacrifices, and persisting through difficulty. Once congregations have established these sustaining habits, they begin to see good fruit from teen worshipers and worshipers of all other ages. However, it is really the final three characteristics that help encourage teens who are engaged in worship to *become* worshipers. This is a shift from doing to being.

Stretching the Adoptive Community

8. Balance excellence with multiple opportunities to lead and experience worship.
9. Equip families to have conversations about worship.
10. Engage all of the arts in worship.

Most churches can find ways within their own traditions and contexts to cultivate the first seven characteristics. The last three, however, can be a stretch for some churches. Congregations that have a good foundation in the top seven habits and then stretch to add these final three have the most vibrant adoptive worship. What is more, their teens are most likely to report that the "good life" in adulthood involves worshiping in church.

Sometimes even the best congregations do not do all of these things, nor do they always do them very well. Cultivating healthy adoptive worship is an ongoing process. While the list above is in a roughly chronological order to help a church make positive change, some churches may already be strong in items further down the list and have little activity around items near the top. For instance, a church may be committed to engaging all of the arts in worship, but their worship may be primarily led by and geared for middle-aged adults. It should also be said that this list is both descriptive and prescriptive. It describes congregations where all ages, especially teenagers, are flourishing in worship. It prescribes a methodology that other congregations might use to enhance intergenerational worship. Like any list, it is worth noting that no congregation can control the movement of the Holy Spirit in the church of all ages. But congregations that use this list can plan worship so that when the Holy Spirit captivates teenagers' souls and employs teenagers' gifts in meaningful ways, the church of all ages flourishes.

A Final Story

For a number of years, I served a congregation that was not averse to imperfect worship, often because we weren't sure who would decide they wanted to go to church and walk in on Sunday morning. A single mother from our neighborhood began attending church, deciding that she wanted her child, whom she had out of wedlock, to grow up in church. She showed up one Sunday morning, and she kept coming to church with her daughter.

When she found out a second baby was on the way, she kept coming to church because she wanted this baby to grow up in church too. The church supported her and helped her. We threw her a baby shower and set her up well, and she kept coming to church with her three-year-old. She had her baby, and two weeks after her birth, she came with the baby and her three-year-old. We had a guest in the pulpit that day, and as luck would have it, the baby started to cry during the sermon. The mother tried to quiet the baby, but she wouldn't stop crying.

The mother spent what felt like an eternity gathering all her children's things, and everyone was watching her. As she stood up from the pew, the three-year-old exclaimed loudly, "No leave, Mommy!" It was about that time that the minister, in the middle of his sermon, said, "Ma'am, we need this baby in here, and we need your daughter, and we need you in here. If you'll come back, I'll bet we could sing this baby to sleep." The minister started singing "Jesus Loves the Little Children," the matriarch of our congregation stood up and got the crying baby while the mother tended to the three-year-old, and a teenager from the front pew took the diaper bag back to the mother's seat. Eventually things settled down and our collective focus returned to the sermon.

Monday morning, our secretary said hi to me when I walked in the door and asked me if I had seen what happened in worship the day before. I thought I was about to get an earful, but she said, "All of that did more to convict my seventy-year-old self than any sermon I've heard or any song I've ever sung."

6
♦ ♦ ♦

Worship and Culture

From the Sanctuary to the Soup Kitchen, from the Mission Field to Summer Camp, and Back Home Again

The beginning of culture and the beginning of humanity are one and the same because culture is what we were made to do. There is no withdrawing from culture. Culture is inescapable. And that's a good thing.

—Andy Crouch, *Culture Making*

Worship in Different Contexts

I was raised in worship services that were rooted in the Southern Baptist tradition of music, prayer, testimony, sermon, and invitation. Worship in the sanctuary, for me, often included music by our choir, an organ, and a piano; a sermon; and an invitation to come to faith.

Worship in our youth room, however, was different. It imitated worship experiences from summer camps and retreats and the Passion conferences that began in the late 1990s. While the music making and messages were not as professionally executed, they all hark back to the worship our youth group participated in during summer camps and mission trips. Fall weekend retreats served as spiritual energizers to remind us of our summer commitments, and winter weekend retreats served to provide hope for what the summer would have in store. Worship in the youth room was a perpetual anamnesis that called us to remember those commitments we made in the summer, recall the ways we had forgotten those commitments at school and at home in the past week, and reflect on how we might do better.

I liked both styles of worship, and I didn't want to choose between the two. All-church worship was formative for me, but it often lacked the experience that the youth room afforded. That said, worship in the youth room presented its own challenges because it could never measure up to the quality of worship in all-church worship or at summer camps, fall and winter retreats, and larger conferences such as Passion and Urbana.

The phenomenon of camps, retreats, conferences, and missions has significantly impacted youth ministry in the twentieth and twenty-first century. So, too, have the worship practices at these events. Teenagers return home from countercultural experiences talking about the passionate, contemplative, energetic, or (insert-adjective-here) worship that was different from the typical worship in their home congregation, and every other form of worship is then measured by that emotionally charged experience. Worship at home often appears lackluster or subpar compared to worship at summer camp, the fall or winter retreat, the Passion conference, or that mission trip to South America. Short-term summer mission trips are full of experiences. Whether the trip is within the United States or on one of the five other continents (assuming Antarctica is not an option), teenagers participate together in a host of activities that range from serving to sightseeing.

Much has been written about the pros and cons of these trips and the church's approach to them in the twentieth century. Mission trips are not without their challenges, but they are also not without their opportunities. Worship is usually a part of these trips, however central or peripheral. In many ways, these trips provide teenagers with an opportunity to experience firsthand the relationship between worship and culture. When they worship in the host culture, they experience worship in a context very different from their "liturgical homeland."[1] Many times, mission trips provide teenagers with opportunities to lead worship in a cross-cultural context. These experiences have the potential to be formative.

1. The term *liturgical homeland* comes from Kathy Black, *Culturally-Conscious Worship* (St. Louis: Chalice, 2000), 4.

The Church in Mission and Worship

The Myth of Normal Worship

There is no such thing as "normal worship." Yet the church has not cultivated well a rhetoric for worship practices that are different from our normative experiences, and this is one of the great crises in ecclesiology. We label worship by style, and one becomes good and one bad, when we are really talking about our preferences. Language about worship practices that are different creeps up in conversations and pits parties against one another, whether we are talking about differences in cultural expressions in worship or differences in musical and homiletical styles. The conversation goes, "*We* are *normal*, but *everyone else* is *other*." We and them. One is normal; the other is not. Sandra Maria Van Opstal says that communities are often "unaware of what it means to be *us* and hyper aware of what it means to be *them*." This ignorance about one's own culture becomes the "biggest barrier Christians face in developing communities hospitable to people of every ethnicity and culture."[2] At its core, this is an ethnocentric issue that suggests "*my* way of worshiping is better than *their* way of worshiping." When our worship vocabulary sounds like this, we are promoting a cultish mentality among our teenagers, who know this mentality from their schools all too well.

In *Gather into One*, C. Michael Hawn warns about giving in to a dichotomy with many of our worship practices. The dichotomy is worship at the center versus worship at the periphery. Worship at the center is worship that follows normative practices for the majority culture, especially those who "share in the wealth, privilege, and power." In contrast, worship at the periphery is the worship exercised by "poor, dispossessed, and marginalized persons" who are not at the center of power.[3] Historically, individuals at the center have tried to pull those on the periphery toward themselves. This was an all-too-familiar scenario and approach to worship and mission in the American church during the twentieth century. It was accompanied by an elitist mentality that suggested that the West is better than the rest. As Hawn notes, this elitist mentality is not without its consequences—namely, a *de facto hegemony* where both sides lose elements of their identities.

2. Sandra Maria Van Opstal, *The Next Worship: Glorifying God in a Diverse World* (Downers Grove, IL: InterVarsity, 2016), 40.

3. C. Michael Hawn, *Gather into One: Praying and Singing Globally* (Grand Rapids: Eerdmans, 2003), 2.

With teenagers, the goal is in many ways the opposite: to move from center to periphery and back again with a greater understanding of what lies at the periphery so that both periphery and center are better appreciated. A challenge is that the church regularly positions "ethnic minority cultures against white cultures" and vice versa, using those positions to define the center and the periphery.[4] In other words, the church cannot divorce notions of normality from individual experiences. Consider Van Opstal's experience training young worshipers and worship leaders. After visiting a congregation or worship gathering different from their own, individuals usually do one of two things. They name the commonalities in worship they found with their home congregation and identify them as normal. Or they name the differences they found and state how those differences were distracting to them—when *distracting* really means *different* or *strange* or *other*. Is there a "normal" way for teenagers to worship? If so, how do we describe it?

No matter how *other* is defined, learning can come from relationships and worship with communities of faith who are different from the teenagers' liturgical homeland, and these contexts can become some of the most generative for teaching about worship, doctrine, and practice. Our teenagers have likely already moved past these biases in the surrounding culture; we can help them move past the biases in worship through diverse expressions of worship and multiple attempts to engage those expressions. At the same time, our different worship practices have an opportunity to instill in our teenagers the values of reciprocity, solidarity, and obligation rather than individualism, selfishness, and pride. All of these are growing edges that we must help our teenagers move past in the conversations about worship and culture, whether the worship practices are from the congregations across the street, in the soup kitchen, or around the world.

Hawn suggests that a healthy starting place for thinking about worship practices in different cultures is distinguishing between a healthy bias, which "is inclusive of other worldviews and presupposes that there are other cultural ways of making meaning that are equally valid" and prejudice, which "assumes an exclusive posture toward other cultural perspectives."[5] Prejudice is something the church found in itself in the worship wars of the 1990s, at least in those congregations where "the ethos of normative cultural values" became "associated with the 'high culture' of the Western classical tradition." Their "preference for a particular style of worship" became "an exclusive prejudice." The struggle between bias and prejudice may always be with us; however,

4. Van Opstal, *Next Worship*, 39.
5. Hawn, *Gather into One*, 7.

"moving from a center-based model to a spectrum-oriented understanding of worship practice is much more challenging than naively embracing the new, exotic, or quaint. Welcoming strangers and aliens in worship requires an intentional process."[6]

The Nairobi Statement on Worship and Culture

In 1996, the Lutheran World Federation's Study Team on Worship and Culture published a series of papers and statements titled *Christian Worship: Unity in Cultural Diversity*.[7] The papers noted the dynamic relationship between worship and culture, highlighting four areas of interest, study, and practice. Now referred to as the "Nairobi Statement on Worship and Culture," the document highlights that worship is transcultural, contextual, cross-cultural, and countercultural.[8] All four of these themes are important for thinking about worship with teenagers, especially in cultural contexts that are not the teenagers' liturgical homeland.[9]

Worship as Transcultural

Worship is *transcultural*; some components of worship are beyond culture. First and foremost, this is the "resurrected Christ whom we worship, and through whom by the power of the Holy Spirit we know the grace of the Triune God." This truth "transcends and indeed is beyond all culture." To worship with the global church is to join in solidarity to proclaim allegiance to the power of Christ in our midst, over against the powers and principalities of governments that oppress, avenge, and require the allegiance of teenagers in the United States. However, teenagers are more likely to be made aware of their freedoms and allegiances when they worship side-by-side with those from a country less fortunate than theirs, where worshipers understand oppression and revenge and thus the significance of the confessional statement "Jesus Christ is Lord." This statement is communicated through Scripture, ecumenical creeds, the Lord's Prayer, and baptism in the name of God the Father, Christ the Son, and the Holy Spirit—practices that are transcultural in their own right.[10]

6. Hawn, *Gather into One*, 9.
7. Lutheran World Federation, "Nairobi Statement on Worship and Culture Full Text," Calvin Institute of Christian Worship, 1996, https://worship.calvin.edu/resources/resource-library/nairobi-statement-on-worship-and-culture-full-text.
8. Lutheran World Federation, "Nairobi Statement," art. 1.1.
9. Black, *Culturally-Conscious Worship*.
10. Lutheran World Federation, "Nairobi Statement," art. 2.1.

Worship as Contextual

Worship is *contextual*; some elements of worship that are related to both nature and culture will vary according to the local situation. This acknowledges that Christ, the one whom we worship, "was born into a specific culture of the world." So Christian worship will also reflect the culture in which it is offered. This principle allows worship to express a "culture's values and patterns" as long as they are "consonant with the values of the Gospel." These values are in turn used to express the "meaning and purpose of worship." All worship practices are contextual, including the worship practices that a teenager engages in from week to week. Contextualization is "a necessary task for the Church's mission in the world, so that the Gospel can be ever more deeply rooted in diverse local cultures."[11]

That said, two methods are particularly helpful for contextualizing worship: dynamic equivalence and creative assimilation. These are important for thinking about worship and culture and for practicing the contextualization of worship with teenagers. The former includes "re-expressing components of Christian worship with something from a local culture that has an equal meaning, value, and function," and the latter is "adding pertinent components of local culture" to the order of worship "to enrich its original core."[12] A youth minister who encourages a teenager to read Scripture in Spanish might be participating in dynamic equivalence. Similarly, a worship minister who learns the hidden songs of a culture from a musician in Brazil or who asks a teenager to learn North American musical resources that remain uncultivated in worship, such as those of the Native Americans, is participating in creative assimilation.[13]

Worship as Countercultural

The third element from the "Nairobi Statement on Worship and Culture" suggests that worship is *countercultural*. To say that worship is countercultural is to challenge "what is contrary to the Gospel in a given culture" by resisting the idolatries of its cultural context. Countercultural worship acknowledges that Christ "came to transform all people and all cultures, and calls us not to conform to the world, but to be transformed with it (Romans 12:2)." This component of the Nairobi Statement also calls for the "transformation of cultural patterns which idolize the self or the local group at the expense of a wider humanity," as well as those patterns that "give central

---

11. Lutheran World Federation, "Nairobi Statement," art. 3.1.
12. Lutheran World Federation, "Nairobi Statement," arts. 3.2–3.3.
13. Hawn, *Gather into One*, 128–29.

place to the acquisition of wealth at the expense of the care of the earth and its poor."[14]

In many ways, countercultural worship may be the deepest and the hardest practice to observe for teenagers, their parents, and their ministers. We all are steeped in the culture of the United States, which has long equated religion with culture, however implicitly or explicitly. The challenge is that now, the "altars where we worship" reflect the values and principles of our surrounding culture rather than the values and principles of Jesus.[15]

Worship as Cross-Cultural

Fourth and finally, worship is *cross-cultural*. To say worship is cross-cultural is to say it is possible to share between local cultures in the same way that Christ "welcomes the treasures of earthly cultures into the city of God." In this understanding of worship, congregations can share liturgical artifacts, such as hymns, arts, prayers, and other elements, to "enrich the whole Church and strengthen the sense of the communion of the Church." Appropriately, the cultural sharing that happens across worship, be it "music, art, architecture, gestures, and postures," should be carefully "understood and respected."[16]

This means that the worship practices our teenagers might bring home with them from a short-term mission trip need to be couched in more than fun, games, and laughter. There should be living evidence that teenagers have come to know the meaning of the artifacts as they exist in another place, that teenagers have found solidarity in some form with the community that utilizes them, and that in sharing those artifacts, the teenagers have an obligation to ongoing communication and contact with the community from which they were received.[17]

A Summer Mission Tour: Four Scenarios

For many summers, I participated in what a congregation I served called a "mission tour" with the student music ministry. The title "mission tour"

---

14. Lutheran World Federation, "Nairobi Statement," arts. 4.1–4.2.

15. See Juan M. Floyd-Thomas, Stacey M. Floyd-Thomas, and Mark G. Toulouse, *The Altars Where We Worship: The Religious Significance of Popular Culture* (Louisville: Westminster John Knox, 2016).

16. Lutheran World Federation, "Nairobi Statement," arts. 5.1–5.2.

17. See Andrew Root, "The Mission Trip as Global Tourism: Are We OK with This?," in *The Theological Turn in Youth Ministry*, ed. Andrew Root and Kenda Creasy Dean (Downers Grove, IL: IVP, 2011), 189–90. Here, Root is reflecting on the work of Karl Barth, "The Community for the World," in *Theological Foundations for Ministry*, ed. Ray S. Anderson (Edinburgh: T&T Clark, 1979), 499–532.

borrows from "mission trip" and "choir tour," models of ministry that are familiar to many. The title is an attempt at honesty, an acknowledgment that both an element of mission from mission trips and an element of performance from choir tours are included. I saw these trips have a significant impact on the teenagers in our congregation, and I remain a proponent of them, even though I am acutely aware of their challenges. I also maintained a deep level of trust for the leaders in my congregation, who understood the complexities of the mission trip as tourism.

Every four years, our mission tour was international, and on one particular summer, we went to Ecuador, where we worked with a missionary organization with which our congregation has an ongoing partnership. Throughout our ten days in Ecuador, four worship scenarios occurred, and I will describe them here. They are common scenarios in student worship ministry.

Scenario 1: We worship for you. We led worship for the congregation that makes up the missionary organization with whom we partnered and for guests from the area which the congregation invited. Our student choir sang songs in Spanish, and our student worship team led songs for the congregation in both English and Spanish. Our staff minister preached a combination of personal testimony and sermon, which were translated by our host, and we ended the time with an opportunity for those gathered to respond to the invitation that had been presented by our minister. Our worship gathering lasted about sixty minutes, during which the gymnasium we were gathered in became very warm. Our students became restless, and the assembled congregation, which included families of all ages, did too. When worship ended, our students quickly left the building for fresh air and water while some of our adults lingered to interact with the congregation from Ecuador.

Scenario 2: You worship for us. We attended worship with the congregation members and church leaders from the missionary organization, and they led worship for us. This happened one day after we had led worship for them in the same gymnasium where our group sat in chairs in the front of the room and the congregation sat on bleachers behind them. Much of the worship service was in Spanish, though the sermon was preached in both Spanish and English so that we could understand. Tired from a day of service, our teenagers became disengaged about halfway through the ninety-minute worship service, which was much longer than usual presumably because of the added element of translation. The single moment that captivated their attention happened when a group of Ecuadorian women and children presented a native dance. Our teenagers were curious. They watched, and they asked questions afterward.

Scenario 3: We perform for you. We visited schools and churches in the area and led worship for them. These schools and churches varied in size and scope, but generally speaking, attendance was strong. I remember one concert in particular. In this concert, we were in a large outdoor arena, and children and teenagers gathered for our presentation of music, testimony, and sermon. The children and teenagers in the school clearly enjoyed being out of class, and they enjoyed seeing members of our group. As soon as we began singing, the students began giggling among themselves and pointing at us. I later learned that most of them had never seen a choir before; the concept of a choir was entirely unfamiliar, nearly a novelty for them. We continued in our presentation, but we never gained their attention for worship. Though we tried cutting our spoken words short to sing more and invite them to sing with us (attempting to recover the moment), our efforts did not work. Our teenagers left the experience frustrated.

Scenario 4: We share our experiences at home. When we returned home from Ecuador, a fourth scenario occurred in our annual "home concert." We presented our music, testimony, Scripture, sermon, and other elements of worship. Throughout the night, we presented a number of these elements in Spanish, though our congregation is primarily English speaking. They did not understand the words our teenagers used, but they were impressed that our teenagers were able to speak Spanish. Our home concert ended, and our congregation no doubt felt good that the money they spent on this mission tour had been invested well.

In the ice cream social following our home concert, I was standing next to Ben, a teenager prone to reflection, recalling some of the experiences we had shared together, when he asked, "As musicians, I know we did well in Ecuador. But do you think we did any good?" I knew he must have asked the question because he feared the answer might be no. Did our work and worship in those ten days matter? Did we make a difference in the lives of others? Did the trip make a difference in our lives? And how do we know? He didn't know it, but he was voicing the question that scholars and ministers and congregations and young people and old people have been asking since the beginning of the twenty-first century. What is the value of our work and worship on short-term trips? Do they matter? And how do we know?

Short-Term Mission Trips

The Popularity of Mission

Throughout the twentieth century, the church has assumed that its mission endeavors matter, that those Christians who give their time and energy to serve

Christ locally and globally, short-term and long-term, do make a difference. This is why more than 1.5 million Christians from the United States travel abroad on short-term mission trips each year.[18] In a broader cultural phenomenon, this is why "more than 55 million Americans have taken some form of volunteer vacation and nearly twice as many are considering doing the same."[19]

The phenomenon of short-term missions has significantly impacted the nature of youth ministry in the twenty-first century. In the 1970s and 1980s, the primary activity of most youth ministries was youth camp. From the late 1980s to the mid-1990s, the activities of most youth ministries included large concert-like events such as contemporary Christian concerts, large denominational youth rallies, and Passion conferences. While all these events are still happening, and many of us have been to those events, the core activity of youth ministries today is the short-term mission trip. It is now the vogue thing to do. Because of this, more than two million teenagers in the United States go on mission trips annually,[20] and approximately one in three American teenagers will participate or have participated in some kind of cross-cultural service project before finishing high school.[21]

Andrew Root, a prominent voice in youth ministry, says, "The mission trip, it appears, has become 'the' youth ministry activity. Whether it is to Mexico, Chicago, Africa, Appalachia, India or South Dakota, every summer the church sends its adolescent children to the ends of the earth. . . . 'To serve, to evangelize, to grow in their faith' are usually the answers we give as we raise money for the trips and justify their central place on our calendars. Service and mission seem more noble and, dare we say, 'holy' than stadium-filled Christian rock concerts sprinkled with funny speakers."[22]

Now, no doubt service and mission do happen on these trips. I'm a believer in short-term and long-term mission trips. I have seen a church birthed and lives changed in the small, rural village of Nava, Mexico, on a short-term mission trip. I have also supported family friends on their three-year mission

18. Robert J. Priest et al., "Researching the Short-Term Mission Movement," *Missiology* 34, no. 4 (October 2006): 432. This data is extrapolated from work done by Robert Wuthnow and is referenced in Kenda Creasy Dean, *Almost Christian: What the Faith of Our Teenagers Is Telling the American Church* (New York: Oxford University Press, 2010), 158.

19. Margaret Jaworski, "Volunteer Vacations: How to Choose an Ethical Program," *Transitions Abroad*, September/October 2006, https://www.transitionsabroad.com/publications/magazine/0609/volunteer_vacations_gain_popularity.shtml.

20. Kurt Ver Beek, "The Impact of Short-Term Missions: A Case Study of House Construction in Honduras after Hurricane Mitch," *Missiology* 34, no. 4 (October 2006): 485.

21. G. Jeffrey MacDonald, "Rise of Sunshine Samaritans: On a Mission or a Holiday?," *Christian Science Monitor*, May 25, 2006, https://www.csmonitor.com/2006/0525/p01s01-ussc.html.

22. Root, "Mission Trip," 183.

excursion to live with, work, teach, and disciple Christ followers in China. On a short-term mission trip to Kenya, I witnessed a close friend make the decision to follow Christ's call on her life to become a full-time vocational missionary to the same country. And my own call to full-time Christian ministry was realized on a short-term mission trip while working with inner-city children in Dallas, Texas. Service and mission happen when the church gives itself to following the work of Christ through missional endeavors.

The Problem with Short-Term Mission Trips

Yet the Ecuador scenarios above, combined with the research, point toward a set of challenges that plague our approach to worship and mission with teenagers in cross-cultural settings. The research says that those of us in the church often approach mission trips as opportunities to "fix" people who are not like us. So we pack our nice suitcases, travel on big planes, and show up in charter buses with boxes of materials. We find ways to help people and enter mission trips thinking that our short-term presence will provide long-term solutions to the problems of people who live daily with realities we can't fathom. But it's been proven again and again that this approach—this mentality—isn't working. As sociologists have researched the nature of missions in the North American church, they have labeled challenges in short-term missions—many of which aren't easy to hear.

First, sociologists have learned that short-term mission projects don't help the recipients of our good intentions. Our short-term projects don't help those people we minister to, because in most cases, the church emphasizes spiritual needs over physical needs. And let's be honest: meeting spiritual needs makes us feel good about ourselves, and those are the reports that congregations want to hear when we return. The problem is that people in need can't receive anything spiritual until their physical needs are met. We don't help people on short-term mission trips because, to use the old adage, we are giving people fish for a day without teaching them how to fish for life.

Second, sociologists have also learned that short-term mission projects don't help the givers or participants. The growth in short-term mission trips among students and adults has not translated into the growth of career missionaries. Going on mission trips hasn't caused participants to give more money to alleviate poverty than they might have otherwise. And participation has not reduced participants' tendencies toward materialism. This has led Root to compare mission trips to a type of global tourism, saying that most of us, when we travel on short-term missions, behave more like tourists than missionaries—and this gets confusing. We live with the poor for a while, then we hit the water park. We serve the hungry a meal, then we spend the afternoon shopping for souvenirs. Kids learn how to pray together, then they learn how to surf. We see poverty and pain as well as local sights. And we should all be asking why these dichotomies exist.[23]

Finally, short-term mission trips have little effect on the long-term spiritual growth of teenagers. Kenda Creasy Dean says that you can "ask teenagers in a church youth group what they mean by mission, and most of them will tell you about a hot week in July when they traveled to a poverty-stricken community to do home repair, lead Bible school, and (theoretically) help those who are culturally and/or economically 'other.'"[24] Teenagers remember short-term trips for the specifics of travel, work, and time with friends. The work of Dean and the NSYR demonstrates that teenagers rarely, if ever, describe short-term missions as significant moments of spiritual transformation.

The Mission Trip as Liturgical Tourism

In the same way that the church has often approached the relationship between teenagers and worship as worship *for* teenagers and worship *by* teenagers, so too have we approached worship on mission trips as worship done *for* another culture or worship done *by* another culture. Worship done for another culture happens when we take our worship practices to another culture while often assuming that the individuals we are engaging are in need of evangelization. So we sing our songs, pray our prayers, present our testimonies, and preach our messages to evangelize the culture we are visiting, and we good-naturedly invite them to participate in worship with us by providing translators.

Worship for Another Culture

The problem with the above invitation is twofold. First, if our initial assumption, that these individuals may not be Christians, is correct, can they worship God with us?[25] The second problem with this approach to worship is that it focuses on what we do rather than who we are. We are Christians, and we do worship. In this model, we do worship for other people rather than finding opportunities to be with them. Once again, worship is reduced to entertainment for those who are not like us. I have been on a number of mission trips where these worship services have turned into ploys to "keep the attention" of the hundreds—and in some cases thousands—who have come to see the

23. Root, "Mission Trip," 183.
24. Dean, *Almost Christian*, 96.
25. See Stephen R. Holmes, "Trinitarian Missiology: Towards a Theology of God as Missionary," *International Journal of Systematic Theology* 8, no. 1 (2006): 89.

Americans. Worship becomes about entertaining the other culture, hoping we can keep their attention long enough to present them with the gospel message.

While this experience may have certain benefits for the teenagers in our youth groups, who get to practice their witness in the world through testimony and song, the message they hear becomes dull and boring. Moreover, they become discouraged when our entertainment, disguised as worship, is not well received in altar calls and responses to the gospel. Beyond that, they silently wonder with the rest of us what will happen to those individuals who respond to the gospel invitation when we depart for home and no one is there to help them worship.

Worship by Another Culture

The reverse of this scenario also happens in short-term mission trips. In many instances, these trips provide opportunities for teenagers to worship in congregational contexts around the world. We enter congregations with our teenagers as tourists, and we often sit together in the back or the front of the worship space. In more noble attempts, we ask our teenagers and adults to spread out and sit in clusters around the room. We try to blend in, but this is impossible. One of two things will happen. Either the host congregation will do worship as is normal for them, and our teenagers will be left to interpret what is happening—at times laughing, giggling, and raising their eyebrows at those things that are unfamiliar to them. Or sometimes the receiving culture will accommodate our presence by providing translators, preaching messages to us, and, in many cases, singing songs that they think Americans will know and enjoy. The problem with this scenario is that our teenagers miss the opportunity to see how a particular culture worships. Again, worship is reduced to entertainment, this time by the other culture *for* us.

When we return home from these trips, we do worship for our congregations as we did worship in the mission context. We sing our songs and preach our messages and share our testimonies just as we did on the mission field, all while boasting about the number of people who responded during the altar calls in the worship services we led for our host culture. In other instances, we attempt to re-create the worship practices of the culture we visited as though we understand and appreciate them, when in reality, neither is the case. Worship for teenagers in the home congregation functions more like a show-and-tell than a formational experience for our congregations.

This kind of worship does not help our teenagers, nor does it help the culture within which they are worshiping. In each scenario, worship is again reduced to a performance by our teenagers for others or a performance by other cultures for us. When we worship in cross-cultural settings, we assume that our usu structures of worship are the ones in which we need to operate, and so we o our worship and ask others to watch us. Then they do their worship, and we watch them. Our usual patterns of worship do not work in cross-cultural settings for our teenagers or for the culture in which we find ourselves as guests, because each side ends up observing worship on the sidelines rather than participating in worship. Both cultures try to *do* the right things in an effort to accommodate each other, and in the end, we miss the opportunity to *be* with each other and learn about each other's worship practices.

Root writes that the secret to avoiding the "tourist trap" on mission trips is to focus "not on doing but on being." Our "adolescents and parents ask, 'What will we do?' But if our purpose for going is not first for doing but for being with, the question becomes, 'Who will we be with?' 'Who will we be encountering?'"[26] Expressed through the lens of worship, our question might shift from "What will we do in worship?" to "Who will we be with as we worship?" This moves our worship practices from something we do for others or something others do for us to "simply being with people." Then our worship becomes "about seeing, hearing and sharing existence with others—others who are living as unwanted vagabonds in our world of tourism."[27]

Mission Trips as Liturgical Pilgrimages

Reforming Our Approach to Mission and Worship

As we work toward a better view of mission and worship, there is some good news: our young people are the ones leading the church to reform its mission practices. They are leading the way for the church. In a survey that asked graduating high school seniors what they wanted more of in their youth groups, FYI reports that the number one answer was "time for deep conversation. Second was mission trips. Third was service projects. Last was games." Sixty percent of those seniors "were motivated to come to youth group because of the ways youth group has helped them learn to serve." Finally, 93 percent of those who were asked to volunteer face-to-face by someone close to them—a parent, a church leader, or a friend—did end up volunteering.[28]

26. Root, "Mission Trip," 188.
27. Root, "Mission Trip," 189.
28. Kara E. Powell, Brad M. Griffin, and Cheryl A. Crawford, *Sticky Faith, Youth Worker Edition: Practical Ideas to Nurture Long-Term Faith in Teenagers* (Grand Rapids: Zondervan, 2011), 101–2.

nducted a nationwide survey to learn why young people are
causes, and they found that "62 percent say the issues that mat-
them are those that have touched them or someone they know."
eventy percent involved in activism report that their parents' encour-
played a major [role] in their choice to get involved." Other students
y would be more involved if they could participate with their friends or
y had more time to volunteer or had more convenient volunteer activities.[29]

What do these statistics mean for the church? That young people are one
of the most hopeful resources for forging a new path of missions in North
America. But it also means that adults need to find ways to right the wrongs
in the world with our children and youth. It means that all of us—young
and old—need to examine more closely how particular injustices relate to
all of our lives at home, not just abroad. It means that all of us need to give
injustice a face and a name. And it means that everyone in the church must
commit to partner together in intergenerational relationships, where every
possible combination of people serve together to make missions a long-term
process, not a short-term event.

This means there can be no "drive-by" mission trips. Rather, having gone
and seen in solidarity, we are called to take these others into our own communities and lives. In other words, when the mission trip is over, we must not
only find ways to continue the partnership but also work to keep bringing the
trip back into the life of the church community.[30]

Learning from Egeria

In the latter part of the fourth century a nun named Egeria, probably from
France or Spain, made a pilgrimage to Jerusalem and wrote to her religious
community about all she saw and observed. Most notable in her writings are
her accounts of worship in Jerusalem. She describes in great detail patterns of
daily prayer, Sunday worship, and festival days such as Easter. Though there are
complications with the history surrounding Egeria's pilgrimage and the documentation of what was and what was not originally hers, her testimony signifies
for us an important lesson. She prepared for her journey by studying Scripture,
and she reported the findings of her journey with her community so they could
improve upon their practices of worship. In her writing, "there is an underlying
emphasis on the learning experience as an essential part of [the pilgrimage]."[31]

29. Reported in Powell, Griffin, and Crawford, *Sticky Faith, Youth Worker Edition*, 131.
30. Root, "Mission Trip," 190.
31. Hagith Sivan, "Holy Land Pilgrimage and Western Audiences: Some Reflections on Egeria
and Her Circle," *Classical Quarterly* 38, no. 2 (1988): 528. See M. L. McClure and C. L. Feltoe,

What if Egeria's example became one for all our mission trips? We could start preparing for mission trips by learning about the places we are visiting before we visit them, including their worship. Doing this would emphasize the importance of learning about worship from the communities we visit in order to understand what makes them meaningful and to improve the worship practices of our own communities.

Informal, Spontaneous, and Extemporaneous Worship

A Fifth Scenario

There is a fifth scenario I have yet to describe from the mission tour to Ecuador. One afternoon we experienced a significant thunderstorm that caused both our group and our partners from Ecuador to wait in the gymnasium for the storm to end. Teenagers from our group chatted casually with teenagers from Ecuador, who happened to be part of the dance troupe mentioned in a scenario above. One teenager from our group asked, "So how do you do that dance?" The young dancers began to teach the dance to a small group of our teenagers, who provided the music. As they learned the dance, the circle of dancers grew from a small handful to a cohort of fifty or more. Both groups danced and sang together, laughing at one another's attempts and failures. That evening, when our travel group had its daily debrief, our leader began with the typical first question, "Where did you experience God today?" The young man who started the shared dance experience said, "Is it weird for me to say I experienced God when we were all dancing together?"

One the one hand, his question articulates the power of the arts to bring disparate cultures together to create, sustain, and nurture a powerful cross-cultural sharing. On the other hand, his question articulates the transcendence of the liminal space the teenagers experienced together that afternoon with their friends from Ecuador. Liminal places are those places that are "betwixt and between," where an attempt is made to exist in two worlds simultaneously.[32] In this case, one foot is in the door of one culture, and the other foot is in the door of another culture. The result of liminal experiences is often a type of inculturation, "the cultural learning process

---

ed. and trans., *The Pilgrimage of Egeria* (London: Society for Promoting Christian Knowledge, 1919), https://www.ccel.org/m/mcclure/etheria/etheria.htm.

32. See Victor Turner, *The Ritual Process: Structure and Anti-structure* (New Brunswick, NJ: Aldine Transaction, 1995), 95.

of the individual, the process by which a person is inserted into his or her culture."[33]

The Power of Curiosity, Play, Failure, and Repetition

What else might we learn from this moment suspended in time? First, this moment began with the curiosity of a teenager who dared to ask questions about the dance from another culture's liturgy. Teenagers who are willing to be curious may experience "an approach to worship where strangers and aliens become full citizens with the saints."[34] Second, curiosity was followed by play, where learning another's liturgical custom became a game. Though we don't often think of it as a game, worship is inherently a game with "its own rules, customs, and etiquette." Melanie Ross writes that "it suspends normal patterns of thought and behavior" and "takes place in its own controlled space and time." She continues to say that worship, like a game, "can nonetheless have widespread benefits in forming, training, and developing its participants."[35] Third, failure was acceptable and even humorous. This particular instance was constituted in the context of sharing and friendship, which prevented those who failed from retreating to familiar patterns, actions, and securities from their normative culture.

Fourth, repetition helped teenagers appreciate the dance from the other culture and also get it right. In a liminal space, there is often a gap between the "authentic experience of the sending culture and the social/psychological structures of the receiving culture."[36] In fact, entering this gap is sure to cause "a sense of instability and insecurity."[37] However, through repetition, participants can move toward "intercultural empathy," where a "deeper, fuller equilibrium between the sending and receiving cultures may take place." Repetition of liturgical practices "decreases the possibility that an encounter with the sending culture will be reduced to musical novelty, sensationalism, or cultural stereotyping."[38]

Curiosity. Play. Failure. Repetition. All four elements are important in worship with teenagers. They appear not in carefully manufactured moments but extemporaneously and spontaneously as characteristics of moments that cannot be planned in advance—and absolutely cannot be manufactured.

33. Aylward Shorter, *Toward a Theology of Inculturation* (Maryknoll, NY: Orbis, 1988), 5.
34. Hawn, *Gather into One*, 4.
35. Melanie Ross, "Liturgy and Spiritual Formation," (lecture, Samford University, Birmingham, AL, January 14, 2013).
36. Hawn, *Gather into One*, 246.
37. Hawn, *Gather into One*, 245.
38. Hawn, *Gather into One*, 246.

Yet the combined effect of these elements may lead to a profoundly intimate moment of being and mutuality, where the receiving culture becomes the giving culture. Could we have had that informal moment without the formal moments described above? I don't know, but this moment had significant ramifications for our worship on the remainder of the trip. It also demonstrated that worship with teenagers on the mission field may need to sacrifice "normal" patterns to favor worship that is unstructured and informal.

Returning Home

Teenagers as Worship Enliveners

Teenagers have a deep interest in and passion for the whole world, and they are interested in worship gatherings that speak to injustices locally and globally. As we saw in chapter 4, researchers from FYI found that interest in "the centrality of Jesus" and the message he proclaimed "offers congregational leaders both clarity and hope." They went on to write, "Jesus is compelling, and the vast majority of young people in churches growing young want to talk about him."[39] We would do well to let our teenagers enculturate us before we attempt to enculturate them. If the church followed this path, teenagers would certainly participate in worship that beckons them to assume the prophetic voice Jesus exhibited in the familiar scene of worship we mentioned above, Luke 4:14–30.

Jesus, Worship, and Culture

As we discussed in chapter 4, Jesus's public ministry proclaims good news to the poor and release of the captives. It demonstrates that God's work is much bigger than just the individual, and it asks all of us to participate in it. When teenagers participate in and experience worship that is different from however they define *normal*, it will call them to take their cue from Jesus, who will expand their vision for the mission of God in the world and for the church's role in it. No worshiping community paints the full picture of the church past and present. A white teenager needs to worship with the African American church and participate with them in their joyful and exuberant expressions of faith. The Baptist teenager needs to worship beside her

---

39. Kara Powell, Jake Mulder, and Brad Griffin, *Growing Young: Six Essential Strategies to Help Young People Discover and Love Your Church* (Grand Rapids: Baker Books, 2016), 138.

Methodist, Presbyterian, and Roman Catholic friends. The wealthy teenager from the city needs to worship with the poor teenager.

By worshiping with Christians from different cultures and traditions, teenagers learn more about the vast history, theology, and practice of Christian worship that characterize the Christian impulse in the past, present, and future. Teenagers also learn more about worship in their own traditions and communities of faith. When they return from these experiences, their curiosity for the worship practices of their own communities inevitably deepens. As they are drawn deeper into their faith traditions, they will actually be pulled outside of their own tendencies toward self-interest and preoccupation. Worship with the whole world helps teenagers become more self-aware, not only of themselves as individuals but also of the faith and worshiping tradition from which they come.

Then, when teenagers return home to report on their travels, they are prepared to call their congregation to join their singing and praying with the worship of the world. Rather than distilling worship into a show-and-tell, they can use their cultural experiences to offer congregations an invitation to lament, confess, and bless the people, the worship, and the culture from which the teenagers have returned. As a teenager invites the congregation to try on new worship practices with understanding and appreciation, the teenager will assume the role of an enlivener in worship who "embodies the traditions of a faith community and attempts to explore its fullness by sharing its faith heritage in poetry, songs, rituals, and artifacts" rather than reducing "the richness of a tradition to programs, ideas, and logical categories of thought."[40]

When a teenager enlivens the worship of the congregation by expanding its understanding of local and global culture, she will experience transformation that comes from mutuality of worship with Christians around the world, the goal toward which all of our worship practices press. Moreover, as she and other teenagers are drawn from their liturgical homeland, their center of worship, and are invited to participate in the periphery of worship across faith traditions, they will be drawn toward God, and they will help the church do the same. In doing so, teenagers become the prophetic voice for their neighbors down the street and across the world, teaching congregations the values of hospitality, solidarity, and mutuality through worship. More importantly, they teach our congregations that we have an obligation to the global church, and in turn, our teenagers learn the same principles for themselves.

40. Hawn, *Gather into One*, 242.

A Final Scenario

Ben and I kept talking during the ice cream social. We eventually discussed how mission trips usually do more for us than for the people we meet, work with, and sing for. I asked him why he thought the trips did him good, and he proceeded to tell me what I already knew: that he lived with his grandparents, that his mom lived further south, that his dad lived in the Northeast and that he hadn't seen his parents in months. He told me how the adults on that trip were like parents to him. He told me how his friends were like his siblings. Then he said, "This week is the closest I get to experiencing family each year. This is one of the few times I really feel like I'm loving God with all my heart, soul, mind, and strength—and my neighbor as myself." I nodded, smiled, and found myself without words, so I didn't say anything. We continued eating our ice cream as the lights in the fellowship hall dimmed and the recap video from our week played on the screen.

As the video played, I found myself in a moment of personal worship, quietly giving thanks to God for all the young people like Ben who aren't afraid to be honest, ask tough questions, and open themselves up to adults like me at the end of a long week. I began to think about all the congregations I know who are participating in the *missio Dei* through worship and mission, especially those congregations who are reimagining worship and mission for the twenty-first century. Finally, I thought about Jesus, who in Matthew 9 travels among all the cities and the villages, teaching in all the synagogues, announcing the good news of the kingdom, and healing every disease and sickness. I thought about how he had compassion for the large and small crowds he met because they were without a shepherd. I thought about his words: "The harvest is plentiful, but the laborers are few." And I remembered that I am that worker. That you are that worker. That we are those workers. That being a disciple of Jesus means doing so locally as well as globally. What Dean says of teenagers is true for all of us. Being a disciple of Jesus

> assumes that [each of us will] take part in the church's mission—that [each of us] is a missionary called to translate the gospel across boundaries, not because [we are] capable or even interested, but because [we are] baptized and [are] therefore sent into the world as Christ's envoy. The more [we] tell this story, the more it starts to "tell [us]." In other words, as the Holy Spirit aligns [our] lives with the gospel and empowers [us] to proclaim and enact Christ's embrace, a missional imagination takes root: [we] begin to view the world as a place where God acts, and to see [our]selves as participants in God's action.[41]

41. Dean, *Almost Christian*, 97.

In worship across cultures, teenagers connect God's story to the whole world. May we better frame our practices of worship with strangers so that when today's teenagers find themselves eating ice cream in the future with a teenager who asks them, "Did we do any good?" they'll be able to smile, nod their heads, and claim, "Yes. Yes, we did."

PART 3

PASTORAL PERSPECTIVES

7

◆ ◆ ◆

Teenagers, Emotions, and Worship

Wisdom from Philosophy, Sociology, and Anthropology

We are discovering that the rational-materialistic worldview handed down to us from the eighteenth, nineteenth and early twentieth centuries has led to lives that are fractured and broken, and has created personal dysfunction on the grand scale.

—John Drane, *The McDonaldization of the Church*

Two Tensions: Education and Emotions

Worship with teenagers holds two things in tension: the reality that worship should form teenagers to be certain kinds of people in the world and the reality that "experiencing God's immediacy in worship is crucial for adolescents."[1] Historically, the former has focused on worship as a disseminator of theology, a posture of Christian education that assumes that when teenagers worship, they learn about the Christian tradition, which prompts them to behave differently in the world. With the rise of Moralistic Therapeutic Deism (MTD), discussed in chapter 1, this approach has not been as successful as many originally believed it to be. The latter has focused on worship as a disseminator of

1. Kenda Creasy Dean, *Practicing Passion: Youth and the Quest for a Passionate Church* (Grand Rapids: Eerdmans, 2007), 214.

experiences, a posture of performance in which, in its most egregious forms, the performance of worship becomes directed at humans rather than God, and the church becomes a "competitor with the entertainment media for Sunday morning programming."[2] An alternative to MTD is Moralistic Therapeutic Pietism (MTP),[3] and it has in many ways revealed that the entertainment approach to worship has not worked either. Is it any wonder that our attempts at worship renewal have been a "bad fax of entertainment genres"?[4]

In recent years, key voices inside and outside the church have written about the importance of emotions during adolescence. In regard to worship, teenagers must perceive or feel God's presence in order to have a significant spiritual experience. Kenda Creasy Dean writes,

> Worship with adolescents never reduces to issues of style. Young people desire a subjective encounter with the Passion of Christ, a sense of divine immediacy that is mediated through God's majesty and mystery as often as through interpersonal identification with Jesus Christ. . . . Without the ability to point beyond itself, to convey God's give-and-take with creation, worship lacks the power to engender an existential surrender. . . . It is too simple to reduce concerns about worship and adolescents to marketing: What will appeal to the youth? How will we get them to come? What should we avoid so they won't leave once they get here? Hundreds of resources are produced each year to answer such questions, all of them obsolete within a week. Media-saturated, information-overloaded, advertising-savvy adolescents don't really care what we do to attract them, or how we do it. They care that when they worship, God is present, and that something "happens" because God is there.[5]

The first half of this chapter will explore the relationship between teenagers, emotions, and worship through the lenses of philosophy, psychology, and sociology, respectively. The second half of this chapter will study the three lenses together for their collective wisdom that might inform how we approach the relationship between teenagers, emotions, and worship.

2. Dean, *Practicing Passion*, 213.
3. Amanda Hontz Drury, "Moralistic Therapeutic Pietism," *The Princeton Seminary Bulletin* 34 (2017): 30–40. MTP has five tenets: (1) A God exists who created and ordered the world and planned out every day of my life before I was even born. (2) God wants people to be holy and obedient, to pray and read their Bibles, and to share their faith. (3) The central goal of life is to make God happy. (4) God wants to be involved in every single aspect of one's life, and if he's not, his feelings are hurt. (5) Saved people go to heaven when they die. These tenets were compiled not from a sociological survey but from interviews with sixteen teenagers, "the kind of kids you want in your youth group" (34).
4. Dean, *Practicing Passion*, 213.
5. Dean, *Practicing Passion*, 214–15.

Philosophy and Worship in Dialogue

Teenagers Learn Best at the Mall

Though he doesn't write specifically about teenagers, in his book *Desiring the Kingdom*,[6] Calvin University philosopher James K. A. Smith emphasizes a particular way of thinking about the human identity as well as the way that worship works. In a nutshell, Smith argues that we are all "affective, desiring, liturgical animals" who are shaped by liturgies we participate in—both in the church and outside the church.[7] When we are at the mall, we are trained in the corporate liturgy of consumerism. When we are at church, we are trained in the corporate liturgy of faith. When we participate in liturgies at the mall or at church, we become certain kinds of people. These liturgies form the innermost core of our beings by telling us what we love and what we do not love.

The challenge for all of us, Smith claims, is that many Christian institutions—schools, colleges, universities, and churches—have misappropriated their understanding of humans as well as their understanding of the way liturgies shape and form the human person. This misunderstanding is rooted in two prominent yet incorrect views of the human person that owe "more to modernity and the Enlightenment" than to "the holistic, biblical vision of human persons."[8] The first of these views is the human person as thinker, and the second is the human person as believer. Briefly, I want to look at these two views and Smith's critiques of them.

The Human as Thinker and Believer

The vision of the human as thinker can be traced back to philosophers such as Descartes. It is evident in the axiom "I think, therefore I am." In a nutshell, this view claims that people are formed through "a steady diet of ideas." The problem with this view is its failure to account for the fact that the human mind exists within a functioning human body that also has a heart and a soul and hands and feet. "It is just this adoption of a rationalist, cognitivist anthropology that accounts for the shape of so much Protestant worship as a heady affair fixated on 'messages' that disseminate Christian ideas and abstract values (easily summarized on PowerPoint slides)."[9]

6. James K. A. Smith, *Desiring the Kingdom: Worship, Worldview, and Cultural Formation* (Grand Rapids: Baker Academic, 2009).
7. Smith, *Desiring the Kingdom*, 24.
8. Smith, *Desiring the Kingdom*, 31.
9. Smith, *Desiring the Kingdom*, 42.

The second misappropriated view of humanity is the human person as believer. This vision is represented by the age-old axiom "I believe in order to understand." This picture of humanity assumes that all of us are "religious creatures." Smith shows how this view came along and taught that "what defines us is not what we think—not the set of ideas we assent to—but rather what we *believe*, the commitments and trusts that orient our being-in-the-world."[10] Again, Smith claims that the problem with this view of human nature is that religion becomes a set of beliefs and doctrines, when in fact, religion is supposed to be a way of life.

The problem with both of these understandings of humans is that they cause many churches and ministers to approach worship as education or as "a heady project concerned with providing *information*." But worship and education aren't as much about providing *in*formation as they are about providing *for*mation, "shaping and creating a certain kind of people."[11] We can know all the right beliefs, but what follows is doing and practicing what we believe: "Being a disciple of Jesus is not primarily a matter of getting the right ideas and doctrines and beliefs into your head in order to guarantee proper behavior; rather, it's a matter of being the kind of person who *loves* rightly—who loves God and neighbor and is oriented to the world by the primacy of that love. We are made to be such people by our immersion in the material practices of Christian worship—through the affective impact, over time, of sights and smell in water and wine."[12] Smith articulates that public Christian worship is at the heart of all practices, rituals, and routines that paint a picture of the good life.

The Human as Lover

Critiquing the views of the human as thinker and believer, Smith offers a third way to think about the person: the human as lover. He argues that when we view human beings first and foremost as lovers, the stakes are drastically raised for how our worship practices form (or malform) disciples of Christ. This sketch of the human person is rooted in the thought of Saint Augustine, and Smith argues that it is the most complete picture for understanding the way humans work in the world. When we understand the human as lover, the heart, the gut—not the mind—becomes the most important part of the human identity. In other words, we do not primarily make our way in the world by thinking or believing ourselves through it. We make our way around the world as affective, embodied creatures who rarely lead with our heads or our

10. Smith, *Desiring the Kingdom*, 43 (emphasis original).
11. Smith, *Desiring the Kingdom*, 26 (emphasis original).
12. Smith, *Desiring the Kingdom*, 32–33 (emphasis original).

minds. Instead, we lead from the deepest, innermost part of ourselves—our hearts, our guts, our souls—and the desires there define and determine the habits and practices we act with in the world.

This understanding of human beings has significant implications for worship with teenagers. Unpacking Smith's model a few steps further shows how worship works to form the human by directing the aim of love. As affective, desiring, liturgical animals, we aim our love in a particular direction. This aim defines who we are as people. We are not talking about trivial loves, like an affinity for cookie dough ice cream. We are talking about larger loves—what we desire above all else or what we worship. The challenge is that we don't always love the same thing. Our loves are often pointed in different directions. These differences are what define us as individuals and as communities.

Not only are we people who love and desire, but we are also intentional people. In other words, our loves, our desires, always have a target—an end goal, a telos.[13] This goal is not necessarily a set of ideas, rules, propositions, or doctrines. Most of the time, the target is a picture of the "good life" that has captured "our hearts and imaginations" by showing us "what it looks like for us to flourish and live well."[14] Hopefully, the telos that we desire is the kingdom of God. On our quest for the end goal, we begin to act a certain way. We pick up habits, dispositions, ways of being in the world.[15] Our habits are those things we do without thinking about it. They "incline us to act in certain ways without having to kick into a mode of reflection."[16] Our habits are often unconscious, such as beginning to bite our fingernails when we get nervous, but they represent our understanding, our picture of the target, the end goal, the kingdom. These habits become "inscribed in our heart through bodily practices and rituals that train the heart . . . to desire certain ends."[17]

Applying this model to worship as Christian practice, we see that implicitly imbedded in all of our worship gatherings is a target, an end goal, a picture of the "good life," or a vision of the kingdom. This picture of the kingdom forms a vision of the world that functions before thinking or believing. Smith calls this the "social imaginary." Drawing on the work of Stanley Hauerwas, Smith illustrates how this vision is painted most powerfully through art: stories and legends and myths and plays and novels and films and music.[18] This social

13. Smith, *Desiring the Kingdom*, 52–55.
14. Smith, *Desiring the Kingdom*, 53.
15. Smith, *Desiring the Kingdom*, 55–56.
16. Smith, *Desiring the Kingdom*, 56.
17. Smith, *Desiring the Kingdom*, 58.
18. Smith, *Desiring the Kingdom*, 53. See Stanley Hauerwas, "A Story-Formed Community: Reflections on *Watership Down* (1981)," in *The Hauerwas Reader*, ed. John Berkman and Michael Cartwright (Durham, NC: Duke University Press, 2001), 171–99.

imaginary is created not by informing people about doctrine and beliefs but by forming disciples who "intuitively [understand] the world in the light of the fullness of the gospel."[19] But, Smith says, if we are primarily lovers, this presents a problem for the way we practice and lead worship. The problem, he says, is that it's time for many congregations to "own up to the fact" that many of our worship practices are missed opportunities to form pictures of the kingdom of God. Smith writes,

> We fail to draw on the formative riches of the [Christian] tradition and thereby shut down channels for the Spirit's work. . . . We may have construed worship as a primarily didactic, cognitive affair and thus organized it around a *message* that fails to reach our embodied hearts, and thus fails to touch our *desire*. Or we may have construed worship as a refueling event—a chance primarily to get what I "need" to make it through the week (perhaps with a top-up on Wednesday night), with the result that worship is more about *me* than about God, more about individual fulfillment than about the constitution of a people. Or we may have reduced gathered worship to evangelism and outreach, pushing us to drop some of the stranger elements of liturgy in order to be relevant and accessible. In all these cases, we'll notice that some key elements of the church's liturgical tradition drop out. Key historical practices are left behind. While we might be inclined to think of this as a way to update worship and make it contemporary, my concern is that in the process we lose key aspects of formation and discipleship. In particular, we lose precisely those worship practices that function as *counter*-formations to the liturgies of the mall, the stadium, and the frat house. We also lose a sense that worship is the "work of the people"—that the "work of praise" is something we can only do *as a people* who are an eschatological foretaste of the coming kingdom of God. In short, we lose the sense in which Christian worship is also political: it marks us out as and trains us to be a peculiar people who are citizens of another city and subjects of a coming King.[20]

Psychology and Worship in Dialogue

Teenagers Crave Emotional Experiences

Developmental psychologist Erik Erikson (1902–94) spent a considerable amount of time and energy studying the maturation process in children, youth, and adults, with a particular focus on how children socialize and how that socialization affects their understanding of self. Erikson developed a theory

19. Smith, *Desiring the Kingdom*, 68.
20. Smith, *Desiring the Kingdom*, 153–54.

of psychosocial development with eight distinct phases, the first five of which occur prior to the age of eighteen (the other three occur later in life).[21] According to Erikson, at each stage of development a crisis occurs as a result of competition between the needs of the individual and the needs of society. Successful completion of each stage results in a healthy personality; failure to complete each phase risks the inability to advance through other stages, an unhealthy personality, and an unclear picture of the self.

Stage 5 applies to adolescence, the period between ages twelve and eighteen, which Erikson defines as "a turning point of increased vulnerability and heightened potential."[22] In other words, adolescence is the time when children learn who they are by becoming more independent from caretakers while also learning to reinvent themselves according to patterns they see from parents, mentors, celebrities, and the like. During this period, teenagers may "try on" and experiment with different identities as though they were different pieces of clothing, ultimately attempting to build their own identities and emerge on solid footing. Successful navigation of this process instills *fidelity*: "truthfulness and consistency to one's core self or faith in one's ideology."[23] If the adolescent does not establish an identity, the result may be role confusion or identity crisis.

In stage 5 of development, Erikson notes that adolescents are drawn to ecstatic emotional experiences, what he labels "locomotion." The most widespread expression of the discontented search of youth is the craving for locomotion. This may be expressed in a general "being on the go," "tearing after something," or "running around" or in locomotion proper, expressed in vigorous work, absorbing sports, rapt dancing, shiftless *Wanderschaft*, and the employment and misuse of speedy animals and machines. But locomotion also finds expression through participation in the movements of the day (whether the riots of a local commotion or the parades and campaigns of major ideological forces), if teenagers appeal to the need for feeling "moved" and for feeling essential in moving something along toward an open future.[24] Locomotion is a physical and an existential need for adolescents who gauge—consciously or unconsciously—every encounter they have with the question, Did it move me? Teenagers go for an emotional high because, for the first time in their lives, they are actually capable of experiencing it.

21. Erik Erikson, ed., *Youth: Change and Challenge* (New York: Basic, 1963). A helpful overview of Erikson's work can be found in James S. Fleming, "Erikson's Psychosocial Developmental Stages," in *Psychological Perspectives on Human Development* (Prescott, AZ: Southwest Psychometrics and Psychology Resources, 2020).
22. Fleming, "Erikson's Psychosocial Developmental Stages," 12.
23. Fleming, "Erikson's Psychosocial Developmental Stages," 12.
24. Erickson, *Youth*, 11.

The Teenage Brain at Worship

Neuroscientists have confirmed the teenage penchant for emotion by examining the frontal lobes of the adolescent brain through magnetic resonance imaging (MRI).[25] During puberty, adolescents experience significant growth in their frontal lobes, a part of the cerebral cortex where executive functions happen: judgment, insight, and impulse control. These functions assist adolescents with tasks such as resisting impulses, determining possibilities in situations, and planning ahead. The new functional MRI (fMRI), which lets doctors see if the areas that fire together are wired together, has shown that "the connectivity of the brain slowly moves from the back of the brain to the front. The very last places to 'connect' are the frontal lobes. In fact, the teen brain is only about 80 percent of the way to maturity. That 20 percent gap, where the wiring is thinnest, is crucial and goes a long way toward explaining why teenagers behave in such puzzling ways."[26]

The part of the brain that develops earliest in this growth spurt is the amygdala, which contains emotional responses such as joy, fear, and anger. The early development of the amygdala has prompted neuroscientists to suggest that adolescents are in a unique place to seek out and experience the emotional. These findings confirm Erikson's more dated claim that adolescents need, and even seek out, locomotion. Could worship be a type of locomotion for teenagers—one of those ecstatic emotional experiences they crave? Melanie Ross has said, "Theoretically, the answer is yes." Worship "moves" us, physically and existentially, toward the awesome nearness of God, as well as to a profound sense of belonging to a larger whole: the body of Christ. This is a gift to the church; it helps adults reclaim subjective aspects of faith undervalued by modernity.[27]

Sociology and Worship in Dialogue

Interaction Ritual Chains

Though the connection between worship and locomotion for teenagers is by no means explicit, Randall Collins's work on interaction ritual chains suggests that worship could be a type of locomotion, to borrow Erickson's

---

25. Frances Jensen, *The Teenage Brain: A Neuroscientist's Survival Guide to Raising Adolescents* (New York: Harper, 2015), chaps. 1–3.

26. Jensen, *Teenage Brain*, 37.

27. Melanie Ross, "Liturgy and Spiritual Formation" (lecture, Samford University, Birmingham, AL, January 14, 2013).

term. Interaction ritual theory proposes that successful rituals, such as worship, create group membership and infuse participants with emotional energy. Given teenagers' ability to experience emotions in uncanny ways, as well as their penchant for locomotion, interaction ritual chains may be a helpful framework for thinking about short- and long-term liturgical and spiritual formation among teenagers. This ritual theory may even be a helpful puzzle piece in the ongoing challenge of instilling a generative faith in teenagers.

Interaction ritual theory acknowledges that "religious commitment originates in ritual assemblies"[28] and that sense of religious commitment is raised or lowered depending on the amount of emotional energy and connection one experiences as a result of the ritual assembly. In the church's case, the ritual assembly is worship. "Whether one is most attracted to a church service, a political rally, or an intimate conversation," Collins states, "is determined by each individual's expectations of the magnitude of [emotional energy] flowing from that situation."[29] Over time, participation in multiple interaction rituals—an interaction ritual chain—becomes "a model of motivation that pulls and pushes individuals from situation to situation, steered by the market-like patterns of how each participants' stock of social resources—their [emotional energy] and their membership symbols (or cultural capital) accumulated in previous [interaction rituals]—meshes with those of each person they encounter."[30] Though not specific to teenagers, interaction ritual chain theory illustrates that "in mainstream churches . . . , teenagers who have the strongest adherence to [their church's] doctrines are those who have the most personal friends who are also members; social ties brings ritual participation, and this brings belief. And those without close ties in a cult or church tend to drop out, and their belief fades away."[31]

The theory of interaction rituals assumes that rituals contain the emotional ingredients capable of intensifying into shared excitement—what Émile Durkheim calls "collective effervescence"—among a group of people.[32] The most positive result to come from the shared excitement is a sense of moral solidarity as well as an "emotional strength from participating in

28. Randall Collins, *Interaction Ritual Chains* (Princeton: Princeton University Press, 2004), 146.
29. Collins, *Interaction Ritual Chains*, 158.
30. Collins, *Interaction Ritual Chains*, xiv.
31. Collins, *Interaction Ritual Chains*, 97.
32. Quoted in Collins, *Interaction Ritual Chains*, 35. See Émile Durkheim, *The Elementary Forms of the Religious Life*, trans. Joseph Ward Swain (1915; Mineola, NY: Dover, 2008).

the group's interaction. This makes one not only an enthusiastic supporter of the group, but also a leading figure in it."[33] In an interaction ritual, the bodily presence of the assembled individuals affects the participants. Closed to outsiders, the group possesses a mutual focus on the same object. This level of mutual focus creates a high degree of emotional entrainment (or enculturation), in which participants share an emotional/cognitive experience that is reinforced by a feedback process that intensifies the emotional experience.

Ritual Outcomes

When the interaction ritual is successful, a set of ritual outcomes can be anticipated. These include a strong sense of group solidarity and belonging; positive feelings in the individual, such as confidence and enthusiasm; shared symbols that define the interaction (and that may define future interactions); and a "desire for action in what they consider a morally proper path."[34] The individuals in the community come to crave the emotional energy that successful interaction rituals create, giving rise to multiple interaction rituals, known as an interaction ritual chain, which has a "circular, self-perpetuating form."[35] Interaction ritual chains influence people over an extended period of time, giving "a theoretical model of how individuals will be motivated, not just in a single situation, but in the longer-run trajectories of their lives; and it shows how cultural symbols are passed along in chains, sometimes acquiring greater emotional resonance, sometimes losing it."[36]

Successful moments of interaction rituals, and their cumulative chains, are critical pieces for forming groups and the individuals that create them. In the end, interaction rituals are "the events that we remember, that give meaning to our personal biographies, and sometimes to obsessive attempts to repeat them. . . . Where these moments have a high degree of focused awareness and a peak of shared emotion, these personal experiences, too, can be crystalized in personal symbols, and kept alive in symbolic replays for greater or lesser expanses of one's life."[37] Although much more could be said about the nuances of philosophy, psychology, and anthropology, in an effort to bring together this work, I have provided a few closing comments below, none of which are intended to be exhaustive.

33. Collins, *Interaction Ritual Chains*, 108.
34. Collins, *Interaction Ritual Chains*, 42.
35. Collins, *Interaction Ritual Chains*, 131.
36. Collins, *Interaction Ritual Chains*, 142.
37. Collins, *Interaction Ritual Chains*, 43–44.

Collective Wisdom of Philosophy, Psychology, and Sociology

Emotions Are Important for Adolescent Worshipers

What might we learn from the collective wisdom of philosophy, psychology, and anthropology? First, emotions are an undeniably important component of spiritual formation in the teenage years, and the church must find a way to address this truth and all the complexities it presents. This does not mean advocating for manufactured spiritual moments where manipulation runs rampant and worshipers are coerced into emotional moments that prioritize immediacy of feeling over depth of emotion. Worship with teenagers should not be defined by the large-scale events that have come to characterize some youth ministries in the twentieth and twenty-first centuries (though those have a noteworthy place in the broader religious climate). Collins himself notes that many religious persons who experience these emotional highs and are "born again" in some way "drop out of religious participation within a year; many persons are born again numerous times. . . . It is the big, intense religious gatherings that bring forth the emotion and the shift in membership attachment; as one settles back into the routine of smaller and less collectively emotional church services, and then drifts away from attending, the identification and the emotional energy also fade."[38]

In order to correct this all-too-familiar scenario, the church must find a way to balance the approach to worship that privileges expressive worship over formative worship. Expressive worship—associated with immediacy of feeling—asks, "Where are the people at, and how can we match that?" In contrast, formative worship correlates with depth of emotion and asks, "What kind of people are our worship practices forming us to be?"[39]

Worship Is Evocative Rather than Logical

Second, teenagers need the church to focus on the right things. This should be done to foster the appropriate means of entrainment among teenagers. Worship planners and leaders must ensure that "mutual focus of attention" is on the right symbols: those things that "make us love, desire, and want the right thing—God!"[40] Ross writes, "The work of worship is evocative rather than logical. We are not gathering in order to have a coherent, intellectually logical experience of tenets. Our actions have a dream-like logic rather than

38. Collins, *Interaction Ritual Chains*, 61.
39. Ross, "Liturgy and Spiritual Formation," 2.
40. Ross, "Liturgy and Spiritual Formation," 2.

a didactic clarity. This is an important point, for in liturgy we are formed in meta-logical ways, through suggestion, resonance, analogy, and metaphor more than through clearly defined, unequivocal actions and words allowing for only one interpretation."[41]

If churches can learn to appropriate affections, acknowledging them at least as much as they do propositions in worship, then teenagers might be drawn more closely into the worshiping community. If worship is a type of locomotion, and teenagers crave locomotion, then the church needs to assist teenagers who are trying to navigate and learn to distinguish between what John Witvliet calls ritual habits ("ritualized expressions that mark every relationship, whether we know it or not") and ritual moments ("those sweet times of profound intimacy, of sincere emotional connection").[42] While habits are the long-term goal for spiritual formation of teenagers, teenagers are more likely to respond *first*, though that is admittedly difficult for some adults to stomach. This presents a challenge for many congregations who have valued the cognitive over the affective. Yet we must find a way to balance these, for we know that moments of "sincere emotional connection" (or feedback in interaction rituals) occur only after a wide range of habits has been developed by the ritual assembly.

The Arts Are Underutilized in Worship with Teenagers

Third, it seems we have all had meaningful artistic moments. But throughout much of the nineteenth and twentieth centuries, the church at large seemed to be plagued by "the tragedy of a starved imagination."[43] This is certainly true for worship with teenagers, where the arts have been reduced to primarily music and preaching. Forces outside and inside the church became suspicious of the arts, intimidated by the emotions that artistic expression can foster and frightened by an inability to explain artistic encounters with cognitive, rational thinking. This is why not long ago, during worship for a large gathering of Christians that included the full display of all the arts, a large disclaimer was printed in the program asking worshipers not to be offended by graphic images and dancing and videography and the art of silence.

41. Ross, "Liturgy and Spiritual Formation," 2.
42. John D. Witvliet, "Liturgy as God's Language School," *Pastoral Music* 31, no. 4 (April–May 2007): 21.
43. Paul Claudel, *Positions et propositions*, in *Oeurves completes*, vol. 15 (Paris: Librairie Gallimard, 1959), 98–99. Quoted in Patrick Sherry, *Spirit and Beauty: An Introduction to Theological Aesthetics*, 2nd ed. (London: SCM, 2002), 44.

In separate studies, however, sociologist Robert Wuthnow and psychologist Alexis Abernethy claim that there seems to be a renaissance in the art world and in the church. Through statistical surveys, spiritual journey interviews, elite interviews, focus groups, and clergy interviews, both have found "that the arts hold potential as a source of religious revitalization, at least insofar as artistic activities help to nurture interest in spiritual growth."[44] Wuthnow writes, "The data reveal that the vast majority of church members in all three traditions [evangelicals, mainline Protestants, Catholics] consider the arts (here, referring to painting, sculpture, music of all kinds, dance, theater, and creative literature) to be important in their personal lives. Among evangelicals, three-quarters do, and among mainline Protestants and Catholics, more than four in five do. This means that the typical pastor, looking out at his or her flock on a given Sunday morning, can be pretty sure that most of the congregation has some appreciation of the arts."[45]

Wuthnow puts use of the arts at the feet of leaders in the church: "Religious leaders need to understand the profound cultural shift that the current interest in the arts represents. It is a move away from cognition and thus from knowledge and belief, a move toward experience and toward a more complete integration of the senses into the spiritual life. It is uncharted territory. Few clergy have learned anything in seminary that will help them to address it."[46] This seems daunting, yet in a world that is full of lies and terrors, we humans (and the worshipers in our pews) long for beauty. And when the church fails to attend to beauty, "the life of faith becomes grim and onerous. We distort the image of God in ourselves and in our understanding of God's character."[47] When we attend more to God's wrath and God's power than God's beauty, we mute the splendor and loveliness of God (Ps. 27:4), reducing our image primarily to "judicial and moral categories."[48]

Teenagers Need to Belong in the Worshiping Community

Fourth, teenagers must have a sense of status and belonging in public Christian worship; this is really about fitting in with the community. Here, it

---

44. Robert Wuthnow, *All in Sync: How Music and Art Are Revitalizing American Religion* (Berkeley: University of California Press, 2006), 77. See also Alexis D. Abernethy, ed., *Worship That Changes Lives: Multidisciplinary and Congregational Perspectives on Spiritual Transformation* (Grand Rapids: Baker Academic, 2008), 17–18. All essays in Part 2 of Abernethy's book directly relate to worship arts as a means of spiritual growth and transformation.

45. Wuthnow, *All in Sync*, 137.

46. Wuthnow, *All in Sync*, 245.

47. Wuthnow, *All in Sync*, 21.

48. Thomas H. Troeger, *Wonder Reborn: Creating Sermons on Hymns, Music, and Poetry* (New York: Oxford University Press, 2010), 20.

is worth remembering that the worship gatherings teenagers participate in are usually the product of adult planning and leadership.[49]

The interaction ritual chain model proposes that people acquire or lose emotional energy in both power and status interactions. Since adults are the order givers in worship, they maintain and sometimes gain emotional energy while the teenagers, who are order takers, lose it. Being the focus of attention and thereby successfully enacting group membership raises emotional energy; experiencing marginality or exclusion lowers it. Interaction rituals are connected in chains over time, with the results of the last interaction (in emotions and symbols) becoming inputs for the next interaction; thus emotional energy tends to cumulate (either positively or negatively) over time.[50]

Two Gaps in Belonging

An Authenticity Gap

In one of a series of programmatic essays completed on worship formation, Witvliet identifies two gaps that occur in worship practices.[51] Although these gaps are not specific to teenagers, they apply to teenagers, especially in the "normative" practices of faith communities where teenagers are the minority. These gaps are often named after worship in the form of critiques, objections, and complaints, and they manifest themselves in comments and conversations in church hallways and on social media and may be either unspoken or articulated with family over a meal, in objections to attending church, or with friends after a retreat.

Witvliet acknowledges that these gaps are nearly universal in experience and also necessary for worship to be formative. The first of them is a "real-time sincerity or authenticity gap." Witvliet explains that this is what might be expressed in worship and what worshipers might feel. He writes, "People may express this sense of disconnect by communicating things like, 'That song is not meaningful to me,' 'I cannot relate to that.'"[52] This gap comes when we cannot pray that prayer, sing that song, or personalize that sermon. Witvliet also notes that this is a necessary experience for worship to be formative. In other words, we all need "to experience a gap between how I have already been

49. As we've discussed throughout, even where teenagers may lead the music or speak or play another leadership role in adult worship or youth room worship, teenagers remain influenced by the adults who mentor them and bear responsibility for their actions.

50. Collins, *Interaction Ritual Chains*, 118.

51. John D. Witvliet, "Mind the Gaps: Responding to Criticisms of a Formative Vision for Worship and Congregational Song," *The Hymn: A Journal of Congregational Song* 67, no. 4 (Autumn 2016): 33–39.

52. Witvliet, "Mind the Gaps," 34.

formed and how I need yet to be formed if I am to grow." Solving the sincerity and authenticity gap, Witvliet notes, is done by "listening to the people
who experience the greatest gap between their experience and the meaning of
[worship], and discerning how we can best equip them with the framework
or perspective that will embrace [worship] as a formative experience."[53]

A Hypocrisy Gap

The second gap is one that comes "between [worshiping] in public assembly
and how we live the rest of our lives."[54] This particular gap asks how an hour
on Sunday is able to compete with the "entire consumerist industrial complex
of modern culture."[55] The recent Broadway musical *Dear Evan Hansen* had
mass appeal to teenagers, who are immersed in a culture that values an inside
to outside expressivity. The song "Waving through a Window," made popular
by that musical, demonstrates how badly teenagers want to be able to express
themselves from the inside out. Its lyrics say, "Can anybody see, is anybody
waving back at me?"[56] If we don't see our weekly worship as training us for
our vocation of discipleship in the world, we run the risk of keeping what
happens at church "locked up in a liturgical box that is only cracked open
on Sundays." This failure fosters the hypocrisy gap in our praying and our
singing: our worshiping becomes incongruent with our being, and the words
of worship fail to match the ways of our lives. Witvliet says one solution to
the hypocrisy gap is "the pastoral practice of knitting together liturgy and
life, weaving together music and every other form of congregational ministry,
finding ways of letting our liturgical song echo throughout life—encouraging
each other to let our liturgical songs become the soundtrack by which we live."[57]

When teenagers are engaged as worshipers and worship leaders with
help from adult mentors, worship apprentices them into a way of being that
transforms them from the outside to the inside. Teenagers are able to try on
practices in worship, and adults give them ways to retain those practices by
developing habits that can be implemented later in life. These kinds of practices, as Witvliet has noted, hit "right at the very places in ecclesial life that
brim with both potential tension and surprising discovery, places that turn
out to be extremely generative."[58]

53. Witvliet, "Mind the Gaps," 35.
54. Witvliet, "Mind the Gaps," 36.
55. Witvliet, "Mind the Gaps," 36.
56. Ben Platt, vocalist, "Waving through a Window," by Benj Pasek and Justin Paul, recorded
2017, track 2 on *Dear Evan Hansen (Original Broadway Cast Recording)*, Atlantic Records, 2017.
57. Witvliet, "Mind the Gaps," 37.
58. Witvliet, "Mind the Gaps," 36.

As discussed above, emotional energy can accumulate negatively over time by experiencing gaps that come from age or a lack of authenticity and honesty, as Witvliet describes. In these cases the participants—here, teenagers—become products of unsuccessful rituals. At least three types of these rituals exist: failed, empty, and forced. Failed rituals show "a low level of collective effervescence, the lack of momentary buzz, no shared entrainment at all or disappointingly little."[59] Empty rituals show "the missing ingredients," usually a lack of shared attention and shared initial emotion. Forced rituals "occur when individuals are forced to put on a show of participating wholeheartedly in interaction rituals. . . . [They are] energy draining, not creating, and the experience of going through many forced rituals will tend to make individuals averse to those kinds of ritual situations, even creating what appear to be anti-sociable personalities. . . . They have to put energy into giving the impression that they are charged up."[60]

As mentioned in the introduction, the end result of the gap between adults who plan and lead worship and teenagers who participate "reveals the failure of initial primary enculturation. . . . The mistaken hope is that this alternative enculturation would in any way lead people to return to the primary enculturating community and its practices. That's just hardly ever how it works."[61]

Two Siblings in Worship

Friends of mine have two teenagers: their son, Sam, is a junior in high school, and their daughter, Emily, is a freshman. Sam is an honor student, is involved in the band, participates fully in worship every Sunday, and is slightly extroverted. Emily is a gifted child who becomes bored easily. She is extremely introverted but participates in worship every Sunday. Both of them read during the sermon on Sundays because they get bored easily and find their books more interesting than the pastor's words.

Not long ago, I went on a youth retreat where Sam and Emily were present. Toward the end of the worship set, the one-hundred-member youth group sang a chorus a cappella at the worship leader's prompting. I was sitting in the back row, and I noticed Sam looking around with an awkward smile on his face as well as a few tears. Curious, I asked him if he was OK after worship and told him I had noticed he had some tears in worship. His response?

---

59. Witvliet, "Mind the Gaps," 51.
60. Witvliet, "Mind the Gaps," 53.
61. Taylor Burton-Edwards, email to the author, September 29, 2015.

"Yeah, I've just never felt anything like that before in worship—when we were all singing together. I wish that would happen all the time."

Two weeks later, Sam and Emily's mom pulled me aside. "So," she said. "Sunday night Emily came home from church in tears telling me she was afraid she didn't have a relationship with God." Concerned, the mom asked, "What makes you think that, Emily?" Emily had said, "When we were singing, our youth minister told us that if we didn't have our hands up and weren't feeling something, then we weren't really worshiping. Mom, is that true? If it is, I'm in trouble, because I never feel anything when I worship."

Teenagers are, without a doubt, learning things from worship in the church. The question is, What?

8
♦ ♦ ♦

Congregational Worship with Teenagers

A Guide for Change

The psalmist could not see himself as an individual apart from Israel. His self-identity was bound up in his participation in the community of faith.

—C. Hassell Bullock, *Encountering the Book of Psalms*

Introduction: A Typical Sunday

Worshipers rushed into the sanctuary of Trinity United Methodist Church as the band wrapped up the gathering music. Fifteen-year-old Ethan walked to the microphone and said, "Young and old, we have gathered today to worship our Lord. Stand and sing with us as you are able—let's lift our voices together in song." The band began the introduction as the congregation stood, and Ethan's twin brother, Daniel, joined him on the platform along with three other teenagers from the student worship team. These five teenagers led the music, responsive readings, and prayers during the first half of worship, and they returned after the sermon to help conclude the service.

After worship, these teenagers were chatting in a circle when Jewel, a long-time church member in her eighties, interrupted their banter, embraced Ethan with a hug, and said with a beam on her face, "I just love the way you lead us in worship. Your energy is contagious!" Jewel chatted with the teenagers for a few more minutes about the service before heading to Sunday school. This Sunday was not a special occasion. It was an ordinary Sunday morning for this congregation that was transitioning after the departure of their last worship pastor and waiting on the arrival of the next worship pastor. Ethan, Daniel, and their peers ably led worship for their congregation during an interim season, but this would not have been possible if their previous worship leader and student minister had not been intentional about engaging them in worship leadership over the past three years. This would not have been possible if their congregation had not been open to worship as a training ground for students to use their gifts in the body of Christ.

Congregations can't manufacture moments like these, just as they can't control the movements of the Holy Spirit in worship. But they can be attentive to those moments when the Holy Spirit moves in their midst. They can prepare the soil so that when the Holy Spirit employs teenagers' gifts in meaningful ways, everyone recognizes the source of the rain.

Trinity United Methodist Church is an intentional congregation. An intentional congregation is a congregation that purposefully decides to engage teenagers as full, conscious, active participants in its worship life. Long before students began leading all-church worship, the church leaders at Trinity saw something among their teenagers and began the process of engaging teenagers more deeply as worshipers and worship leaders. Their student pastor began teaching teenagers about worship in the church and worship in all of life, and their worship pastor began actively inviting students into worship planning and worship leadership. Teenagers like Ethan and Daniel embraced these roles with willing hearts and open minds.

The question is, What happened before this Sunday? Did Trinity Church simply get lucky with a group of teenagers who were interested, gifted, and mature worshipers and leaders at just the time their church needed them?

Animate

A Laboratory for Worship with Teenagers

This chapter is the fruit of work with teenagers and congregations and of research models grounded in ethnography and practical theology conducted over a period of seven years. Principles from ethnography have allowed me to engage congregations' faith practices through theological reflection and to better understand the faith of the people. Mary Clark Moschella has said, "Sometimes, we can't even know what a congregation's theology really is until we look at what the people there do—how they practice their faith."[1] The same is true of teenagers at worship. We don't really know their theology until we look at what they do and examine how they practice their faith. This particular chapter represents work with congregations, youth ministers, and worship ministers who have thriving models of worship with teenagers.

In the summer of 2014, I began a summer program at Samford University in Birmingham, Alabama, called Animate. Animate was a summer worship leadership program for teenagers and their adult mentors. I liked to think that it was more than a one-off summer camp. I often said, "Animate is not a product; it is an invitation to a process." Animate was intergenerational and highly relational, mostly peer-to-peer. Over five days, teenagers were invited into a process of worshiping, reflecting on the experience of worship, acquiring worship leadership skills, planning and leading worship, and celebrating their gifts for the church. Teenagers were equipped and encouraged to find their voices in their local congregations in the weeks following Animate.

Animate averaged sixty-five participants every summer. These teenage participants ranged in ages from twelve to nineteen, with a sixty-to-forty ratio of females to males and a seventy-to-thirty ratio of teenagers to adults. Participants represented multiple races and ethnicities, and they came from Protestant and Roman Catholic traditions from as many as sixteen states in the United States. Though implicit to the average teenager, the Animate schedule followed a pattern borrowed and expanded from practical theology: prepare, experience, reflect, transfer, act.[2] This pattern happened on a macro and micro level as students participated in worship, afternoon workshops, panel discussions, small groups, innovative pedagogies, and other formative activities.

There are other programs around the country like Animate, and like Animate, many of them were sponsored by Lilly Endowment. The first wave of these summer programs in Protestant circles started in the late '90s and early 2000s in seminaries such as Duke, Yale, Princeton, and Candler. There, high school youth theology institutes had the central goal of teaching teenagers theology, and worship was a daily experience in many of them. In the early

1. Mary Clark Moschella, *Ethnography as Pastoral Practice: An Introduction* (Cleveland: Pilgrim, 2008), 40.
2. Andrew Root and Kenda Creasy Dean, *The Theological Turn in Youth Ministry* (Downers Grove, IL: IVP, 2011), 45–46.

2000s, Roman Catholic communities birthed liturgical programs: One Bread, One Cup (Saint Meinrad Seminary and School of Theology in Indianapolis) and Music Ministry Alive (with David Haas). More recently, programs like Animate at Samford, Awakening at Hope College, Worship Arts Lab at Azusa Pacific University, and the Worship Lab at Baylor have come into existence with the specific goal of training teenage worship leaders. I anticipate more programs such as these will appear in the years ahead, and I'm excited about it.

Characterizing these programs in a plenary at the Hymn Society conference in 2016, John Witvliet noted, "One fascinating part of many of these mentoring or apprenticeship programs is that they work with dozens of high school and college-age students who grow up immersed in a culture that values *inside out* expressivity and introduce them to a world of [spiritual formation that works] *outside-in* to shape new experiences. These are the young people who live, it appears, at the epicenter of our culture's concern for immediate gratification and yet show such openness to a formative vision for worship."[3]

What captured my attention since beginning Animate in 2014 was teenagers' love for the church, their eagerness to engage in its ministry, and their openness to (and I might say hunger for) a formative vision for worship. In the process of developing and running Animate, I began learning from these teenagers, their parents, their adult ministers, and their congregations alongside my colleagues and a small handful of Samford undergraduate and graduate students. We surveyed more than four hundred teenagers—some multiple times over a period of three or four years—and conducted fieldwork with eighteen congregations from different denominational, geographical, ethnic, and liturgical traditions and sensitivities. Some of these were Animate participants, and some were not.

Worship and Change in a Congregational Context

One of the challenges Animate encountered was helping youth ministers, worship ministers, and teenagers incorporate the principles from Animate into their congregations when they returned home. This was not unlike the challenge that many church leaders and teenagers face after attending a conference or camp. In those experiences, they were transformed, had a new way of seeing things, and felt the need to share that transformation with their

3. John D. Witvliet, "Mind the Gaps: Responding to Criticisms of a Formative Vision for Worship and Congregational Song," *The Hymn: A Journal of Congregational Song* 67, no. 4 (Autumn 2016): 36.

congregations. After Animate, many church leaders and teenagers wanted to make changes in their approach to all-church worship and youth group worship. The lesson we learned from history, however, is that change in any congregation requires careful thought, reflection, and planning.

Trinity United Methodist Church—the church in my opening story—is one of those congregations that participated in Animate every year since its inception. This congregation was an example of what we called an intentional congregation. Trinity was an intentional congregation because it made intentional decisions in the planning and leading of worship where teenagers were concerned. Long before the Sunday experience in the opening story, the church leaders at Trinity began to respect the talent and sincerity of the young Christians in their midst and engage them more deeply in the worship life of the church. Through their slow, careful, deliberate planning, this congregation incorporated teenagers into the leadership of the entire congregation, beginning with worship.

Congregations wanting to make this change, or other changes, would do well to follow the example of Trinity Church, a church that worked to engage teenagers as worshipers and leaders for multiple years. Congregations must be in it for the long haul. They must acknowledge that lasting change requires a marathon, not a sprint. This is true because worship is but one part of a much larger whole.

The Worship System

Understanding Worship in Congregational Contexts

Lawrence Hoffman has illustrated that worship is a system that belongs to a larger system: the church or synagogue (see fig. 8.1).[4] Within the church or synagogue system, worship is a first-generation system. Other first-generation systems include ministries for education, children, and youth. Each of these first-generation systems affects the others. So a change in one system might affect the worship system and so on. For instance, if the children's ministry adds children's church on Sunday mornings, the larger worship system feels it when children are absent from all-church worship. If the larger worship system adds a children's sermon, the children's system feels it in the volunteers and lessons they may need to coordinate. Similarly, problems in the worship system can often be addressed through another system. For instance, if teenagers

4. Lawrence A. Hoffman, *The Art of Public Prayer: Not for Clergy Only*, 2nd ed. (Woodstock, VT: SkyLight Paths, 2009).

Figure 8.1
Congregational System

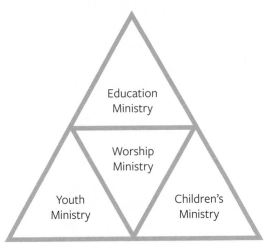

Adapted from Hoffman, *Art of Public Prayer*, 69.

fail to engage the worship system, the youth system might help by teaching teenagers about worship.

Worship is a first-generation system composed of at least three second-generation systems: the individual at worship, the worshiping group, and the physical environment in which worship occurs (see fig. 8.2). The first second-generation system is the individuals who come to worship. They come from a system external to the church, such as a family, occupation, or economic system, and these and other factors influence the concentration, participation, and comprehension of the individuals at worship. They will possess different personalities, aptitudes, and moods.

Individuals who come to worship give rise to the second second-generation system: the worshiping group. The worshiping group possesses a common worship language and familiar liturgical structure that help meet the needs of the individuals who make up the group. Because individuals depend on the group to meet needs, the group also develops needs: to sense that God is somehow present in worship and to identify with those things that bind worshipers together and relate their identities to God. As the group worships, it defines who God is, and it defines who it is. It also defines who God is not, and it defines who it is not. Worship reinforces the group's view of God and the identity of the group. Worship also forms boundaries between worshiping communities that may be theological, musical, cultural, technological, or otherwise.

The third second-generation system is the physical environment in which worship occurs, or "the set of worship props."[5] The prop system contains all those items with which the worshiping group identifies, such as prayer books, hymnals, screens, pews, crosses, clothing, or other items. Props "remind us of who we are, tell us that our group and its values are supremely important, and suggest the possibility of God's presence among us." So "when a group finds its self-image changing, the first thing it generally does is change the props, since it identifies them as 'just things,' and it is easier to tamper with things than with the group members, who are people."[6] The goal is for the entire system to find harmony between its beliefs about God and its attitudes toward people.

Figure 8.2
Worship System

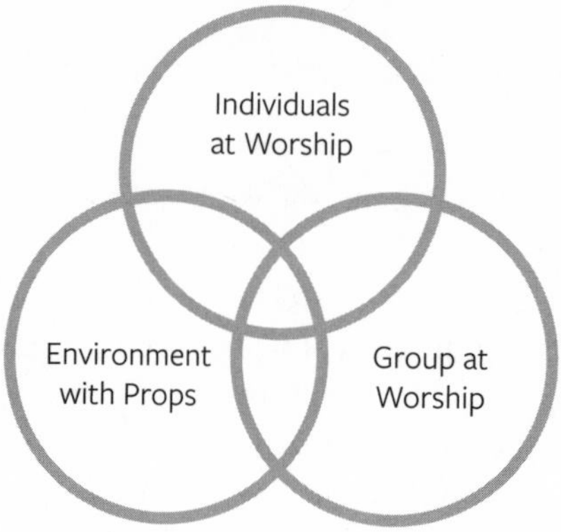

Difficulty in the Worship System

When our worship does not find harmony, we increase our risk of conflict or of creating a dysfunctional worship system that competes with rival systems. Rival systems minimize God and ignore the gathered community and the church's mission in the world. When they do this, worship becomes "an empty vessel into which a host of extraneous activities have been poured."[7] In youth ministry, an example of a rival system might be games that water

5. Hoffman, *Art of Public Prayer*, 83.
6. Hoffman, *Art of Public Prayer*, 84.
7. Hoffman, *Art of Public Prayer*, 91.

down the work of worship, though the spirit they embody, of play and improvisation, might be helpful ingredients for the worship system with teenagers.

A more challenging rival system might be arguments about worship. Although conflict can be "unhealthy and destructive" and "should not be baptized as good by virtue of its ability to engender the passions of the congregation and its young people," some moments of argument and conflict where worship is concerned may be helpful, even to teenagers. Reflecting on her work with two congregations, Joyce Ann Mercer writes that "if young people are privy to adults fighting with passion about issues that matter, they will come away with a sense of Christianity not as a crowd of bickering rabble-rousers, but as a living, changing, growing entity, ever renewing itself to better reflect the image of God."[8]

Worship Pathology

Hoffman labels two ways that rival systems manifest themselves: pathology and dysfunction. Pathology is "when a single worshiper ruins worship for everyone else."[9] Hoffman labels four types of individuals at worship: watchers, regulars, movers, and professionals (see fig. 8.3). Any one of these individuals might do harm to the worship system by allowing "their own needs to encroach on successful public prayer."[10]

Watchers almost never come to worship. When they are present, it is usually for a reason other than to worship, such as their teenager being honored at graduation. They rarely hurt the worship system, but their presence changes the dynamics within the worship system. For instance, if a father attends Senior Sunday and the minister makes worship about evangelizing the father, the opportunity to name God in an important moment for teenagers is lost, and dysfunction has occurred.

The second group is the regulars, and they are the opposite of watchers. They "come all the time, not only to worship services, but to almost everything else." Regulars have internalized worship communications and, what may be worse, possess or believe they possess the authority to "influence them for better or worse."[11] The third group is the movers, individuals who sit between the watchers and the regulars, moving between the two extremes

---

8. Joyce Ann Mercer, "Calling amid Conflict: What Happens to the Vocations of Youth When Congregations Fight?," in *Greenhouses of Hope: Congregations Growing Young Leaders Who Will Change the World*, ed. Dori Grinenko Baker (Herndon, VA: Alban Institute, 2010), 187–88.

9. Hoffman, *Art of Public Prayer*, 99.

10. Hoffman, *Art of Public Prayer*, 107.

11. Hoffman, *Art of Public Prayer*, 103.

Figure 8.3
Individuals at Worship

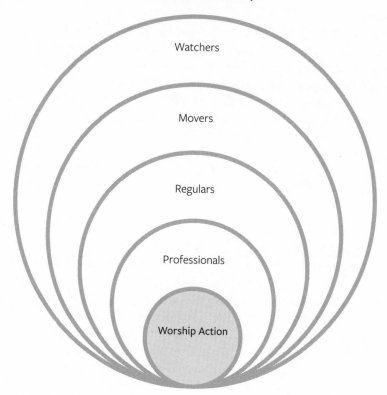

of barely attending or attending all the time. "It is the group of increasingly marginalized regulars, the people who resent being moved away from the center of power, which most often generates malignant behavior, especially at times of change when the rules are not taken for granted by almost everyone."[12]

The fourth group is the professionals, the ministers who bear responsibility for worship and other ministries of the church. They are "not completely free to decide how worship should proceed" because they "can be hired and fired." This group has studied and understood "the boundaries governing worship." Serving as "parental figures," they know what is right and what is wrong, what can be changed and what must be kept the same. At times, their innovations "can fail and become pathological."[13]

12. Hoffman, *Art of Public Prayer*, 106.
13. Hoffman, *Art of Public Prayer*, 107.

Worship Dysfunction

Worship pathology is easily identifiable because it points to a specific person or small group. The second issue, worship dysfunction, is much more difficult to identify. Hoffman describes this way: "Everyone seems to be doing everything right, but worship doesn't happen."[14] The challenge of worship dysfunction is that "dysfunctional systems often function very well at doing things that we do not claim we want them to do. . . . The worship system may be functioning quite well, then, at something other than worship."[15]

Worship may become a place for entertainment, like a Christian *American Idol*, where we socialize with friends, award people, and recognize civic events and holidays but do not worship. Hoffman claims that worship dysfunction is too prevalent among churches today: "Worship dysfunction has been going on for so long that people are not even sure they can or should pray. So, changing the worship system to facilitate worship will require, first and foremost, the recognition that worship moments are desirable and possible."[16] When dysfunction occurs, worship becomes ritualization that is routine, empty, and hollow—or glitzy, glamorous, and marketable.

When dysfunction happens, Hoffman claims, it is time for church leaders to lead the congregation to change. "Ritual is not the result of faith, but one of its causes—that is why we need good rituals. Ritual's power lies in its artistic capacity to present an alternative world where time and space unfold in structured ways that indicate pattern, plan, and purpose. Faith derives from trusting that the universe in which we live is meaningful and ordered, as opposed to being random, chaotic, and accidental."[17]

Four Congregational Models of Worship with Teenagers

While there is no single size or shape of youth worship in the United States, some common trends and patterns do prevail. In my work with congregations, teenagers, youth ministries, and worship ministries, I have found that one of the easiest ways to think about teenage worship is to use Hoffman's understanding of the worship system. This begins by studying worship ministry and youth ministry, which are both first-generation systems within the larger congregational system. We then gather information about all-church worship and student

14. Hoffman, *Art of Public Prayer*, 108.
15. Hoffman, *Art of Public Prayer*, 109.
16. Hoffman, *Art of Public Prayer*, 112.
17. Hoffman, *Art of Public Prayer*, 117.

worship by considering the second-generation systems: individuals, groups, and props. Who is leading, and who is worshiping? Adults or teenagers? Laypersons or professionals? What are their dispositions? What are the props of worship?

Four models emerge from approaching teenage worship in this way, as illustrated in figure 8.4. In one scenario, adults lead all-church worship, where all ages are worshipers, and teenagers represent a minority in the worshiping community. In another scenario, adults lead worship as professionals, where students are worshipers and teenagers are a majority in the worshiping community, such as at a conference, camp, or retreat weekend. In a third scenario, teenagers lead all-church worship on an occasion such as Youth Sunday, and in a fourth scenario, teenagers lead student worship for their peers. This final scenario is a prevalent model for worship in the youth room on a Sunday or Wednesday evening. Hoffman's system theory is useful for thinking about promises and possibilities with these models.

Figure 8.4
Models of Worship with Teenagers

	All-Church Worship	Student Worship
Adult Leaders	**Model 1: All-Church Worship** Adults lead all-church worship, where all ages are worshipers, and teenagers represent a minority in the worshiping community.	**Model 2: Camps, Conferences, and Retreats** Adults lead students in worship for a special event, such as a conference or retreat. Teenagers represent a majority in the worshiping community.
Student Leaders	**Model 3: Youth Sunday Worship** Teenagers lead all-church worship, where all ages are worshipers, and teenagers represent a minority in the worshiping community.	**Model 4: Youth Group Worship** Teenagers lead student worship for their youth group, Christian school, or a small group, and teenagers represent a majority in the worshiping community.

Model 1: All-Church Worship

We will refer to this first model as "all-church worship," where presumably all ages are worshipers, and teenagers represent a minority in the worshiping community. In this model, teenagers are participants in intergenerational worship, wherever they may fall on the spectrum as watchers, movers, regulars, or professionals. Adult worshipers and worship leaders model worshiping and worship leadership for teenagers. They teach about worship from the authority and experience they bring naturally as worship leaders, and teenagers conceive of them as professionals because of their age or training. They are perceived as parental figures who know what is right in worship. And an official meaning about what the congregation or its leadership believes about worship is placed on the props of worship.

Dysfunction or pathology in this model is that the "product" of all-church worship is usually a result of adult planning and adult leadership in a church of many ages. The voice of teenagers, as far as worship is concerned, may not always be heard. When it is heard, teenagers may not feel heard because they are not involved in leadership. Worship is seen by these teenagers as an activity led by adults, and it is presumably for adults. Whether this is true or not, it is how it is perceived, and this means teenagers who attend worship regularly are more likely to function as movers who consistently vacillate toward or away from the primary action of worship. If teenagers don't see their age group providing worship leadership in all-church worship, they are unlikely to imagine themselves as members in the community of faith when they are twenty-five, thirty, or thirty-five, meaning they may function as watchers by the time they graduate from high school.

Model 2: Camps, Conferences, and Retreats

The second scenario applies to camps, retreats, and conferences where adults lead student worship and teenagers represent a majority of the worshiping community. Like with all-church worship, in this model adult "professional" worship leaders model worshiping and worship leadership for teenagers. They teach about worship from the authority and experience they bring as adults. In this scenario, teenagers are free to worship with their peers, as well as spend more time in fellowship with them before and after worship, because they don't have leadership responsibilities. Because teenagers are the majority in this worship setting, they are likely to move closer to the liturgical action than they might in the first scenario.[18]

Dysfunction and pathology might come from the fact that the "product" of this worship is a result of adults planning and leading worship. Adults in leadership, especially a professional band, can be out of the loop regarding teenagers' current life situations, be prone to sentimentality ("When I

---

18. An exception to this is those congregations where teenagers sit in the front pews during all-church worship.

was your age . . ."), and hinder teenagers' honest expressions in worship (bodily posture, engagement in song, etc.). More often, however, the real challenge to worship is that it may be primarily entertainment. Hoffman writes, "Dysfunctional systems often function very well at doing things that we do not claim we want them to do. They are dysfunctional only from the perspective of our own arbitrary definition of what they are supposed to do."[19]

Model 3: Youth Sunday Worship

In the third model, teenagers lead all-church worship, where all ages are worshipers, and teenagers represent a minority of the worshiping community. The congregation participates in intergenerational worship, which we know has a lasting impact. Here, teenagers serve as the professionals and have opportunities to add their voice to the church's worship life. Teenage worship leaders from this scenario are more likely to be mentored by an adult on the worship team or a minister in the church. Teenage worshipers are interested when their peers lead them in worship, and they function more like regulars. In this scenario, both teenage worshipers and worship leaders join an intergenerational community of worshipers and worship leaders. Teenagers might see worship leadership as something they can do when they're older, and they might begin to imagine themselves as members in the community of faith when they are twenty-five, thirty, or thirty-five.

Pathology and dysfunction in this model can come from the amount of time that is needed for planning and rehearsing so that teenagers can lead well. Not all teenagers have the necessary time to give to preparation, and not all adults are willing to give time to mentor teenagers. When worship is led by teenagers out of necessity, teenagers may not have an adult mentor, and as a result, their own spiritual formation may suffer or differences in worship style among the generations may be more pronounced in worship planning and leading. Teenagers may also become a "token" or "security blanket" to older members in the congregation who may be concerned about the longevity of the church, and in this case, worship is again reduced to entertainment.

Model 4: Youth Group Worship

In this fourth and final model, teenagers lead worship for their youth group, Christian school, small group, or another group where they represent a major-

19. Hoffman, *Art of Public Prayer*, 109.

ity of the worshiping community. The teenage worship leader, the "professional," will likely be more in touch with the group's current life situation, less prone to adult sentimentality, and able to encourage other teenagers' honest expressions in worship as they model it for their peers. Teenage worship leaders are also more likely to be mentored by an adult in youth ministry and have more opportunities to add their voices to the church's worship life. Teenage worshipers in this scenario will function more as regulars, though movers and watchers will inevitably exist. Younger teenagers might see worship leadership as something they can do when they're twenty-five, thirty, or thirty-five.

Pathology and dysfunction here come from teenage worshipers who may not respect the peer leading them in worship, and the authority of the teenage worship leader may be challenged by the teenage worshiper. In one scenario, the worship leader may become a local celebrity, and worship becomes a time to perform. On the flip side, teenage worshipers may not respect the teenager up front and claim something like, "She made me mad at school today; I can't believe they let her up front."

Not all youth ministers or adults who supervise teenagers have had training in worship, and as a result, one person—often a teenager—becomes responsible for choosing the music, planning the transitions, determining the spoken words, creating the slides, printing the music, planning the rehearsal, leading the rehearsal, and communicating with the speaker. A particular challenge that comes from this scenario and is common among teenage worship leaders is burnout. For instance, Scott, a recent high school graduate, reported that he led worship as many as four times a week his senior year: twice for his high school chapel services, once for his church youth group on Wednesday night, and once again for all-church worship on Sunday morning. Though Scott was gifted as a worship leader, by the time he arrived at the college campus where I once taught, he was burned out from the intense schedules of rehearsing and leading, and in his words, he was "ready to take a break for a while." Scott changed his major from worship leadership to business and has yet to resume the role of worship leader.

Dysfunction in the System

In many of the congregations I work with, I have noticed that religiously engaged teenagers participate in multiple worship gatherings each week and year. These gatherings may take the shape and form of any of these models. Teenagers worship with the whole church on the weekend, and they worship with the youth group during the week. This is not to imply that youth ministry worship is bad or that Sunday morning worship is bad, but in many cases, these worship practices compete with one another.

If teenagers consistently experience one style or form of worship with the whole church, another style or form on Wednesday nights, and perhaps yet other styles when youth ministries and worship ministries and preaching ministries are all operating in silos, then teenagers are bound to receive mixed theological messages, prefer one service over the other, and experience uncertainty about what worship actually is. In Hoffman's language, these worship practices become rival systems to one another so that when it comes to worship, our teenagers "don't even know what to look for!"[20] Taken together, the various worship practices display a conceptually brittle theological framework, nebulous boundaries between culture and faith, and blurred conceptions of God. Is it any wonder our teenagers' faith has not been able to weather the secularization of society?

Impact of Teenage Engagement

Impact on the Teenager

What is the impact of congregations who work to engage teenagers as worshipers and worship leaders? Truthfully, it is difficult to tell. Kathleen Cahalan says, "Impact is a way of talking about how the project activities affect people, particularly the people who face the problem, need, question, or opportunity."[21] While impact is important, it is often intangible. That said, a number of impact areas have arisen in the exploration of these models. Models 3 and 4 may have the most significant impact on teenagers in the faith community because they put teenagers in a position of leadership, and the best versions of these models encourage mentoring relationships with adults in the worshiping community.

What follows are some of the long-term effects that can happen as a result of models 3 and 4. This is not to say that these effects fail to happen in models 1 and 2, but they are significantly more pronounced in models 3 and 4. First, all teenagers find a sense of place and identity. Youth worshipers who see their peers in leadership more readily see people in their age group as valid members of the body of Christ. Worship isn't something that only adults do; it's something that teenagers in the church do too. Teenage worship leaders

20. Hoffman, *Art of Public Prayer*, 112.
21. Kathleen A. Cahalan, *Projects That Matter: Successful Planning and Evaluation for Religious Organizations* (Herndon, VA: Alban Institute, 2003), 17.

realize they belong in the church as worshipers and that their gifts are needed. Teenage worship leaders find agency and become further rooted in the life of the church because of that agency. Adult ministers and volunteers are interested in mentoring them, investing in them, and helping them use their gifts for the common good. These teenage worship leaders are more likely to imagine themselves as members of the church in the future.

By engaging teenagers as leaders in all-church worship and in student worship, adults are "making the accidental intentional."[22] Teenagers often attend worship because their parents make them or because their friends are there, making them movers in the congregational system. They are also often interested in leading worship because they realize they enjoy music, they are good at public speaking, or someone sees their skills and invites them to participate. In each case, teenagers aren't programmed to think first about the long-term value of what they are doing in their own faith lives. Teenagers aren't programmed to think about the mechanics—the nuts and bolts—of worship unless someone encourages it and takes time to explain it to them. When teenagers lead worship, the significance of their role as worshipers is highlighted, and adults make the accidental act of going to church very intentional.

When teenagers are brought into leadership roles in worship, they develop an expanded vision of leadership, with the help of adults. Because of leadership in worship, teenagers are drawn into other areas of leadership, such as ecclesial and civic leadership. Multiple roles in worship leadership develop many leaders, and congregations with multiple leaders in worship have teenagers who are more likely to see themselves leading in the present or in the future. In fact, it is more important for teenagers to see many diverse leaders than to see peers near their age in leadership. In contrast, congregations with only a few leaders in worship have teenagers who are less likely to see themselves leading in the present or future.

Worship that happens in the church also begins to happen in life. Teenagers who are regulars and who say worship is relevant to them often describe their personal spiritual formation (Bible study, prayer, etc.) as lacking. Put another way, the practices of worship (prayer, Scripture, response) that teens might experience on Sunday are missing from their lives Monday through Saturday. This is true because teenagers are immersed in a culture that values an inside to outside expressivity. When teenagers are engaged well as worshipers and worship leaders and when they have help from adult mentors, worship apprentices them into a way of being that transforms them from the outside to

22. My colleague Charles E. Stokes introduced this phrase to apply to our work.

the inside. Teenagers "try on" practices in worship, and adults give them ways to retain those practices, developing habits so they can improvise in life. This creates an identity schema that can be awakened later in life.

Additionally, teenagers learn to appreciate and innovate. In other words, when teenagers learn about and appreciate the worship life of the church, they then help the church innovate out of the tradition they have created. Teenagers—when given an opportunity to provide input—have some strong thoughts and opinions about what happens in the worship life of the church. Sometimes, and even often, those opinions are not informed by a congregation's local history or the church's global history. When these traditions are explained, teenagers engage them, are eager to embrace them, and are interested in adopting and adapting them in new ways.

Teenagers are at a critical point, and if they find their place in the church, they are more likely to imagine themselves in the church in the future. They develop a sort of ecclesial imagination, which is important in light of research that shows an approximate 50 percent attrition rate for teenagers between high school and college. I have asked a number of teenage worshipers and worship leaders, "What will get your thirty-year-old self up and to church when no one else is there to wake you?" (Several students have said they'd like to find a church with services at night, but that is a story for another day.) Many of them have responded to that question by saying, "I'll be most likely to go to church if I have a responsibility." Worship leadership is one of those possible responsibilities.

Many teenagers express a curiosity about worship, and some even like the idea of planning or leading it. Worship leadership provides teenagers with the opportunity to experience and reflect on the psychological concept of "flow." Flow is commonly described as a moment when an individual's performance excels and they are "in the zone." Flow occurs when an individual's skill level and the challenge at hand are equal, though the latter often increases the former.[23] For our purposes, flow is when teenagers meet a difficult task, such as worship leadership, and rise above their abilities to nail it. This is an interesting inverse to an emotional high that teenagers may experience as worshipers in a camp, retreat, or conference. What teenagers come up with can be very interesting and at times wonderfully creative and brilliant. On other occasions, their solutions can be less than theologically or biblically sound, but this is fine. Those moments are great opportunities for teaching and asking questions that reveal the teenagers' perceptions about worship.

23. Mike Oppland, "8 Ways to Create Flow according to Mihaly Csikszentmihalyi," Positive Psychology.com, https://positivepsychology.com/mihaly-csikszentmihalyi-father-of-flow/.

This activity is about engaging those teenagers who are primarily worshipers to think more critically about worship. There are other ways to engage those teenagers who are active as worship leaders—leading music, prayer, reading, and even preaching. All along the way, teenagers need guidance and confidence from adult mentors.

Finally, worship becomes a portal for becoming a more faithful disciple of Jesus Christ. I have seen a number of students attend our summer worship leadership program to talk about worship. Inevitably, deeper theological questions always arise. University students who lead small groups of teenagers have repeatedly said that a conversation about worship evolves into a conversation about theological concepts that are implicitly related to worship. During a discussion panel about worship, a Catholic priest was present to talk about worship in the Catholic tradition, and he happened to mention that he was formerly Baptist. That whole panel evolved into a conversation about switching denominations, and there was nothing we could do to get back on track.

Impact for the Church

What may be the impact of engaging teenagers as worshipers and worship leaders in congregations for the church? First, this will create an established network of teenagers, students, congregations, leaders, and lay leaders with a sense of understanding, buy-in, vision, and empathy toward the promises and challenges of worship practices among generational cohorts in specific congregations. Finding a balance between being too centered on youth and ignoring youth is important to a healthy intergenerational church.

Second, I hope to cultivate in individual teenagers and groups of teenagers the ability to practice and experiment with worship leadership. Through worship leadership, we have created opportunities to reframe the way teenagers participate, engage, see, and are seen in the lives of congregations, especially where worship is concerned. In the end, this is about not isolating teenagers but encouraging them and promoting their agency within the context of intergenerational community. This, however, is a countercultural approach and model because negotiating the messiness of worship practices and styles where teenagers are concerned is difficult for most communities of faith. A youth worship subculture already exists; our goal is to enter that world and bring teenagers into a broader world.

The long-term impact of engaging teenagers intentionally will promote the full, active, conscious participation of teenagers in the worship life of the church. More importantly, it is cultivating within young people the capacity and respect necessary to understand worship in all its fullness and to be agents of positive change in the liturgical life of the communities in which they reside. We are working to reframe the historical conversation of youth ministry and worship and innovation from a fear-based approach that argues, "We must invent new worship styles to keep teenagers in the church," to an approach that says, "By engaging the broad tradition of Christian worship through intergenerational gatherings, individual practices, transferrable leadership models, and multiple opportunities to connect, we can foster the full, active, conscious participation of teenagers in the worship life of the church."

Shifting Assumptions

Wendell Berry writes, "We have lived our lives by the assumption that what was good for us would be good for the world. . . . We have been wrong. We must change our lives so that it will be possible to live by the contrary assumption, that what is good for the world will be good for us. And that requires that we make the effort to know the world and learn what is good for it."[24] I often wonder what would happen if we replaced the phrase *the world* with the word *teenagers*: "We have lived our lives by the assumption that what was good for us would be good for [teenagers]. We have been wrong. We must change our lives so that it will be possible to live by the contrary assumption, that what is good for [teenagers] will be good for us." And that requires that we make the effort to know teenagers and learn what is good for them. My hope is that the church will continue in the effort to know teenagers and learn what is good for them—how we might offer prayers, songs, and spiritual formation with them for the good of the whole church.

---

24. Wendell Berry, "A Native Hill," in *The Long-Legged House* (Berkeley: Counterpoint, 2012), 220.

9
♦ ♦ ♦

Youth Group Worship with Teenagers

A Guide for Formation

> Do not depend on the hope of results. . . . The big results are not in your hands or mine, but suddenly happen, and we can share them, but there is no point in building our lives on this personal satisfaction, which may be denied us and which after all is not that important.
>
> —Thomas Merton, *Letter to a Young Activist*

The Rhythm of Worship in Youth Ministry: A Personal Testimony

The year was 2007. I was fresh out of seminary, and I was in my first full-time youth ministry position. I had inherited a youth ministry that followed a weekly calendar that included Sunday night Rendezvous, which was a time of fellowship and worship. The fellowship part of this was easy. Worship included a time of song, Scripture, and prayer. On Wednesday nights we hosted Refuge, a time of worship and Bible study that included twenty-five minutes of song, Scripture, prayer, and teaching, followed by small group discussion. I oversaw the planning of these youth-specific worship times, which included a band composed of high school student worship leaders who helped with the planning. Beyond this weekly schedule, the youth ministry's annual calendar included a fall retreat and a midwinter retreat, and we did these retreats in collaboration with two local youth groups. Our church's responsibility, which I inherited, was to plan worship for these events in concert with guest musicians and speakers.

No one told me that as a youth minister I would be responsible for overseeing all of this worship planning and leadership, not to mention worship at summer camps and other retreats. Planning worship—whether by myself or with others—became challenging for me in the context of an otherwise quite full youth ministry. Empowering teenagers to engage in worship and provide leadership set up an equally difficult challenge. Combined, both caused significant tension. On the one hand, I believed worship was important—very important—for these teenagers. On the other hand, I had only a limited number of hours in my week to do the administration, preparation, pastoral care, and other tasks required by youth ministry. Worship became a last-minute attempt to pull it together on Sundays and Wednesdays as best I could. I would leave church afterward thinking that our time in worship as a youth group could have been so much better.

My seminary education taught me about the history and theology of worship in the church, but it failed to adequately address the nuts and bolts of worship planning and leadership. I studied worship planning and leadership while pursuing my church music degree, but none of my classes equipped me to think adequately about worship through the eyes of a teenager. Like in my experience, many youth ministers find themselves responsible for planning and implementing worship gatherings with teenagers on a regular basis. Yet few youth ministers have formal training in worship planning and leadership. And many worship ministers are already responsible for planning one or more weekly worship gatherings, balancing multiple priorities as well as congregational demographics.

This chapter is written for both of those individuals: youth ministers who want to be more intentional with worship in the youth room and worship ministers who want to better engage teenagers with worship in the sanctuary. My aim is to present a rich model of adolescent spiritual formation through the regular patterns of worship teenagers engage and participate in on a weekly basis. These weekly patterns of worship are in contrast to the mountaintop experiences that many of us think about when we think about teenage worship practices—those moments teenagers experience at youth camps, denominational gatherings, or large-scale events such as Passion or Urbana. These mountaintop experiences create problems of reentry into a congregation's normative worship life and are not sustainable as a means of ongoing adolescent spiritual formation. The real spiritual formation for teenagers—where worship is concerned—happens week in and week out. With the church of all ages on Sunday morning and with the youth group on Sunday and Wednesday evenings, or whenever the youth group gathers.

An Ecology of Worship for Youth Ministry

Lawrence Hoffman's work, which was unpacked in the previous chapter, has shown us that the worship system in congregational contexts is complex. [1] The worship system functions much like an ecological system, where changes in one area affect every other area. In an ecological system, for example, when the population of bees drops in an area, the diversity and health of plants are affected by the resulting decrease in pollination. In a congregation, when teenagers are disengaged or absent during the main Sunday morning worship service, other areas of worship suffer. Fortunately, ecosystems also work in the positive direction. When one area becomes healthier, other areas benefit; growth is contagious. When teenagers are engaged in all-church worship and beyond, other areas benefit.

Understanding the worship patterns of teenagers through the lens of an ecological approach means churches are not required to fix everything, or even most things, to see positive change. Simply helping teenagers become more engaged worshipers will boost the health of other areas of congregational life. And teens are particularly well positioned in most churches to impact other age groups. So how can a church begin to more deeply integrate teenagers into community worship?

In my work with teenagers, I have begun using an ecological model for understanding and thinking about teens' engagement in Christian worship inside and outside the church. The model is based on reciprocity, where positive changes in any of the areas improve the health of the others. There is no best starting place in the model, because teenagers can start at any one place and still see success. An easy starting place for youth ministries, however, might be examining where teenagers, congregations, and ministries are already strongest. The goal is eventually complete coverage, because the healthiest ministries for teenagers at worship are the ones that are effectively addressing all five areas in the ecology, as noted in figure 9.1: intergenerational worship, portable worship practices, diverse expressions and experiences of worship, multiple attempts to engage worship expressions, and transferrable leadership

1. My former Samford University colleague Charles E. Stokes helped me develop and write about the ecology described in this section and in fact influenced my thinking on many of the ideas in this chapter.

roles. As congregations pursue a fully orbed worship system with this model as their guide, teenagers begin to experience spiritual integration in their everyday lives. Their Sunday-morning lives start to infiltrate their Monday-through-Saturday lives. And that's because worship moves from being "just something they do" to something that defines them as disciples of Christ.

Moreover, the healthier the ecological system becomes over an extended period of time, the more transformative the effect will be on the spiritual lives of its teenagers as well as the congregation in which they reside. As worship leaves its imprint, young people are more likely to lean into the liturgical process of the church, and they are more likely to imagine themselves as worshipers and members of the church when they are older. Such ecclesial imagination naturally blossoms into adolescent identity. Teens begin to see themselves not

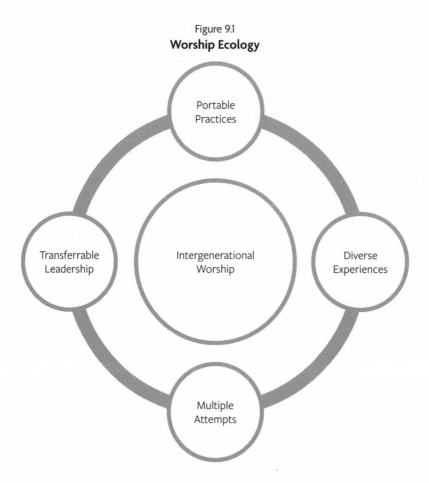

Figure 9.1
Worship Ecology

just as worshiping but as worshipers, and there is a difference between those two things: one is doing; one is being. While activities of worship can easily be exchanged or discarded, choked out or snatched away by the cares of a busy world, the identity of being a *worshiper* is more durable for teenagers.

Worship with the Church of All Ages

At the center of this ecological system is an adoptive, intergenerational community that gathers together regularly for worship that is focused on the right things. Whether made up of mostly young adults, midlife families, or retirees, the most fertile soil for nourishing worshiping teens today is unquestionably worship that includes all the ages of the church community (see chap. 5).

It is important to reiterate here that healthy intergenerational worship is not about finding the perfect style of worship. The goal is that people of every age feel included and important in all-church worship gatherings. Changing all-church worship to accommodate young people at the expense of distancing senior adults will lead to pathology; it will not produce good fruit. Blending styles in a way that leaves the worship disconnected from all ages equally might have the same effect. And segregating worship by age groups alleviates an immediate, practical need to please everyone, but it creates a series of long-term problems, especially for teenagers. If the youth minister wants to start change in all church worship, it is better done by working with the senior pastor and worship minister. Otherwise, mistakes could be made. Trying to engage teenagers in all-church worship who are not also being mentored in leadership roles and worshiping in diverse contexts, for instance, can lead to tokenism (putting teens on display during worship as a sort of self-congratulatory exercise for older church members). It can also create tensions between ministry areas.

This being said, showing up for church on Sunday, even if worship is intergenerational and healthy, is not enough to deepen and reinforce the short-term or the long-term spiritual formation of teenagers wanting to follow Christ in the world. There must be real and consistent investment in them as worshipers and as worship leaders beyond all-church worship. Teenagers need to know God with their whole beings, and they need to connect worship with school, work, family, and friends. The following four areas can help make that happen.

Portable Worship Practices

The first piece in this ecology is portable worship practices. Portable practices are the signs, symbols, and gestures of worship—songs, prayers, handshakes, meals, messages, and hugs—that can go anywhere: to the house, school, soup kitchen, hospital, courthouse, park, funeral home, prison, cemetery, or anywhere else Christians can be the hands, feet, and voice of God. Do teens realize that all of these things are related to church worship? Yes, song, prayer, and Scripture are clearly associated with worship, but what about practices of serving and caring about others? These are the natural manifestations of the very words and melodies of our worship.

If we fail to provide teenagers with portable worship practices, we run the risk of keeping what happens at church "locked up in a liturgical box that is only cracked open on Sundays." This understanding fosters the hypocrisy gap (a term borrowed from John Witvliet and described in chapter 7) in our praying and singing: when our worship is incongruent with our being and the words of worship don't match the way we live our life.[2] Examples of portable practices might include finding new ways to read Scripture, centering prayer, reading a hymn text, practicing morning or evening prayer, or praying through news headlines.

Diverse Expressions and Experiences of Worship

In any ecological environment, diversity is necessary for health, growth, and sustainability—and this applies to church worship as well. To cultivate diverse worship experiences, teenagers must be invited out of their own liturgical homelands to explore unfamiliar expressions of worship, be they down the street, in the soup kitchen, or across the world. A mainline Protestant youth minister might take his teenage worshipers to learn to dance and sing with a more charismatic congregation down the street. A teenage contemporary worshiper might be encouraged to ask a senior adult about his favorite song from the hymnbook so that she can learn it on the guitar and sing it with him in his nursing home. By participating in worship practices that differ from their preferences, priorities, or normative experiences, teenagers learn to appreciate their own worship traditions. Only when they engage practices different from their normal preferences do teenagers earn the right to ask someone to participate in an expression of worship that they know and love themselves. And teenagers gain a larger picture of God in the process.

To use a culinary metaphor, health in this area involves both home cooking and adventure eating. Many of us have had the experience of traveling and experimenting with new kinds of cuisine, only to return home eager to enjoy

2. John Witvliet, "Mind the Gaps: Responding to Criticisms of a Formative Vision for Worship and Congregational Song," *The Hymn: A Journal of Congregational Song* 67, no. 4 (Autumn 2016): 36. See also Matthew Kaemingk and Cory B. Willson, *Work and Worship: Reconnecting Our Labor and Liturgy* (Grand Rapids: Baker Academic, 2020).

our favorite dish. If teens can learn to think of the worship style of their home congregation as a kind of home cooking, they are more likely to appreciate it, even when they encounter other styles of worship that they may find more fulfilling, exotic, or meaningful.

While observing churches that have engaged diverse expressions well and allowed teenagers to reflect on them, I have seen teenagers have aha moments: "Oh, that is why my church worships like this!" As they come to understand that Christians have worshiped in many different ways throughout time and across spaces, teenagers are more likely to develop a rooted yet flexible worship identity, one that can remain strong in a diverse and rapidly changing world. As they confront differing belief systems, variant doctrines, and countless Christian traditions, their adventure eating through worship prepares them for respectful dialogue, from their own home-cooking perspective, with others.

Multiple Attempts to Engage Worship Expressions

Leading worship or trying something new in worship is often intimidating. Adolescents are hyperaware of the image they are projecting, so the prospect of "failing" in worship is enough to keep many teens on the sidelines. That's why it is important to encourage teenagers not to give up on an experience of worship after one try. This "try" might be a song they have written and played for the youth group, a prayer they've composed or want to offer extemporaneously, or an attempt at a different style of worship. Those singular experiences need to be repeated; the prayer needs to be prayed again and that song sung multiple times, all in different contexts, until the expression becomes a known element and maybe even a foundational part of the teenager's faith journey. We are not completely formed by the things we say and do in worship until they become *normative* in our own worship and life experience. Sometimes, of course, new experiences and expressions simply don't work; not every good try leads to a solid win. But congregations can help teenagers sort that out in community. And anything that's producing good fruit should be given a chance to yield in all seasons.

Three areas and questions are important for congregations to assess how well they encourage multiple attempts to engage in worship. First, does the congregation repeat worship elements, especially in different contexts? For example, is the benediction that is offered at the end of each Sunday morning service also prayed after a church picnic? What about a song that is regularly sung in a worship service? Is that song also sung during a small group meeting?

And do teenagers know how that song might help them follow Christ on Monday afternoon when life isn't as they want it to be?

Second, does the congregation offer multiple entry-level opportunities for worship leadership? A youth choir can be a great precursor to singing a solo. Composing and praying a prayer before a meal at church camp prepares a teenager to pray in an all-church setting. Leading little ones in singing during VBS week can get the jitters out and give a teen the courage to lead adults in singing too.

Third, and most importantly, how well does the congregation encourage risk and comfort failure? If a teen stumbles over the words during a prayer, does the congregation respond in a way that will encourage her to try again? If a teen says something while leading worship that isn't exactly right doctrinally, do other church members take offense? Or do they allow the pastor or youth pastor to gently mentor him? In the case of encouraging multiple attempts at worship, the best soil is soft soil—where it doesn't hurt to fall down.

Transferable Leadership Roles

Describing teen leadership opportunities as *transferable* means two things. First, their leadership skills gained at church need to transfer to other areas of their lives, and vice versa. Most teenagers lead busy lives, and those who do not probably wish they had something interesting to do. In school, sports, band, clubs, and work, teens have multiple chances to be leaders. In their social and dating lives, they lead as well (hopefully in a wholesome direction). Many of the leadership talents these teens develop and utilize in their weekday worlds can also be employed at church. Musical talent is the most obvious transferable skill, but physical, social, and technical skills are also part of worship. When teens are given the opportunity to employ their talents in church, they not only begin to connect Sunday with the rest of the week, but critical elements of their identities (things they are good at) start to have a place at church.

The second component of transferable leadership is that teenagers transfer leadership among themselves. They need to see their peers engaging in or leading worship regularly to eventually make it part of who they are in the present and the future. Teenagers might attend intergenerational worship, but if adults are the only ones on the platform each week, teenagers subliminally receive the message that they don't belong. Or at the very least, that they don't belong *yet*. In contrast, teenagers who see their peers engage as worshipers and worship leaders are more likely to engage as worshipers or look for ways to use their own gifts in worship or other areas of the church.

This model has become a diagnostic tool for considering the health of a congregation's soil when it comes to nurturing growth in teenagers' worship lives as well as in the tender shoots of worship experiences as they emerge. Teenagers who participate in *portable worship practices*, worship *in diverse contexts*, and are given opportunities to engage worship through *multiple attempts* in a variety of contexts will develop in *transferable leadership roles*, and they will naturally grow. To repeat the metaphor, they will pollinate the growth all around them as they are prepared to fully participate in all-church intergenerational worship times. More importantly, teenagers will experience the magic of spiritual integration in their everyday lives.

A Theology of Worship with Teenagers

When it comes to planning worship with teenagers, a basic philosophy or theology for approaching worship planning should be present. My own approach to worship planning with teenagers has been one rooted in principles of traditioned innovation, and it borrows heavily from the work of Robert Webber, Constance Cherry, and Todd Johnson. The work of Webber has been expounded upon at length already in this text, so I will start here with the work of Johnson and his model of liturgical theology for the Free Church tradition.[3]

His method suggests that our worship gatherings must include (1) congruence between the way we believe and the way we worship, (2) a narrative that tells the story of God and the story of God's people, and (3) an identification with the life of Christ and his disciples.[4] Attaining congruence between our beliefs and our worship requires asking two questions: What do we believe as a body of worshipers? And does the communication that worshipers receive in our worship practices align with our stated beliefs? Every element of worship, not just the sermon, needs to align with the beliefs of the congregation—including the songs we sing, the words we speak, the gestures we make, the actions we perform, and the props in the room.[5]

The second element, narrative, requires two components of worship gatherings: a construction with a logical beginning, middle, and end, and the public reading of Scripture. Worship should also situate personal stories within God's

3. Todd E. Johnson, "Liturgical Links: Toward a Theology of Free Church Worship," (unpublished address, installation of Todd E. Johnson to the Brehm Chair for Worship, Theology, and the Arts at Fuller Theological Seminary, Pasadena, CA, May 22, 2007).

4. T. Johnson, "Liturgical Links," 7–11.

5. T. Johnson, "Liturgical Links," 7–8.

cosmic story.[6] As Hoffman reminds us, "Each worship service is a rereading of a sacred script and the establishment of a new sacred reality, a world that did not exist until we willed it to, one that we established anew with every sacred performance. Part of the script rehearses history as we choose to see it, the people of the past as we care to recollect them, and a selective perception of the events that made us what we are."[7]

The third element suggests that worship must identify with the life of Christ and Christ's disciples. Here it will be necessary to make a sacrifice in praise of God. The liturgy of Christ and his disciples involved worshiping God, supporting the church, and serving the world. If worship practices invite teenagers to affirm their baptismal pledge as well as offer their lives in sacrificial service to the Triune God, they will not only be rich historically, biblically, and theologically but also have relevance within the context in which they find themselves.[8]

I employ these three principles from Johnson's approach and add a fourth element from Cherry's convergence approach to worship: "the combining of the historical and the contemporary at every level of worship to create maximum opportunities for engaging worshipers with the presence of God."[9] Cherry articulates strongly that convergence worship is a model, not a style, of worship: "Convergence worship should not be considered a worship style in that it does not arise out of a specific context and is not identifiably influenced by any particular culture. In fact, convergence worship transcends particular worship styles and is applicable to a myriad of styles." The convergence model is useful in that it explicitly "urges the complementary use of worship elements of biblical and historical practice with contemporary expressions suitable for many cultures." As shown throughout this text, worship with teenagers can happen in a number of places, and inherently, those styles will likely change. The convergence model of planning worship acknowledges style and encourages "stylistic nuances that identify it with a particular context."[10] That said, note that style comes after the other three parts: congruence, structure, and narrative.

This approach requires teenagers to engage the depth and breadth of the worship tradition as they have come to understand it, but it centers them in our historically limited ways of thinking about worship—ways that use labels like traditional, contemporary, and blended. Worship is more complex

6. T. Johnson, "Liturgical Links," 8–9.
7. Hoffman, *Art of Public Prayer*, 156.
8. T. Johnson, "Liturgical Links," 10–11.
9. Constance Cherry, *The Worship Architect: A Blueprint for Designing Culturally Relevant and Biblically Faithful Services*, 2nd ed. (Grand Rapids: Baker Academic, 2021), 263.
10. Cherry, *Worship Architect*, 245.

than an individual's or a congregation's either/or mentality, which often accompanies it. Many times the solution to our worship problems can be found in the complex middle, not in the oversimplified extremes. Put another way, "It is the task of prophetic ministry to bring the claims of the tradition and the situation of enculturation into an effective interface."[11] This approach to worship situates teenagers between memory and hope: memory of what God has done in the past and hope of what God will do in the future. This allows them to live with confidence in the present.

A Framework for Worship with Teenagers

Youth ministry is a theological task just as worship is a theological task. Youth ministers are worship leaders, and both youth ministers and worship leaders are theologians. Whether planning, leading, or worshiping alongside teenagers, the youth minister and the worship leader must engage together in the task of theology. This will be necessary as these two ministries collaborate with each other for the sake of the spiritual formation of teenagers through worship. Bridging the divide that has existed between youth ministry and worship ministry is not enough; ministry leaders must think about and reflect critically on the outcome. As they "enter into mutually significant conversation beyond [their] isolation," it will become apparent that these ministries and these individuals "are not seeking to justify [themselves] but rather are trying to construct deep theological articulations of how God is at work within the world."[12]

To understand worship with teenagers as a theological task is to move both worship ministry and youth ministry "beyond utilitarianism" and demand "that we do real reflection on the practice of ministry and the young people to and with whom we minister."[13] This will move both youth minister and worship minister beyond the pragmatism that often surrounds worship with teenagers and promote thoughtful, reflective approaches to worship that situate teenagers' stories in God's story. Approaching worship with teenagers as a theological task will also help us "move past much of the fragmentation of ministries within the church." The arguments and suggestions found in this book call for youth ministry and worship ministry to work in tandem toward the flourishing of congregational life. This will help both youth minister and

11. Walter Brueggemann, *The Prophetic Imagination*, 40th anniversary ed. (Minneapolis: Fortress, 2018), 2.

12. Andrew Root, "God Is a Minister," in *The Theological Turn in Youth Ministry*, ed. Andrew Root and Kenda Creasy Dean (Downers Grove, IL: IVP, 2011), 39.

13. Root, "God Is a Minister," 41.

worship minister "see the adolescent from a contextual perspective, as one who is affected by multiple forces," and approach worship as something to be done not by teenagers or for teenagers but with teenagers.[14] Additionally, in this theological approach, "theory and practice are held together," demanding that both sides engage the framework of experience, reflection, and action.[15]

Experience asks the question, What is happening? Reflection and evaluation analyze the process through theology and sociology. Action is the result of an experience, reflection, and evaluation. Action produces a new experience and continues the process. It is important for all ministers to engage in these three areas, for in order to do well, one must think well. Over time, the church has privileged one of these three over the other. For instance, academics have often neglected experience and action in favor of theology. Youth and worship ministry have often neglected reflection and evaluation in favor of experience.[16]

Where teenage worship is concerned, evangelicals tend to privilege experience and mainline Protestants tend to privilege action, and both sides privilege experience and action over reflection. I once overheard a teenager remark about worship, "I'm always told what to do but rarely how to do it or even why I'm doing it." In the words of practical theology, this student was saying, "You don't care about helping me *reflect* on my *experience* as a worshiper or worship leader; you care only about my *action*: that I'm doing something" (in this case, reading Scripture). I overheard another student say to his dad after worship one Sunday, "I got goosebumps when we sang the chorus of that song without instruments this morning." His dad responded flippantly, "Well, we must have been doing something right." In terms of practical theology, this teenager was trying to make sense of an *experience*, but the dad missed the opportunity to reflect on the action of what can happen when we sing together.

I think we can do real reflection on the practice of ministry and the young people to and with whom we minister by reclaiming the holistic picture that practical theology calls ministers to engage in: experience that leads to reflection that leads to action that leads to new experience.

Teenagers as Worshipers and Practical Theologians

Many individuals—including me—have advocated for Youth Sunday every Sunday. This would mean including youth in planning and leadership every

14. Root, "God Is a Minister," 42.
15. Root, "God Is a Minister," 43.
16. Root, "God Is a Minister," 45–46.

week. While that might be good, it is not enough for teenagers to experience only worship planning and leadership. Just as we are called to be practical theologians as ministers, we are also called to train teenagers—whether worshipers or worship leaders—to be practical theologians. They need to engage in the process of experience, to reflect, and to act just as much—if not more—than adults do. Neuroscience tells us that framing and processing what teenagers experience is absolutely necessary to help teenagers' critical judgment skills and understanding. What might that look like if we engage teenagers' experience of worship, reflection on worship, and action from worship as a theological process? The following list might serve as a helpful starting place.

Experience of Worship

- Create meaningful experiences of worship for teenagers; this cannot be accomplished at the last minute.
- Plan ahead to use interactive prayers, tactile objects, and cohesive ideas.
- Engage the whole person—body, mind, spirit, and voice.
- Frame the worship experience for teenagers before it happens.
- Talk with them about differences they may encounter in different places.
- Be clear about what they should expect from leaders and worshipers.
- Help teenagers anticipate worship gatherings they will participate in.
- Social media and text-based services can be useful tools for communicating.
- Talk with teenagers about what to expect from worship leadership.
- Be clear about your expectations for teenagers during worship.
  - › Where do they sit?
  - › What do they do with their phones?

Reflection on Worship

- Provide teenagers with times and opportunities to reflect on worship; this can happen inside or outside of worship.
- Place teenagers into small groups after a sermon and provide questions as prompts to help them reflect with their peers.
- Ask teenagers questions about the worshiping community; this will prompt them to engage those around them.
- Invite teenagers to complete a questionnaire about worship; this lets you hear their voice, and it asks them to reflect quietly.
- Actively plan a time for worship leaders to debrief a service they led; do this a few days after the service, or at the next planning session.

Action from Worship

- End worship by asking students to name a thought, attitude, action, or behavior they might change as a result of God speaking to them in worship.
- Begin worship by asking students to recall the commitment they made, celebrating when the commitment is accomplished, and offering grace when it's needed.
- Choose a worship habit each week and teach about it briefly.
- Let worship speak boldly and prophetically to world events.
- Talk about worship gatherings during youth activities that are not worship.
- Connect teenagers' work and play and service to worship in all of life.

A Planning Process with Teenagers

There are a number of approaches congregations use in worship planning: the random approach, the blank slate approach, the thematic approach, the fill-in-the-blank approach, the prescribed approach, the dialogical approach, and the fourfold-order approach. The *random* approach makes a list of things that need to be in the service, and places them at random. The *blank slate* approach is an attempt to arrive at something fresh every week. Those who use the *thematic* approach have a certain word or theme in mind and then select and arrange materials around this theme. The *fill-in-the-blank* approach is the same week after week; just the elements change. The *prescribed* approach requires books that specify what is to happen in worship. The *dialogical* approach is rooted in Scriptures, such as Moses at the burning bush, Isaiah during his vision, Mary at the annunciation, or the disciples on the road to Emmaus. In these models a sequence of events happens: God approaches, the person experiences discontinuity, God speaks, the person responds, and God sends. Another common approach is the *fourfold-order* approach, which moves through gathering, Word, Table, and sending.

How, then, should one approach worship planning with teenagers? For me, it begins with a *collaborative* approach, which adapts to the particular context. In many ways, the collaborative way of planning worship is the most difficult with teenagers because schedules must be coordinated. Despite this, the possibility of finding good ideas is much greater, more people own the outcome of worship, and more people are invested in and able to facilitate carrying out plans. Additionally, team planning provides opportunities for more connections to the lives of teenagers, and it also allows teenagers to try their hands at different leadership roles in worship. Finally, team planning avoids placing attention on a single teenager during worship.

To implement the collaborative approach, start a student worship team in the fall and enlist their help in late spring or early summer so they can plan for their role. Pay attention to the makeup of the group, and make it intergenerational when possible. Schedule an end-of-summer retreat with the team that includes eating a meal, building culture, and creating a vision for the team. Also, adopt a purpose statement for worship that uses the theological approach above. Then, set a seasonal trajectory for your planning that runs September through January and February through June.

During or before your planning retreat, prepare a worship repertoire or menu for your ministry that includes core resources for worship planning, core songs for worship, sample worship structures, and carefully determined ordinaries (things that will happen every week) and propers (things that will change according to season). During the retreat, plan the first two weeks of worship and assign tasks for those two weeks so your group will have an early start on their work. Then set a regular sixty-minute planning time that works for everyone. This can be weekly, monthly, or quarterly, and it works best if it is tied to a time teenagers are already at church. Meet with them regularly, and follow a standard procedure such as the one in figure 9.2, which has been adapted from Debra Rienstra and Ron Rienstra's *Worship Words*.[17]

Figure 9.2
Worship Planning Process

Action	Description
Previse	Solicit as much input as possible from as broad a group as possible. Brainstorm with grace about themes, songs, drama, art, dance, everything.
Devise	Plan a first draft. Begin to filter down to the best ideas. Make use of people with specialized expertise in particular areas (music, art, drama).
Revise	Make use of both individual and group input to improve the service plan.
Realize	Communicate the vision for the service to all participants.
Analyze	Review previous services periodically. Analyze less for technical miscues or taste preferences than for theological content.
Assign	Delegate work that needs to be completed.
Close	Small talk and prayer.

17. Debra Rienstra and Ron Rienstra, appendix 2 of *Worship Words: Discipling Language for Faithful Ministry* (Grand Rapids: Baker Academic, 2009).

Here are other things to remember in your planning with teenagers: Accept all ideas, but realize that everything is up for discussion. Establish a comfortable space that has the room and tools you need. Remember that the best ideas rarely end up in their original form. Process is more important than product, and relationships are more important than performance.

In the overall worship cycle, introduce new materials in early fall (September) and early winter (January). Use familiar things closer to holidays (November/December and April/May). If you don't have any worship within your youth ministry and want to incorporate it, begin slowly and gradually with portable practices, with an aim to make these practices part of students' personal worship or to make them the ordinaries of worship down the road. To start a youth worship team, invest in junior high students, and be patient.

A Final Story

When I lived in Los Angeles, I regularly visited the Cathedral of Our Lady of Angels. I attended their annual Easter vigil one year, which included the baptism of several teenagers who had just completed confirmation in the diocese. The baptistry was in the back, and I watched as several teenagers waded through the baptistry to receive their baptism with their parents and families standing nearby. After the teens were baptized, they walked with their families to the Communion table down front to receive the bread and the cup for the first time. As they proceeded, I could see in the distance huge tapestries hanging on the cathedral walls that depicted the communion of saints. On the tapestries were people of all ages, races, occupations, and vocations from around the world. Biblical figures were intermingled with canonized saints and children, youth, and adults who lived in Los Angeles.

As the teenagers walked past these tapestries, the congregation sang, "Radiant risen from the water, robed in holiness and light; male and female in God's image, male and female, God's delight. Let us bring the gifts that differ and in splendid varied ways, sing a new church into being, one in faith and love and praise."[18] As I watched this unfold, I couldn't help but remember Paul's words to the Ephesians, "I pray that the God of our Lord Jesus Christ, the Father of glory, will give you a spirit of wisdom and revelation that makes God known to you. I pray that the eyes of your heart will have enough light

18. Delores Dufner, "Sing a New Church," in *Worship and Rejoice* (Carol Stream, IL: Hope Publishing, 2003).

to see what is the hope of God's call, what is the richness of God's glorious inheritance among believers, and what is the overwhelming greatness of God's power that is working among us believers" (Eph. 1:17–19 CEB).

May we all take to heart these words from Paul and lean into worship practices that encourage our teenagers to see the hope of God's call, the richness of God's inheritance, and the overwhelming greatness of God's power that is working among us believers. More importantly, may our reflections here cause all of us to reevaluate the worship practices in each of our faith traditions to ensure that the kingdom of God finds a way to flourish beyond this generation into the next.

APPENDIX 1

A Letter to Teenage Worship Leaders

Dear Teenage Worship Leader,

You have a unique position in the body of Christ, and as a worship leader, you play an important role in the faith community that cannot be overestimated.

Because you are young, you prompt adults, who were once teenagers, to remember their youth, which probably included a certain zeal and passion for faith. You remind adults that God is still about the business of revitalizing and renewing the church and that the gospel will continue into the next generation. Your mere presence encourages children to look ahead—to that time when they will mature into the faith as you have done. And perhaps most importantly, you set a standard for your peers whom you lead in worship. This is an extraordinary gift, but it also brings a tremendous responsibility.

Passing along wisdom is a time-honored Christian tradition, and in that spirit, I would like to pass along a few proverbs to you. I hope that you will continue to lead in your communities of faith not only in your teenage years but for many years to come.

Wise is the teenage worship leader who

- invests in their personal relationship with God and their call to be a disciple of Jesus Christ and pursues spiritual growth through the dedicated study of Scripture, prayer, and meditation to listen carefully for the voice of the Holy Spirit;

- realizes the significance of their unique leadership position in the church among their peers and exhibits confidence, humility, and conviction on and off the platform;
- searches for one or more adult mentors who can provide teaching, accountability, encouragement, and opportunities for reflective learning;
- builds meaningful relationships with others, including those on the worship team and those in the broader worshiping community;
- pursues excellence in their craft as a musician, speaker, and minister through practice and purposeful learning;
- acknowledges the time demands that come from school, family, extracurricular activities, church, and more and yet still reserves concentrated time for the tasks of planning and leading worship;
- leans into mistakes, learns from them, and adheres to a gospel of grace when worship does not go as planned;
- incorporates disciplined play into the worshiping community;
- addresses serious issues of the day with careful, thoughtful language informed by examples found in Scripture, such as in the book of Psalms;
- commits to learn from different cultures and represent their voices in worship;
- promotes contagious leadership among all ages in the church by regularly sharing a personal testimony of why they like worship or why they like church; and
- teaches the who, what, why, and how of worship when called upon with grace, passion, and poise.

May the Lord bless you and keep you. May the Lord make his face to shine upon you and be gracious to you so that all may know the presiding conviction of your worship leadership: that Jesus Christ is Lord.

Worship Planning Toolbox

A Template for Planning Worship with Teenagers

Gathering Information

A. Basic information: the date, time, and place
   When and where will worship take place?

B. Main idea: overarching topic of worship
   What is the main idea of worship?

C. Scripture: the starting place for worship
   What Scripture passage(s) will be guiding worship?

D. Other information: special notes about this worship gathering
   Are there other important things to note about this worship service?
   Will something special be happening (Communion, etc.)?
   Are there certain elements that have to be present?

E. Sermon: the theme
   Will there be a sermon, and, if so, what theme will it have?

Planning Worship

A. Pray for wisdom.
   Ask God to help you make good choices as you plan this worship
   service. You may want to write a prayer.

B. Reflect on Scripture.

Read the Scripture passages serving as the guide for the worship gathering.

What do they say?

What themes do you see?

What words and phrases stick out?

C. Observe the world.

Spend time thinking about the world outside of worship.

What is happening in the lives of worshipers? The church? The local community? The county? The state? The country? The world?

D. Brainstorm all the possibilities.

Now you are ready to begin brainstorming. Use the Scripture passage(s), the sermon, and other components of worship as a guide.

With the following categories in mind, brainstorm all the possibilities that could happen in this worship service. The sky is the limit!

Later, you can choose what to keep and what to save for another time.

- A special space for worshiping: How might you prepare the space for worship?
- Make art for seeing: What paintings, photos, or other visual images might you use for worship?
- Create drama for hearing: How might you present Scripture in an inviting and engaging way?
- Choose music for singing: What songs match the themes of worship?
- Write poetry for praying: What might worshipers need to say to God? What might God want to say to worshipers?
- Live worship for doing: How might worshipers live their lives differently after this time of worship?

Make Decisions for Implementing

Look at your brainstorming work above. Circle ideas you think align with Scripture and the theme of worship. Cross out ideas that may distract from Scripture, detract from worship, or be impossible to implement. On a blank sheet of paper, determine a structure and order for worship. You might use the structures below as a guide.

Structure 1
A four-part structure used in many traditions.

- Gathering
- Word
- Response or Table
- Sending

Structure 2
A four-part structure based on Isaiah 6.

- Praise
- Confession
- Word
- Sending

Structure 3
A two-part pattern used in many traditions.

- Word
- Table

Structure 4
Create your own structure!

Bibliography

Abernethy, Alexis D., ed. *Worship That Changes Lives: Multidisciplinary and Congregational Perspectives on Spiritual Transformation*. Grand Rapids: Baker Academic, 2008.

Anderson, Herbert, and Edward Foley. *Mighty Stories, Dangerous Rituals: Weaving Together the Human and the Divine*. San Francisco: Jossey-Bass, 1998.

Arnett, Jeffrey Jensen. *Adolescence and Emerging Adulthood: A Cultural Approach*. 5th ed. Upper Saddle River, NJ: Pearson Education, 2012.

Basden, Paul. "Something Old, Something New: Worship Styles in the Nineties." In *Ties That Bind: Life Together in the Baptist Vision*, edited by Gary A. Furr and Curtis W. Freeman, 171–90. Macon, GA: Smyth and Helwys, 1994.

Bauckham, Richard. *The Theology of the Book of Revelation*. Cambridge: Cambridge University Press, 1993.

Bergler, Thomas E. *From Here to Maturity: Overcoming the Juvenilization of American Christianity*. Grand Rapids: Eerdmans, 2014.

———. *The Juvenilization of American Christianity*. Grand Rapids: Eerdmans, 2012.

Berry, Wendell. *The Long-Legged House*. Berkeley: Counterpoint, 2012.

Black, Kathy. *Culturally-Conscious Worship*. St. Louis: Chalice, 2000.

Bradley, C. Randall. "Desegregating Worship." *Creator*, September 9, 2013. https:// creatormagazine.com/desegregating-worship.

———. *From Memory to Imagination: Reforming the Church's Music*. Calvin Institute of Christian Worship Liturgical Studies Series. Grand Rapids: Eerdmans, 2012.

Branch, John, and Campbell Robertson. "Meet the Covid Class of 2020." *New York Times*, May 30, 2020. https://www.nytimes.com/interactive/2020/05/30/us /coronavirus-class-of-2020.html.

Brueggemann, Walter. *Israel's Praise: Doxology against Idolatry and Ideology*. Philadelphia: Fortress, 1988.

———. *Out of Babylon*. Nashville: Abingdon, 2010.

———. *The Prophetic Imagination*. 40th anniv. ed. Minneapolis: Fortress, 2018.

———. *The Spirituality of the Psalms*. Minneapolis: Fortress, 2002.

Buggeln, Gretchen. "Spaces for Youth in Protestant Churches." In *Making Suburbia: New Histories of Everyday America*, edited by John Archer, Paul J. P. Sandul, and Katherine Solomonson, 227–39. Minneapolis: University of Minnesota Press, 2015.

Cahalan, Kathleen A. *Introducing the Practice of Ministry*. Collegeville, MN: Liturgical, 2010.

———. *Projects That Matter: Successful Planning and Evaluation for Religious Organizations*. Herndon, VA: Alban Institute, 2003.

———. *The Stories We Live: Finding God's Calling All around Us*. Grand Rapids: Eerdmans, 2017.

Cahalan, Kathleen A., and Bonnie J. Miller-McLemore. *Calling All Years Good: Christian Vocation throughout Life's Seasons*. Grand Rapids: Eerdmans, 2017.

Canedo, Ken. *Keep the Fire Burning: The Folk Mass Revolution*. Portland, OR: Pastoral Press, 2009.

Carroll, Jackson W., and Wade Clark Roof. *Bridging Divided Worlds: Generational Cultures in Congregations*. San Francisco: Jossey-Bass, 2002.

Cherry, Constance. "Merging Tradition and Innovation in the Life of the Church: Moving from Style to Encountering God in Worship." In T. Johnson, *Conviction of Things Not Seen*, 19–32.

———. *The Worship Architect: A Blueprint for Designing Culturally Relevant and Biblically Faithful Services*. 2nd ed. Grand Rapids: Baker Academic, 2021.

Chesnut, Ashley. "Q&A with the Brook Hills Worship Team." The Church at Brook Hills, March 17, 2015. http://www.brookhills.org/blog/qa-with-the-brook-hills -worship-team/.

Clark, Chap. *Adoptive Church: Creating an Environment Where Emerging Generations Belong*. Grand Rapids: Baker Academic, 2018.

———. *Hurt 2.0: Inside the World of Today's Teenagers*. Grand Rapids: Baker Academic, 2011.

Clark, Francis E. *The Children and the Church, and the Young People's Society of Christian Endeavor, as a Means of Bringing Them Together*. Boston: Congregational Sunday School and Publishing Society, 1882.

———. *Ways and Means*. Boston: Lothrop, 1900.

Collins, Randall. *Interaction Ritual Chains*. Princeton: Princeton University Press, 2004.

Cooke, Bernard J. *The Distancing of God: The Ambiguity of Symbol in History and Theology*. Minneapolis: Augsburg Fortress, 1990.

Corrie, Elizabeth W. "Christian Liturgy Spilling Out into the World: Youth as Public Theologians." *Liturgy* 29, no. 1 (January–March 2014): 13–22.

Courtoy, Charles Webb. "A Historical Analysis of the Three Eras of Mainline Protestant Youth Work in America as a Basis for Clues to Future Youth Work." DMin project, Divinity School of Vanderbilt University, 1976.

Crouch, Andy. "How Is Art a Gift, a Calling, and an Obedience?" In *For the Beauty of the Church: Casting a Vision for the Arts*, edited by W. David O. Taylor, 29–43. Grand Rapids: Baker Books, 2010.

Davis, Josh, and Nikki Lerner. *Worship Together in Your Church as in Heaven*. Nashville: Abingdon, 2015.

Dean, Kenda Creasy. *Almost Christian: What the Faith of Our Teenagers Is Telling the American Church*. New York: Oxford University Press, 2010.

———. "Losing Our Scales: The Adolescent Experience of Joy." In *Delighted: What Teenagers Are Teaching the Church about Joy*, by Kenda Creasy Dean, Wesley W. Ellis, Justin Forbes, and Abigail Visco Rusert, 1–15. Grand Rapids: Eerdmans, 2020.

———. "The New Rhetoric of Youth Ministry." *Journal of Youth and Theology* 2, no. 2 (2003): 8–19.

———. *Practicing Passion: Youth and the Quest for a Passionate Church*. Grand Rapids: Eerdmans, 2007.

Dean, Kenda Creasy, Chap Clark, and Dave Rahn, eds. *Starting Right: Thinking Theologically about Youth Ministry*. Grand Rapids: Zondervan, 2001.

DeSilver, Drew. "The Concerns and Challenges of Being a U.S. Teen: What the Data Show." Pew Research Center, February 26, 2019. https://www.pewresearch.org /fact-tank/2019/02/26/the-concerns-and-challenges-of-being-a-u-s-teen-what-the -data-show/.

DeVries, Mark. *Family-Based Youth Ministry*. Rev. ed. Downers Grove, IL: InterVarsity, 2004.

Dimock, Michael. "Where Millennials End and Post-Millennials Begin." Pew Research Center, January 17, 2018. http://www.pewresearch.org/fact-tank/2018/03/01/defining -generations-where-millennials-end-and-post-millennials-begin/.

Drane, John. *The McDonaldization of the Church: Consumer Culture and the Church's Future*. London: Darton, Longman & Todd, 2000.

Drury, Amanda Hontz. "Moralistic Therapeutic Pietism." *The Princeton Seminary Bulletin* 34 (2017): 30–40.

———. *Saying Is Believing: The Necessity of Testimony in Adolescent Spiritual Development*. Downers Grove, IL: IVP Academic, 2015.

Edie, Fred P. *Book, Bath, Table, and Time: Christian Worship as Source and Resource for Youth Ministry*. Cleveland: Pilgrim, 2007.

———. "Liturgy and Adolescents: Introduction." *Liturgy* 29, no. 1 (2014): 1–3.

Edwards, Randy. *Revealing Riches and Building Lives: Youth Choir Ministry in the New Millennium*. St. Louis: Morningstar, 2000.

Eisenstadt, S. N. *From Generation to Generation*. London: Free Press of Glencoe, 1956.

Ellis, Christopher J. *Approaching God: A Guide for Worship Leaders and Worshippers*. London: SCM, 2009.

———. *Gathering: A Theology and Spirituality of Worship in Free Church Tradition*. London: SCM, 2004.

Elmore, Tim, and Andrew McPeak. *Generation Z Unfiltered: Facing Nine Hidden Challenges of the Most Anxious Population*. Atlanta: Poet Gardner, 2019.

Empereur, James. "Worship Wars in the Roman Catholic Church." *Liturgy* 19, no. 4 (2004): 15–24.

Erikson, Erik, ed. *Youth: Change and Challenge*. New York: Basic, 1963.

Fenwick, John, and Bryan Spinks. *Worship in Transition*. New York: Continuum, 1995.

Fleming, James S. "Erikson's Psychosocial Developmental Stages." In *Psychological Perspectives on Human Development* (Prescott, AZ: Southwest Psychometrics and Psychology Resources, 2020).

Floyd-Thomas, Juan M., Stacey M. Floyd-Thomas, and Mark G. Toulouse. *The Altars Where We Worship: The Religious Significance of Popular Culture*. Louisville: Westminster John Knox, 2016.

Fowler, James W. *Stages of Faith: The Psychology of Human Development and the Quest for Meaning*. San Francisco: Harper & Row, 1981.

Fromm, Jeff, and Angie Read. *Marketing to Gen Z: The Rules for Reaching This Vast and Very Different Generation of Influencers*. New York: Amacom, 2018.

Gibbs, Eddie, and Ryan K. Bolger. *Emerging Churches: Creating Christian Community in Postmodern Cultures*. Grand Rapids: Baker Academic, 2005.

Gould, Meredith. *Transcending Generations: A Field Guide to Collaboration in Church*. Collegeville, MN: Liturgical, 2017.

Graf, Nikki. "A Majority of U.S. Teens Fear a Shooting Could Happen at Their School, and Most Parents Share Their Concern." Pew Research Center, April 18, 2018. https://www.pewresearch.org/fact-tank/2018/04/18/a-majority-of-u-s-teens-fear-a-shooting-could-happen-at-their-school-and-most-parents-share-their-concern/.

Gratton, Carolyn. *The Art of Spiritual Guidance*. New York: Crossroad, 1993.

Grit, Betty. "Vertical Habits: Worship and Our Faith Vocabulary." Calvin Institute of Christian Worship, January 10, 2012. https://worship.calvin.edu/resources/resource-library/vertical-habits-worship-and-our-faith-vocabulary/.

Hall, G. Stanley. *Adolescence: Its Psychology and Its Relations to Physiology, Anthropology, Sociology, Sex, Crime, Religion, and Education*. New York: Appleton and Company, 1904.

Hamilton, Michael S. "The Triumph of the Praise Songs: How Guitars Beat Out the Organ in the Worship Wars." *Christianity Today*, July 12, 1999. https://www.christianitytoday.com/ct/1999/july12/9t8028.html.

Hardesty-Crouch, Brian, ed. *Holy Things for Youth Ministry: A Guide to "Book, Bath, Table, and Time."* Cleveland: Pilgrim, 2010.

Hawn, C. Michael. *Gather into One: Praying and Singing Globally.* Grand Rapids: Eerdmans, 2003.

Hine, Thomas. *The Rise and Fall of the American Teenager: A New History of the American Adolescent Experience.* New York: Perennial, 2000.

Hoffman, Lawrence A. *The Art of Public Prayer: Not for Clergy Only.* 2nd ed. Woodstock, VT: SkyLight Paths, 2009.

Holmes, Stephen R. "Trinitarian Missiology: Towards a Theology of God as Missionary." *International Journal of Systematic Theology* 8, no. 1 (2006): 72–90.

Horowitz, Juliana Menasce, and Nikki Graf. "Most U.S. Teens See Anxiety and Depression as a Major Problem among Their Peers." Pew Research Center, February 20, 2019. https://www.pewsocialtrends.org/2019/02/20/most-u-s-teens-see-anxiety-and-depression-as-a-major-problem-among-their-peers/.

Hughes, Graham. *Worship as Meaning: A Liturgical Theology for Late Modernity.* Cambridge: Cambridge University Press, 2003.

Hustad, Donald P. *Jubilate II: Church Music in Worship and Renewal.* Carol Stream, IL: Hope, 1993.

Ingalls, Monique M. *Singing the Congregation: How Contemporary Worship Music Forms Evangelical Identity.* New York: Oxford University Press, 2018.

Jacober, Amy E. *Redefining Perfect: The Interplay between Theology and Disability.* Eugene, OR: Cascade, 2017.

Jaworski, Margaret. "Volunteer Vacations: How to Choose an Ethical Program." *Transitions Abroad,* September/October 2006. https://www.transitionsabroad.com/publications/magazine/0609/volunteer_vacations_gain_popularity.shtml.

Jensen, Frances E., and Amy Ellis Nutt. *The Teenage Brain: A Neuroscientist's Survival Guide to Raising Adolescents and Young Adults.* New York: Harper, 2015.

Jiang, Jingjing. "How Teens and Parents Navigate Screen Time and Device Distractions." Pew Research Center, August 22, 2018. https://www.pewresearch.org/internet/2018/08/22/how-teens-and-parents-navigate-screen-time-and-device-distractions/.

Johnson, Maxwell. "Is Anything Normative in Contemporary Lutheran Worship?" In *The Serious Business of Worship: Essays in Honour of Bryan D. Spinks,* edited by Melanie Ross and Simon Jones, 171–84. London: T&T Clark, 2010.

Johnson, Steven. "Milestones of Faith: Creating Rhythms through Rites of Passage." Fuller Youth Institute, accessed February 19, 2013, http://www.studyinglifelongfaith.com/uploads/5/2/4/6/5246709/milestones_of_faith_creating_rhythms_through_rites_of_passage__sticky_faith.pdf.

Johnson, Todd E., ed. *The Conviction of Things Not Seen: Worship and Ministry in the 21st Century.* Grand Rapids: Brazos, 2002.

————. "Disconnected Rituals: The Origins of the Seeker Service Movement." In T. Johnson, *Conviction of Things Not Seen*, 53–66.

Joncas, Jan Michael. *From Sacred Song to Ritual Music: Twentieth Century Understandings of Roman Catholic Worship Music*. Collegeville, MN: Liturgical, 1997.

Kimball, Dan. *Emerging Worship: Creating Worship Gatherings for New Generations*. Grand Rapids: Zondervan, 2004.

King, Mike. *Presence-Centered Youth Ministry: Guiding Students into Spiritual Formation*. Downers Grove, IL: IVP, 2006.

Koulopoulos, Thomas, and Dan Keldsen. *The Gen Z Effect: Six Forces Shaping the Future of Business*. New York: Bibliomotion, 2014.

Labberton, Mark. *The Dangerous Act of Worship: Living God's Call to Justice*. Downers Grove, IL: IVP, 2007.

LaCugna, Catherine Mowry. *God for Us: The Trinity and Christian Life*. San Francisco: Harper & Row, 1991.

Lamott, Anne. *Plan B: Further Thoughts on Faith*. New York: Riverhead, 2006.

Lang, Bernhard. *Sacred Games: A History of Christian Worship*. New Haven: Yale University Press, 1998.

Lee, Hak Joon, ed. *Intersecting Realities: Race, Identity, and Culture in the Spiritual-Moral Life of Young Asian Americans*. Eugene, OR: Cascade, 2018.

Levine, Madeline. *The Price of Privilege: How Parental Pressure and Material Advantage Are Creating a Generation of Disconnected and Unhappy Kids*. New York: Harper Perennial, 2008.

Lightfoot, Cynthia. *The Culture of Adolescent Risk-Taking*. New York: Guilford, 1997.

Long, Thomas G. *Testimony: Talking Ourselves into Being Christian*. San Francisco: Jossey-Bass, 2004.

Lyberg, Tom. "Singing a New Song: Lutheran Artists at the 2012 Youth Gathering." Living Lutheran, Evangelical Lutheran Church in America, June 20, 2012. https://www.livinglutheran.org/2012/06/singing-new-song/.

MacDonald, G. Jeffrey. "Rise of Sunshine Samaritans: On a Mission or a Holiday?" *Christian Science Monitor*, May 25, 2006. https://www.csmonitor.com/2006/0525/p01s01-ussc.html.

Maldonado, Samantha A. "Will Millennials Return to Religion?" *Publisher's Weekly*, February 28, 2018. https://www.publishersweekly.com/pw/by-topic/industry-news/religion/article/76179-will-millennials-return-to-religion.html.

Mathis, Eric L. "Is It Time to Rethink the 'Conventional Model' of the Youth Choir?" *Choral Journal* 56, no. 11 (June/July 2016): 18–27.

McIntosh, Gary L. *One Church, Four Generations: Understanding and Reaching All Ages in Your Church*. Grand Rapids: Baker Books, 2002.

Mercer, Joyce Ann. "Calling amid Conflict: What Happens to the Vocations of Youth When Congregations Fight?" In *Greenhouses of Hope: Congregations Growing Young Leaders Who Will Change the World*, edited by Dori Grinenko Baker, 165–90. Herndon, VA: Alban Institute, 2010.

Moore, Mary Elizabeth, and Almeda M. Wright, eds. *Children, Youth, and Spirituality in a Troubling World*. St. Louis: Chalice, 2008.

Morgenthaler, Sally. *Worship Evangelism: Inviting Unbelievers into the Presence of God*. Grand Rapids: Zondervan, 1999.

Moschella, Mary Clark. *Ethnography as Pastoral Practice: An Introduction*. Cleveland: Pilgrim, 2008.

Moss, Kermit, and Jacob Sorenson. "Deep Rhythms of Faith Formation: Separation and Reintegration in Summer Camp and Retreats." In *Cultivating Teen Faith: Insights from the Confirmation Project*, edited by Richard R. Osmer and Katherine M. Douglass, 67–88. Grand Rapids: Eerdmans, 2018.

Nikondeha, Kelley. *Adopted: The Sacrament of Belonging in a Fractured World*. Grand Rapids: Eerdmans, 2017.

Okholm, Dennis. *Learning Theology through the Church's Worship*. Grand Rapids: Baker Academic, 2018.

Ospino, Hosffman, ed. *Our Catholic Children: Ministry with Hispanic Youth and Young Adults*. Huntington, IN: Our Sunday Visitor Institute, 2018.

Pahl, Jon. *Youth Ministry in Modern America: 1930 to the Present*. Peabody, MA: Hendrickson, 2000.

Parker, Kim, Nikki Graf, and Ruth Igielnik. "Generation Z Looks a Lot Like Millennials on Key Social and Political Issues." Pew Research Center, January 17, 2019. https://www.pewsocialtrends.org/2019/01/17/generation-z-looks-a-lot-like -millennials-on-key-social-and-political-issues/.

Peacock, Charlie. "Charlie Peacock Predicts the Future of Christian Music." *CCM Magazine*, April 1, 2008. https://www.ccmmagazine.com/features/charlie-peacock -predicts-the-future-of-christian-music/.

Pecklers, Keith F. *The Unread Vision: The Liturgical Movement in the United States of America, 1926–1955*. Collegeville, MN: Liturgical, 1998.

Pecklers, Keith F., and Bryan D. Spinks. "The Liturgical Movement." In *New Westminster Dictionary of Liturgy and Worship*, ed. Paul Bradshaw, 283–89. Louisville: Westminster John Knox, 2002.

Piper, John. *Desiring God: Meditations of a Christian Hedonist*. Rev. ed. Colorado Springs: Multnomah, 2011.

Powell, Kara E., and Chap Clark. *Sticky Faith: Everyday Ideas to Build Lasting Faith in Your Kids*. Grand Rapids: Zondervan, 2008.

Powell, Kara E., Brad M. Griffin, and Cheryl A. Crawford. *Sticky Faith, Youth Worker Edition: Practical Ideas to Nurture Long-Term Faith in Teenagers*. Grand Rapids: Zondervan, 2011.

Powell, Kara, Jake Mulder, and Brad Griffin. *Growing Young: 6 Essential Strategies to Help Young People Discover and Love Your Church*. Grand Rapids: Baker Books, 2016.

Priest, Robert J., Terry Dischinger, Steve Rasmussen, and C. M. Brown. "Researching the Short-Term Mission Movement." *Missiology* 34, no. 4 (October 2006): 431–50.

Redman, Rob. *The Great Worship Awakening*. San Francisco: Jossey-Bass, 2002.

Reynolds, William J., and Milburn Price. *A Survey of Christian Hymnody*. 5th ed. Carol Stream, IL: Hope, 2010.

Rienstra, Debra. *Worship Words: Discipling Language for Faithful Ministry*. Grand Rapids: Baker Academic, 2009.

Roberts, Robert C. *Spiritual Emotions: A Psychology of Christian Virtues*. Grand Rapids: Eerdmans, 2007.

Root, Andrew. *The Children of Divorce: The Loss of Family as the Loss of Being*. Grand Rapids: Baker Books, 2010.

———. *Faith Formation in a Secular Age: Responding to the Church's Obsession with Youthfulness*. Grand Rapids: Baker Academic, 2017.

———. "God Is a Minister." In Root and Dean, *Theological Turn in Youth Ministry*, 37–47.

———. "The Mission Trip as Global Tourism: Are We OK with This?" In Root and Dean, *Theological Turn in Youth Ministry*, 182–91.

Root, Andrew, and Kenda Creasy Dean. *The Theological Turn in Youth Ministry*. Downers Grove, IL: IVP, 2011.

Rosenblatt, Kalhan. "Teen Climate Activist Greta Thunberg Delivers Scathing Speech at U.N." NBC News, September 23, 2019. https://www.nbcnews.com/news/world/teen-climate-activist-greta-thunberg-delivers-scathing-speech-u-n-n1057621.

Ross, Melanie C. *Evangelical versus Liturgical? Defying a Dichotomy*. Grand Rapids: Eerdmans, 2014.

———. "Joseph's Britches Revisited: Reflections on Methodology in Liturgical Theology." *Worship* 80, no. 6 (2006): 528–50.

Ruth, Lester. "*Lex Agendi, Lex Orandi*: Toward an Understanding of Seeker Services as a New Kind of Liturgy." *Worship* 70, no. 5 (September 1996): 403–5.

———. "A Rose by Any Other Name." In T. Johnson, *Conviction of Things Not Seen*, 85–104.

Ruth, Lester, and Swee Hong Lim. *Lovin' on Jesus: A Concise History of Contemporary Worship*. Nashville: Abingdon, 2017.

Savage, Jon. *Teenage: The Creation of Youth Culture*. New York: Penguin, 2007.

Scheer, Greg. "Shout to the Lord: Praise and Worship from Jesus People to Gen X." In *New Songs of Celebration Render: Congregational Song in the Twenty-First Century*, edited by C. Michael Hawn, 175–205. Chicago: GIA, 2013.

Schmemann, Alexander. *Introduction to Liturgical Theology*. Translated by Ashleigh E. Moorehouse. Crestwood, NY: St. Vladimir's Seminary Press, 1966.

Seemiller, Corey, and Meghan Grace. *Generation Z: A Century in the Making*. New York: Routledge, 2019.

———. *Generation Z Goes to College*. San Francisco: Jossey-Bass, 2016.

———. *Generation Z Leads: A Guide for Developing the Leadership Capacity of Generation Z Students*. North Charleston, SC: CreateSpace, 2017.

Seibel, Cory. "From *Multi*generational to *Inter*generational." In *Intergenerate: Transforming Churches through Intergenerational Ministry*, edited by Holly Catterton Allen, 87–96. Abilene, TX: Abilene Christian University Press, 2018.

Senter, Mark H. *When God Shows Up: A History of Protestant Youth Ministry in America*. Grand Rapids: Baker Academic, 2010.

Sherry, Patrick. *Spirit and Beauty: An Introduction to Theological Aesthetics*. 2nd ed. London: SCM, 2002.

Shitama, Jack. *Anxious Church, Anxious People: How to Lead Change in an Age of Anxiety*. Earleville, MD: Charis Works, 2018.

Shorter, Aylward. *Toward a Theology of Inculturation*. Maryknoll, NY: Orbis, 1988.

Sivan, Hagith. "Holy Land Pilgrimage and Western Audiences: Some Reflections on Egeria and Her Circle." *Classical Quarterly* 38, no. 2 (1988): 528–35.

Smith, Christian, Kari Christoffersen, Hilary Davidson, and Patricia Snell Herzog. *Lost in Transition: The Dark Side of Emerging Adulthood*. New York: Oxford University Press, 2011.

Smith, Christian, and Melinda Denton. *Soul Searching: The Religious and Spiritual Lives of American Teenagers*. New York: Oxford University Press, 2005.

Smith, Christian, Kyle Longest, Jonathan Hill, and Kari Christoffersen, eds. *Young Catholic America: Emerging Adults in, out of, and Gone from the Church*. New York: Oxford University Press, 2014.

Smith, Christian, and Patricia Snell. *Souls in Transition: The Religious and Spiritual Lives of Emerging Adults*. New York: Oxford University Press, 2009.

Smith, James K. A. *Awaiting the King: Reforming Public Theology*. Grand Rapids: Baker Academic, 2017.

———. *Desiring the Kingdom: Worship, Worldview, and Cultural Formation*. Grand Rapids: Baker Academic, 2009.

———. *Imagining the Kingdom: How Worship Works*. Grand Rapids: Baker Academic, 2013.

Solarz, Andrea. *Developing Adolescents: A Reference for Professionals*. Washington, DC: American Psychological Association, 2002.

Sorenson, Jacob. "A Theological Playground: Christian Summer Camp in Theological Perspective." PhD thesis, Luther Seminary, 2016. https://digitalcommons.luthersem.edu/phd_theses/4/.

Spiegelman, Paul. "You're Contagious, and That's a Good Thing." *Forbes*, December 12, 2018. https://www.forbes.com/sites/paulspiegelman/2018/12/12/youre -contagious-and-thats-a-good-thing/.

Spinks, Bryan D. *The Worship Mall: Contemporary Responses to Contemporary Culture*. New York: Church Publishing, 2010.

Steinberg, Laurence. *Age of Opportunity: Lessons from the New Science of Adolescence*. New York: Mariner, 2014.

Stucky, Nathan T. *Wrestling with Rest: Inviting Youth to Discover the Gift of Sabbath*. Grand Rapids: Eerdmans, 2019.

Tapscott, Don. *Grown Up Digital: How the Net Generation Is Changing Your World*. New York: McGraw Hill, 2009.

Taylor, Barbara Brown. *An Altar in the World: A Geography of Faith*. New York: HarperOne, 2009.

Taylor, W. David O. *Open and Unafraid: The Psalms as a Guide to Life*. Nashville: Nelson, 2020.

Tisdale, Leonora Tubbs. *Preaching as Local Theology and Folk Art*. Minneapolis: Fortress, 1997.

Tolstoy, Leo. *A Confession*. Originally published 1882. Christian Classics Ethereal Library, July 11, 1998. https://www.ccel.org/ccel/tolstoy/confession.html.

Turner, Victor. *The Ritual Process: Structure and Anti-structure*. New Brunswick, NJ: Aldine Transaction, 1995.

Twenge, Jean M. *iGen: Why Today's Super-Connected Kids Are Growing Up Less Rebellious, More Tolerant, Less Happy—and Completely Unprepared for Adulthood; And What That Means for the Rest of Us*. New York: Atria, 2017.

Underhill, Evelyn. *Worship*. New York: Harper, 1937.

Vanderwell, Howard, ed. *The Church of All Ages: Generations Worshiping Together*. Herndon, VA: Alban Institute, 2008.

———. "A New Issue for a New Day." In Vanderwell, *Church of All Ages*, 1–15.

Van Opstal, Sandra Maria. *The Next Worship: Glorifying God in a Diverse World*. Downers Grove, IL: InterVarsity, 2016.

Ver Beek, Kurt. "The Impact of Short-Term Missions: A Case Study of House Construction in Honduras after Hurricane Mitch." *Missiology* 34, no. 4 (2006): 477–95.

Vogel, Dwight W., ed., *Primary Sources of Liturgical Theology: A Reader*. Collegeville, MN: Liturgical, 2000.

Wainwright, Geoffrey. *Doxology: The Praise of God in Worship, Doctrine, and Life; A Systematic Theology*. New York: Oxford University Press, 1984.

Walls, Andrew. "The Old Age of the Missionary Movement." *International Review of Mission* 77 (1987): 26–32.

Wannenwetsch, Bernd. *Political Worship*. New York: Oxford University Press, 2009.

Ward, Pete. *Selling Worship: How What We Sing Has Changed the Church*. Bletchley, UK: Paternoster, 2005.

Webber, Robert E. *Ancient Future Worship: Proclaiming and Enacting God's Narrative*. Grand Rapids: Baker Books, 2008.

———. *The Younger Evangelicals: Facing the Challenges of the New World*. Grand Rapids: Baker Books, 2003.

Wells, Amos R. *The Officers' Handbook: A Guide for Officers in Young People's Societies, with Chapters on Parliamentary Law and Other Useful Themes*. Rev. ed. Boston: United Society of Christian Endeavor, 1900.

Westermeyer, Paul. *Te Deum: The Church and Music*. Minneapolis: Augsburg Fortress, 1998.

White, James Emery. *Meet Generation Z: Understanding and Reaching the New Post-Christian World*. Grand Rapids: Baker Books, 2017.

White, James F. *A Brief History of Christian Worship*. Nashville: Abingdon, 1992.

———. *Protestant Worship: Traditions in Transition*. Louisville: Westminster John Knox, 1989.

Williams, D. H. *Evangelicals and Tradition: The Formative Influence of the Early Church*. Grand Rapids: Baker Academic, 2005.

Wills, Garry. *Bare Ruined Choirs: Doubt, Prophecy, and Radical Religion*. New York: Doubleday, 1972.

Witvliet, John D. *The Biblical Psalms in Christian Worship: A Brief Introduction and Guide to Resources*. Grand Rapids: Eerdmans, 2007.

———. "Liturgy as God's Language School." *Pastoral Music* 31, no. 4 (April–May 2007): 19–23.

———. "Mind the Gaps: Responding to Criticisms of a Formative Vision for Worship and Congregational Song." *The Hymn: A Journal of Congregational Song* 67, no. 4 (Autumn 2016): 33–39.

———. "On Three Meanings of the Term Worship." *Reformed Worship* 56 (June 2000). https://www.reformedworship.org/article/june-2000/three-meaning-term -worship.

———. "Teaching Worship as a Christian Practice." In *For Life Abundant: Practical Theology, Theological Education, and Christian Ministry*, edited by Dorothy C. Bass and Craig Dykstra, 117–49. Grand Rapids: Eerdmans, 2008.

———. "Vertical Habits: Missional Churches at Worship." Paper presented at the Calvin Symposium on Christian Worship, Grand Rapids, January 2006. https://stor age.googleapis.com/cicw/microsites/worshipsymposiumorg/files/2006/witvliet.pdf.

Wolterstorff, Nicholas. "The Contours of Justice: An Ancient Call for Shalom." In *God and the Victim: Theological Reflections on Evil, Victimization, Justice, and Forgiveness*, edited by Lisa Barnes Lampman and Michelle D. Shattuck, 107–30. Grand Rapids: Eerdmans, 1999.

Wright, Almeda M. *The Spiritual Lives of Young African Americans*. New York: Oxford University Press, 2017.

Wuthnow, Robert. *All in Sync: How Music and Art Are Revitalizing American Religion*. Berkeley: University of California Press, 2006.

Yaconelli, Mark. *Contemplative Youth Ministry: Practicing the Presence of Jesus*. Grand Rapids: Zondervan, 2006.

———. "Focusing Youth Ministry through Christian Practices." In Dean, Clark, and Rahn, *Starting Right*, 155–65.

York, Terry W. *America's Worship Wars*. Peabody, MA: Hendrickson, 2003.

Zschech, Darlene. "The Role of the Holy Spirit in Worship." In *The Spirit in Worship—Worship in the Spirit*, edited by Teresa Berger and Bryan D. Spinks, 285–92. Collegeville, MN: Liturgical, 2009.

Index